Reading Epistemology

Reading Philosophy

Reading Philosophy is a series of textbooks offering interactive commentaries on selected readings, and covering the major sub-disciplines of the field. Each volume contains a number of topical chapters each containing primary readings, accompanied by an introduction to the topic, introductions to the readings as well as the commentary. Edited by leading scholars, the aim of the books is to encourage the practice of philosophy in the process of engagement with philosophical texts.

Reading Philosophy
Samuel Guttenplan, Jennifer Hornsby and Christopher Janaway

Reading Philosophy of Language
Jennifer Hornsby and Guy Longworth

Reading Aesthetics and Philosophy of Art
Christopher Janaway

Reading Epistemology
Sven Bernecker

Reading Epistemology

*Selected Texts with
Interactive Commentary*

Sven Bernecker

Blackwell
Publishing

BLACKWELL PUBLISHING
350 Main Street, Malden, MA 02148-5020, USA
9600 Garsington Road, Oxford OX4 2DQ, UK
550 Swanston Street, Carlton, Victoria 3053, Australia

First published 2006 by Blackwell Publishing Ltd

1 2006

Library of Congress Cataloging-in-Publication Data

Reading epistemology : selected texts with interactive
commentary / Sven Bernecker.
    p. cm. – (Reading philosophy)
Includes bibliographical references and index.
  ISBN-13: 978-1-4051-2763-9 (hardback : alk. paper)
  ISBN-10: 1-4051-2763-5 (hardback : alk. paper)
  ISBN-13: 978-1-4051-2764-6 (pbk. : alk. paper)
  ISBN-10: 1-4051-2764-3 (pbk. : alk. paper)
1. Knowledge, Theory of. I. Bernecker, Sven. II. Series.
  BD161.R3414 2006
  121–dc22

                   2005017016

A catalogue record for this title is available from the British Library.

Set in 10.5/12.5 pt DanteMT
by SPI Publisher Services, Pondicherry, India
Printed and bound in the United Kingdom
by TJ International, Padstow, Cornwall

For further information on
Blackwell Publishing, visit our website:
www.blackwellpublishing.com

Contents

Preface

This book combines two bibliographic genres – anthology and textbook – by offering a thematic introduction to the contemporary theory of knowledge *and* providing a selection of seminal articles in the field. The book presupposes no special background knowledge in philosophy and is meant to be fully understandable by any attentive reader. It could be used as a set reading in seminars and lecture courses, but it is also suitable for individual readers studying without a teacher.

I am grateful to the editors of the series in which this book appears for giving me the opportunity to write it. I am indebted to Peter Bauman, Chris Daly, and Jennifer Hornsby for comments and advice on various parts of the book. Work on this book has been supported by a Heisenberg-Stipendium from the Deutsche Forschungs-gemeinschaft; I am glad to have the chance to extend my thanks. Finally, affectionate thanks to my wife, to whom the book is dedicated.

Sven Bernecker

Sources and Acknowledgements

The author and publisher gratefully acknowledge the permission granted to reproduce the copyright material in this book:

John L. Pollock, 'The Gettier Problem', pp. 180–2 from *Contemporary Theories of Knowledge* (Totowa, NJ: Rowman & Littlefield, 1986). Copyright © 1986 Rowman & Littlefield Publishers, Inc. Reprinted by permission of Rowman & Littlefield Publishing Group.

Robert Nozick, 'Conditions for Knowledge', pp. 172–7, 178–9 from *Philosophical Explanations* (Cambridge, MA: Harvard University Press, 1981). Copyright © 1981 by Robert Nozick. Reprinted by permission of Harvard University Press and Georges Borchardt, Inc.

Alvin I. Goldman, 'What is Justified Belief?', pp. 1–3, 9–14, 14–15, 18–20, 22–3 from George S. Pappas (ed.), *Justification and Knowledge* (London: D. Reidel, 1979). Copyright © 1979 by D. Reidel Publishing Company. Reprinted by permission of Springer Science and Business Media and the author.

Richard Foley, 'What's Wrong with Reliabilism?', pp. 188–91, 192–3, 194–5, 195–7, 199–202 from *The Monist* 68, 1985. Copyright © 1985 by *The Monist: An International Quarterly Journal of General Philosophical Inquiry*, Peru, IL, 61354, USA. Reprinted by permission of the journal.

Matthias Steup, 'A Defense of Internalism', pp. 373–82, 383–4 from Louis P. Pojman (ed.), *The Theory of Knowledge: Classical and Contemporary Readings*, 2nd edn (London: Wadsworth, 1999). Copyright © 1997 by Matthias Steup. Reprinted by permission of the author.

Ernest Sosa, 'Reliabilism and Intellectual Virtue', pp. 131–2, 138–40, 140–5 from *Knowledge in Perspective: Selected Essays in Epistemology* (Cambridge: Cambridge University Press, 1991). Copyright © 1991 by Cambridge University Press. Reprinted by permission of the publisher and the author.

Elizabeth Fricker, extracts from 'Against Gullibility', pp. 125–61 from Bimal Krishna Matilal and Arindam Chakrabarti (eds), *Knowing from Words: Western and Indian Philosophical Analysis of Understanding and Testimony* (Dordrecht: Kluwer, 1994). Copyright © 1994 by Kluwer Academic Publishers. Reprinted by permission of Springer Science and Business Media and the author.

Tyler Burge, extracts from 'Content Preservation', pp. 457–88, from *The Philosophical Review* 102, 1993. Copyright © 1993 by Cornell University. Reprinted by permission of the publisher and the author.

William P. Alston, 'Two Types of Foundationalism', pp. 165–74, 182–5 from *The Journal of Philosophy* 73, 1976. Copyright © 1976 by *The Journal of Philosophy*. Reprinted by permission of the journal and the author.

Laurence BonJour, extracts from 'The Coherence Theory of Empirical Knowledge', pp. 281–312, from *Philosophical Studies* 30, 1976. Copyright © 1976 by *Philosophical Studies*. Reprinted by permission of Springer Science and Business Media and the author.

Fred Dretske, extracts from 'The Pragmatic Dimension of Knowledge', pp. 363–78, from *Philosophical Studies* 40, 1981. Copyright © 1981 by *Philosophical Studies*. Reprinted by permission of Springer Science and Business Media and the author.

Michael Williams, 'Realism and Scepticism', pp. 193, 197, 202, 203–9 from John Haldane and Crispin Wright (eds), *Reality, Representation, and Projection* (Oxford: Oxford University Press, 1993). Copyright © 1993 by The Mind Association. Reprinted by permission of Oxford University Press, Inc.

I am also grateful to the publisher and Fred Dretske for permission to reuse some material from the brief synoptic introductions in my anthology *Knowledge: Readings in Contemporary Epistemology* (Oxford: Oxford University Press, 2000), co-edited with Fred Dretske.

Every effort has been made to trace copyright holders and to obtain their permission for the use of copyright material. The publisher apologizes for any errors or omissions in the above list and would be grateful if notified of any corrections that should be incorporated in future reprints or editions of this book.

Introduction

The term 'epistemology' goes back to the two Greek words, *episteme*, meaning 'knowledge', and *logos*, meaning 'science' or 'rationale'. So 'epistemology' means roughly 'theory of knowledge'. However, knowing what the term 'epistemology' means still doesn't tell us what epistemology is about. What is the theory of knowledge, and why is there a need for it? One way to approach this question is to examine the kinds of issues which epistemology addresses. Five main questions of epistemology can be distinguished.

1. What is knowledge? What does the term 'knowledge' mean? Traditionally philosophers have defined 'knowledge' as meaning 'justified true belief'. But how exactly is knowledge related to justification and belief? Why should it not be possible to know something that is really false? Couldn't one know something without believing it? Maybe knowledge is a basic mental state and instead of analysing knowledge in terms of belief, the concept of knowledge should be used to elucidate the concept of belief. Of what kind is the justification that transforms true belief into knowledge? How much evidence must one have before one can be said to know something? These and related issues are the topic of Chapter 1 and will also crop up in Chapters 2 and 3.

2. What is the value of knowledge? There is no doubt that knowledge is a precious good. Educational institutions charge tuition fees for the imparting of knowledge. Some people earn a lot of money because they are specialists in some field of knowledge. But why exactly is knowledge worth having? Why don't we simply strive for true belief? Could it be that the goal of epistemic endeavours is not only truth but that there are other goals such as understanding, rationality, and utility? But does that mean that one cannot know something without understanding it or being able to make use of it? Is knowledge valuable even if one is ignorant of the fact that one knows something? These are the kind of questions that will be examined in Chapters 2 and 3.

3. *What are the sources of knowledge?* Traditionally there are two sources of knowledge: sense experience and reason. Rationalists maintain that all knowledge derives from reason whereas empiricists hold that knowledge originates through sense experience, that is, through seeing, hearing, touching, tasting, and smelling. But are there only these five senses? Consider, for example, introspection. That seems to be a sense that enables me to know what I am currently thinking and feeling. Chapter 4 is concerned with the question of whether testimony qualifies as a basic source of knowledge and how knowledge is acquired by testimony. There is no doubt that many of the things we know, we know because we accept the word of others. Testimony allows knowledge to be spread throughout the community and to be passed on through generations. But does testimony generate knowledge or is it merely a way of transmitting knowledge which has been obtained by some other source? And, to acquire knowledge by testimony, is it necessary that one ensure that the attester is trustworthy?

4. *What is the structure of our body of knowledge?* Many of the things we believe and know are based on other things we believe and know. For example, I know that I got a telephone call while I was out of the office because I see the flashing 'new message' light on the answering machine. The belief that someone called depends on the belief that the light is flashing. Such dependencies also exist between classes of beliefs. Beliefs about the future, for example, depend on beliefs about the present and the past. This naturally raises questions about the structure of the body of justified belief on the part of any given person. Does the body of justified belief rest on a bottom level of beliefs that is not itself based on any more basic beliefs? Or is a person's body of knowledge structured more like a spider's web where each strand supports all the other strands, which in turn support it? These and related issues will be investigated in Chapter 5.

5. *Can we know anything at all?* This question is pressing because there are powerful arguments to the effect that we can't know anything about the external world. Perhaps things only appear the way they do because we are wired up to computers which are force-feeding us the experiences we have. If so, then all we can really know about are our own private thoughts and experiences. Scepticism is the position that we don't have any knowledge or at least that we don't know most of the things that we claim to know. Chapter 6 tries to come to terms with arguments for scepticism and discusses contextualist strategies to avoid scepticism.

Each chapter starts with an introduction to the relevant epistemological problem and contains two texts. Each text is preceded by a brief introduction to the author and is followed by an extensive commentary. The introductions and commentaries outline the philosophical train of thought, explain terminology, provide background information, and locate particular positions and arguments in the field. By pointing out connections between ideas within the book, and between the ideas here and the wider literature, the book as a whole can impart some overall feel for the concerns of epistemology. The 'Essay/Examination Questions' section is meant to help readers assess their grasp of the material. For those readers wishing to delve more deeply into the issues and pursue ideas not directly discussed here, there is a briefly annotated 'Further Reading' section.

The texts reprinted in this book are abridged versions of journal articles or book chapters. In some cases, large portions of the articles or chapters are omitted. Every omission (including cuts in footnotes) is made explicit by ellipses replacing the deleted material. My use of ellipses is the conventional one. Where material at the end of a paragraph (plus the subsequent paragraphs) is taken out, ellipses are inserted on the same line as the last word quoted. Where a whole new paragraph (or several paragraphs) are deleted, the ellipses are placed on a separate line. Where an entire footnote has been deleted, an asterisk (*) has been inserted in the text to indicate the missing material. In some cases, because of abridgement, the numbering of propositions and of footnotes has been changed. The numbering of subsections has not been altered. Due to abridgement, some texts have insequentially numbered subsections.

Since textbooks in philosophy written from a neutral point of view tend to be stale and boring, I don't try to conceal my own stand on the issues under consideration. Although I do my best to give each argument and theory a fair hearing, in many places I offer my own view.

The process of philosophizing is a dialectical one, consisting of proposals and objections and further proposals and further objections back and forth among the different views on a given problem. To fully understand this dialectical development one must become a participant rather than a mere observer. To kindle the dialogue so essential to real learning, the two texts per chapter often express opposing views. To further aid understanding of the dialectical character of philosophy in general and of epistemology in particular, the commentaries are *interactive*. First, they make use of a system of arrow markers, $\boxed{a} \mapsto$, $\boxed{b} \mapsto$ and so on, which link the commentaries with definite portions of a particular text and invite careful study of selected parts of it. When the arrow marker stands at the beginning of a paragraph it serves to label the entire paragraph; when it stands in the middle of a paragraph it labels a particular sentence. Second, the commentaries contain questions or tasks in boxes, which prompt the reader to think through a specific question for himself.[1] The interactive nature of the commentaries should enable the reader to deepen his understanding of the views expressed in the texts and to develop his own lines of thought in the area.

I envisage the reader using a chapter in something like the following way. Start with the chapter's introduction. The texts should be tackled one at a time. First read it through to gain a general idea of the argument, then read it a second time more carefully, pausing and taking a few notes, if that is helpful. Then turn to the commentary on that text, and take it slowly, stopping at the boxed questions. 'Zoom in' on each question in its own right, and try to answer it before moving on to what I say about it. Approach each idea or theory with the aim of deciding what *you* think about it.

---

[1]   Here and throughout the book gender-unspecific reference is made with 'he' and its cognates, which may then be read as 'she or he', 'her and him', etc.

1

Defining Knowledge

Introduction to the Problem

Epistemology attempts to identify the properties by virtue of which a belief (or set of beliefs) is justified or counts as knowledge. One way of conceiving of this identification of properties is as a conceptual analysis of the concepts of knowledge and justified belief. The aim of a conceptual analysis is to provide a set of conditions, each of which is necessary for the truth of the concept and which collectively are sufficient. 'A is a necessary condition of B' means that B cannot be true unless A is true. 'A is a sufficient condition of B' means that if A is true, then B must be true too. The question 'What is knowledge?' asks for the necessary and sufficient conditions under which a person knows something.

To get a feeling for the kinds of problems connected with conceptual analysis, let's begin with a concept that is considerably simpler than that of knowledge.[1]

> Give a conceptual analysis of the concept of bachelor.

You might want to say that 'S is a bachelor if and only if (i) S is male, and (ii) S is unmarried'. Yet a little thought reveals that while conditions (i) and (ii) are necessary for being a bachelor, they are not sufficient for being a bachelor. For there are cases where S is an unmarried male but is not a bachelor. Suppose, for example, that S is a dog that is male but unmarried. So we need to add a further condition to our conceptual analysis. Suppose we also require that a bachelor be human: (iii) S is human. Are conditions (i), (ii), and (iii) jointly sufficient to identify all and

---

[1] The following example is taken from N. Everitt and A. Fisher, *Modern Epistemology* (McGraw-Hill, 1995), pp. 14–15.

only bachelors? One might object that an unmarried human male who is a newly born baby meets these conditions but still would not be considered a bachelor. So maybe we need a fourth condition: (iv) S is of marriageable age. But what counts as being of marriageable age will, of course, vary across societies. Is this a weakness of the analysis or does it only show that the concept of bachelor is culturally relative?

The above example illustrates that there are at least two kinds of problems connected with conceptual analysis. First, conceptual analysis depends on linguistic intuitions. Linguistic intuitions may differ between people and among societies. For example, people can be of different opinions on whether to call a monk or a baby a bachelor. Linguistic intuitions may also undergo change across time within the same individual. Second, when one tries to analyse complex theoretical concepts, it is often difficult to find a set of necessary and sufficient conditions which will accommodate all the various intuitions we have about the usage of the concept.

Traditionally, epistemologists have held that the concept of knowledge has three individually necessary and jointly sufficient conditions: justification, truth, and belief. Knowledge is said to be justified true belief. This view, which can be traced back to Plato's *Theaetetus*, claims that what distinguishes knowledge from mere true belief and lucky guessing is that it is based on some form of justification, evidence, or supporting reasons.

The traditional analysis of knowledge applies primarily to propositional knowledge (also referred to as 'knowing that' or 'factual knowledge'). Propositional knowledge takes the form 'S knows that p' where S stands for a subject and p stands for a declarative sentence expressing some proposition. 'Proposition' is a technical term of philosophers used to denote what it is that is said or asserted by an utterance, a sentence, or a thought. A proposition is something like a meaning. It is important to distinguish the proposition from the event in which that proposition is expressed. Unlike propositions, events happen at a certain time and at a certain place. One must also distinguish a proposition from the words, sounds, symbols, or brain states that express a proposition. When, for example, you say 'S is a bachelor' and when I say 'S ist ein Junggeselle' we utter different sentences but express the same proposition. Because propositions are either true or false, only declarative sentences can express propositions. A question or a demand is neither true nor false. And there are even some declarative sentences (e.g., 'Picasso is the greatest painter', 'God is benevolent') where it is debatable whether they have clear truth values. So the class of propositional knowledge is relatively small.

Apart from propositional knowledge, philosophers recognize two main kinds of knowledge, namely practical knowledge (or 'knowing how') and non-propositional knowledge of people, places, and things (or 'knowledge by acquaintance'). Within propositional knowledge one can distinguish between inferential (or demonstrative) and non-inferential (or direct, basic, immediate) knowledge. Inferential knowledge is the product of suitable deductive or inductive inferences from other propositions that serve as evidence or justification. An example of inferential knowledge is when you come to know that today is Tuesday on the basis of observing your garbage being collected and knowing that your garbage is collected every Tuesday.

The truth condition of the justified-true-belief analysis of knowledge states that if you know that p, then p is true. You cannot, for example, know that Bert is a bachelor unless, in fact, Bert is a bachelor. But, of course, p can itself be a claim that something else is false. You can, for example, know that it is false that Bert is married. The belief condition claims that knowing that Bert is a bachelor implies believing that he is a bachelor. A person need not be absolutely certain that something is true in order to know that it is. The belief condition only requires some kind of acceptance in the interest of obtaining truth. Finally, the justification condition requires that a known proposition be evidentially supported. The justification condition is there in order to prevent lucky guesses from counting as knowledge when the guesser is sufficiently confident to believe his own guess. Epistemic justification for a belief is justification for the belief's truth, not its usefulness or its social respectability. According to the tradition, a belief can be justified in a way sufficient for knowledge even if the justification is not conclusive – even if it is the sort of justification one can have for a false proposition (though, of course, one could not know a false proposition to be true by having such a justification for it). Thus the necessity for an independent truth condition.

In 1963 the philosopher Edmund Gettier published a three-page paper challenging the traditional analysis of knowledge as justified true belief.[2] Gettier does not dispute the claim that belief, justification, and truth are necessary for knowledge, but rather he argues that these alone are not sufficient for knowledge. He presents two examples of justified true belief that are not cases of knowledge. One such example, which is less complex to describe than Gettier's own examples, is the following scenario from Keith Lehrer[3]: two agents, the ubiquitous S and Mr Nogot, work in the same office. Nogot has given S evidence that justifies S in believing that Nogot owns a Ford car. Imagine that S has seen Nogot driving a Ford, S has been told by persons who have in the past been reliable that Nogot owns a Ford, and so on. From the proposition that Nogot owns a Ford, S then infers the proposition p: 'Someone in the office owns a Ford'. But unsuspected by S, Nogot has been shamming and p is only true because another person in the office, Mr Havit, owns a Ford. Thus S has a true belief, namely the belief p that someone in the office owns a Ford. Moreover, S is justified in believing that p. But we wouldn't want to say in this case that S has knowledge. He has simply been lucky. It just so happened that someone in the office owns a Ford, but not the person S thinks owns a Ford. The kind of reasons S possesses don't seem to be of the right sort.

There is an abundance of Gettier-type examples in the literature. The common feature among all these cases is that the things that justify a subject in believing p are distinct from the things that make p true. What accounts for the justification of the belief is not what accounts for its truth. To see this, reconsider the above example: S clearly has reasons for believing that someone in the office owns a Ford. Yet if we were to explain why this belief is true, we would refer not to Nogot, but rather to

---

[2]   E. Gettier, 'Is Justified True Belief Knowledge?', *Analysis* 23 (1963), pp. 121–3.
[3]   K. Lehrer, 'Knowledge, Truth and Evidence', *Analysis* 25 (1965), pp. 168–75.

Havit. So S's justification doesn't direct us to what accounts for the truth of his belief. There is a gap between the satisfaction of the justification condition and the satisfaction of the truth condition. With respect to S's justification, it is merely good fortune or a happy accident that the belief is true. For all he knows, it might have been false that anyone, including Havit, owns a Ford.

> Construct your own Gettier-type counterexample to the justified-true-belief an-
> alysis of knowledge.

The response to Gettier's short paper, 'Is Justified True Belief Knowledge?', was overwhelming. Some suggested that Gettier-type counterexamples were somehow defective or overlooked some obvious point about justification; others accepted the counterexamples and amended the justified-true-belief analysis by proposing additional conditions on knowledge designed to block Gettier-type cases; still others, instead of adding conditions, suggested changes in how existing conditions (e.g., justification) were to be understood. The section by Pollock discusses the first two kinds of response. Nozick's solution to the Gettier problem belongs to the third group.

Introduction to Pollock

John L. Pollock is professor of philosophy at the University of Arizona at Tucson and works primarily in epistemology, philosophical logic, and artificial intelligence. He not only tries to understand how the mind works but also attempts to build a mind. Pollock directs the OSCAR project, whose purpose is to formulate a general theory of rationality and to implement it in an artificial rational agent. The computer system OSCAR seems already capable of intellectual feats surpassed only by human beings, and Pollock hopes that the time will come when even humans cannot compete with OSCAR on some kinds of intellectual tasks. He has written books about artificial intelligence with such intriguing titles as *How to Build a Person: A Prolegomenon* (1990) and *Cognitive Carpentry: A Blueprint for How to Build a Person* (1995).

'The Gettier Problem' is the introductory section of an appendix to Pollock's *Contemporary Theories of Knowledge* (1986). In this piece he explains the Gettier problem and critically discusses some of the responses to the Gettier problem found in the literature. In the later sections of the appendix, not reprinted in this volume, Pollock set forth his own solution to the Gettier problem. In 1999 Pollock (together with Joseph Cruz) published a second edition of *Contemporary Theories of Knowledge*. The second edition does not contain the appendix on the Gettier problem. Other epistemological books by Pollock are *Knowledge and Justification* (1974), *Subjunctive Reasoning* (1976), and *Nomic Probability and the Foundations of Induction* (1990).

John L. Pollock, 'The Gettier Problem'

It is rare in philosophy to find a consensus on any substantive issue, but for some time there was almost complete consensus on what is called 'the justified true belief analysis of knowing'. According to that analysis:

> S knows p if and only if:
> (1) p is true;
> (2) S believes p; and
> (3) S is justified in believing p.

In the period immediately preceding the publication of Gettier's (1963) landmark article "Is justified true belief knowledge?", this analysis was affirmed by virtually every writer in epistemology. Then Gettier published his article and single-handedly changed the course of epistemology. He did this by presenting two clear and undeniable counterexamples to the justified true belief analysis. Recounting the example given in chapter one, consider Smith who believes falsely but with good reason that Jones owns a Ford. Smith has no idea where Brown is, but he arbitrarily picks Barcelona and infers from the putative fact that Jones owns a Ford that either Jones owns a Ford or Brown is in Barcelona. It happens by chance that Brown is in Barcelona, so this disjunction is true. Furthermore, as Smith has good reason to believe that Jones owns a Ford, he is justified in believing this disjunction. But as his evidence does not pertain to the true disjunct of the disjunction, we would not regard Smith as *knowing* that either Jones owns a Ford or Brown is in Barcelona.

Gettier's paper was followed by a spate of articles attempting to meet his counterexamples by adding a fourth condition to the analysis of knowing. The first attempts to solve the Gettier problem turned on the observation that in Gettier's examples, the epistemic agent arrives at his justified true belief by reasoning from a false belief. That suggested the addition of a fourth condition something like the following:

> S's grounds for believing p do not include any false beliefs.[1]

It soon emerged, however, that further counterexamples could be constructed in which knowledge is lacking despite the believer's not inferring his belief from any false beliefs. Alvin Goldman (1976) constructed the following example. Suppose you are driving through the countryside and see what you take to be a barn. You see it in good light and from not too great a distance, it looks the way barns look, and so on. Furthermore, it is a barn. You then have justified true belief that it is a barn. But in an attempt to

---

[1] See, for example, Michael Clark (1963).

appear more opulent than they are, the people around here have taken to constructing very realistic barn facades that cannot readily be distinguished from the real thing when viewed from the highway. There are many more barn facades around than real barns. Under these circumstances we would not agree that you know that what you see is a barn, even though you have justified true belief. Furthermore, your belief that you see a barn is not in any way inferred from a belief about the absence of barn facades. Most likely the possibility of barn facades is something that will not even have occurred to you, much less have played a role in your reasoning.

We can construct an even simpler perceptual example. Suppose S sees a ball that looks red to him, and on that basis he correctly judges that it is red. But unbeknownst to S, the ball is illuminated by red lights and would look red to him even if it were not red. Then S does not know that the ball is red despite his having a justified true belief to that effect. Furthermore, his reason for believing that the ball is red does not involve his believing that the ball is not illuminated by red lights. Illumination by red lights is related to his reasoning only as a defeater, not as a step in his reasoning. These examples, of other related examples,[2] indicate that justified true belief can fail to be knowledge because of the truth values of propositions that do not play a direct role in the reasoning underlying the belief. This observation led to a number of "defeasibility" analyses of knowing.[3] The simplest defeasibility analysis would consist of adding a fourth condition requiring that there be no true defeaters. This might be accomplished as follows:

> There is no true proposition Q such that if Q were added to S's beliefs then he would no longer be justified in believing p.[4]

But Keith Lehrer and Thomas Paxson (1969) presented the following counterexample to this simple proposal:

> Suppose I see a man walk into the library and remove a book from the library by concealing it beneath his coat. Since I am sure the man is Tom Grabit, whom I have often seen before when he attended my classes, I report that I know that Tom Grabit has removed the book. However, suppose further that Mrs. Grabit, the mother of Tom, has averred that on the day in question Tom was not in the library, indeed, was thousands of miles away, and that Tom's identical twin brother, John Grabit, was in the library. Imagine, moreover, that I am entirely

---

[2]   See, for example, Brian Skyrms (1967).
[3]   The first defeasibility analysis was that of Keith Lehrer (1965). That was followed by Lehrer and Thomas Paxson (1969), Peter Klein (1971), (1976), (1979), (1980), Lehrer (1974), (1979), Ernest Sosa (1974), (1980), and Marshall Swain (1981).
[4]   This is basically the analysis proffered by Klein (1971).

ignorant of the fact that Mrs. Grabit has said these things. The statement that she has said these things would defeat any justification I have for believing that Tom Grabit removed the book, according to our present definition of defeasibility. . . .

The preceding might seem acceptable until we finish the story by adding that Mrs. Grabit is a compulsive and pathological liar, that Tom Grabit is a fiction of her demented mind, and that Tom Grabit took the book as I believed. Once this is added, it should be apparent that I did know that Tom Grabit removed the book.   (p. 228)

A natural proposal for handling the Grabit example is that in addition to there being a true defeater there is a true defeater defeater, and that restores knowledge. For example, in the Grabit case it is true that Mrs. Grabit reported that Tom was not in the library but his twin brother John was there (a defeater), but it is also true that Mrs. Grabit is a compulsive and pathological liar and John Grabit is a fiction of her demented mind (a defeater defeater). It is difficult, however, to construct a precise principle that handles these examples correctly by appealing to true defeaters and true defeater defeaters. It will not do to amend the above proposal as follows:

If there is a true proposition Q such that if Q were added to S's beliefs then he would no longer be justified in believing p, then there is also a true proposition R such that if Q and R were both added to S's beliefs then he would be justified in believing p.

The simplest difficulty for this proposal is that adding R may add new reasons for believing p rather than restoring the old reasons. It is not trivial to see how to formulate a fourth condition incorporating defeater defeaters. I think that such a fourth condition will ultimately provide the solution to the Gettier problem, but no proposal of this sort has been worked out in the literature.[5]

References

Clark, Michael (1963) Knowledge and grounds: A comment on Mr. Gettier's paper. *Analysis* 24: 46–48.

Gettier, Edmund (1963) Is justified true belief knowledge? *Analysis* 23: 121–23.

Goldman, Alvin (1976) Discrimination and perceptual knowledge. *Journal of Philosophy* 73: 771–91.

Klein, Peter (1971) A proposed definition of propositional knowledge. *Journal of Philosophy* 68: 471–82.

Klein, Peter (1976) Knowledge, causality, and defeasibility. *Journal of Philosophy* 73: 792–812.

[5]   A good survey of the literature on the Gettier problem, going into much more detail than space permits here, can be found in Shope (1983).

Klein, Peter (1979) Misleading "misleading defeaters". *Journal of Philosophy* 76: 382–86.

Klein, Peter (1980) Misleading evidence and the restoration of justification. *Philosophical Studies* 37: 81–89.

Lehrer, Keith (1965) Knowledge, truth, and evidence. *Analysis* 25: 168–75.

Lehrer, Keith (1974) *Knowledge*. Oxford: Oxford University Press.

Lehrer, Keith (1979) The Gettier problem and the analysis of knowledge. In *Justification and Knowledge: New Studies in Epistemology*, ed. George Pappas, pp. 65–78. Dordrecht: Reidel.

Lehrer, Keith, and Thomas Paxson (1969) Knowledge: Undefeated justified true belief. *Journal of Philosophy* 66: 225–37.

Shope, Robert K. (1983) *The Analysis of Knowing*. Princeton: Princeton University Press.

Sosa, Ernest, (1974) How do you know? *American Philosophical Quarterly* 11: 113–22.

Sosa, Ernest, (1980) Epistemic presupposition. In *Justification and Knowledge: New Studies in Epistemology*, ed. George Pappas. Dordrecht: Reidel.

Swain, Marshall (1981) *Reasons and Knowledge*. Ithaca, NY: Cornell University Press.

Commentary on Pollock

In the paragraph marked $\boxed{a}$→ Pollock recounts one of the two original Gettier examples. The example is a cousin of the one discussed in the 'Introduction to the Problem': suppose that Smith is justified in believing that Jones owns a Ford car. On the basis of the belief that

Jones owns a Ford

Smith comes to believe that

either Jones owns a Ford or Brown is in Barcelona.

The inference from the first to the second belief relies on the deductive rule according to which if one is justified in believing a proposition one can disjoin it with any other proposition.[1] Now Smith simply picks the second disjunct (that Brown is in Barcelona) out of thin air. As it turns out, Jones does not own a Ford but Brown happens to be in Barcelona. So it is the first disjunct that Smith has reasons for believing but it is the second disjunct which renders the disjunctive belief true. (A disjunction is true if at least one of its disjuncts is true.) Even though Smith is justified in believing the true disjunction that either Jones owns a Ford or Brown is in Barcelona, we wouldn't say that he knows it.

One thing to notice with this example is that it assumes that a person can be justified in believing a proposition that is in fact false. So even though a justified belief is more likely to be true than an unjustified belief, justification does not

---

[1] In ordinary discourse, the operator 'or' is sometimes used in an exclusive sense, to say that exactly one of the two disjoint sentences is true. In logic and epistemology, however, 'or' is always given an inclusive interpretation according to which at least one and possibly both of the two disjoined sentences are true.

guarantee truth. For this reason Smith can be justified in believing falsely that Jones owns a Ford.

> Given that Smith has no evidence for believing that Brown is in Barcelona, why does Pollock (following Gettier) think that Smith is justified in believing that either Jones owns a Ford or Brown is in Barcelona?

Gettier defends this idea by appeal to the following principle: if *S* is justified in believing *p*, and *p* entails *q*, and *S* believes *q* because he deduces *q* from *p*, then *S* is justified in believing *q*. Some philosophers have challenged this principle.[2] Can you think of reasons for denying this principle?

As Pollock explains in the passage marked $\boxed{\text{b}}\!\!\rightarrow$, some philosophers think that Gettier-type counterexamples to the justified-true-belief analysis of knowledge can be ruled out by stipulating that the belief that *p* must not be based on a false premise. In the preceding example, the true belief that either Jones owns a Ford or Brown is in Barcelona is inferred from the false belief that Jones owns a Ford. So maybe one needs only to add a fourth condition to the justified-true-belief analysis, requiring that the justification does not depend on any false premise. The idea of the 'no-false-premise' approach is that to rule out Gettier examples one needs to stipulate that the justification may not depend on any false premises.

Pollock objects to the no-false-premise condition on the grounds that it is too weak to rule out Gettier-type counterexamples.

> Modify the Gettier example discussed by Pollock in such a way that *S*'s belief to the effect that someone owns a Ford does not rely on a false premise.

Suppose *S*'s reason for believing that someone owns a Ford is that Nogot told *S* that he owns one. Let *q* stand for the proposition

   (*q*) Nogot said that he owns a Ford.

From *q* Smith infers proposition *p*

   (*p*) Someone in the office owns a Ford.

Proposition *p* is true, *S* believes that *p* is true and he has reasons for believing *p*, namely *q*. Yet *S* doesn't know that *p* because it is not Nogot who owns a Ford but Havit. The crucial difference between this example and the previous version is that here *S* does not rely on a false premise. For even though Nogot did not tell the truth when he said that he owns a Ford, he did say it. Proposition *q* is indeed true.[3]

---

[2]   For example I. Thalberg, 'In Defense of Justified True Belief', *Journal of Philosophy* 66 (1969), pp. 794–803.

[3]   This example is a variation of an example given by R. Feldman in 'An Alleged Defect in Gettier Counter-Examples', *Australasian Journal of Philosophy* 52 (1974), pp. 68–9.

In the paragraph marked by $\boxed{c} \rightarrow$ Pollock presents another Gettier-type example in which no false belief is present: S is driving in the country and correctly identifies a barn in the distance. Unbeknownst to S, the area is full of barn façades which, from a distance, cannot be distinguished from real barns. Pollock concludes that S cannot be said to know that he is seeing a barn even though he has a justified true belief. The truth of the belief is just a matter of luck. But since S's failure to know is not attributed to any false premise on which the belief is based, the no-false-premise condition does not succeed in saving the justified-true-belief analysis.

Some epistemologists think that the no-false-premise condition is too strong for knowledge rather than too weak.

> Develop an argument to the effect that the no-false-premise condition is too strong for knowledge.

Consider the following variation on the original Gettier example: Smith correctly believes that Jones owns a Ford. Smith's belief is based on his having seen Jones drive a Ford and having seen the registration papers. Suppose that Smith also holds the false belief that Jones bought his Ford in March 2005. However, Jones purchased the car in December 2004. Now Smith infers that someone in the office owns a Ford on the basis of his belief that Jones bought a Ford in March 2005. Since it doesn't matter in which month the car was purchased, we seem to be entitled to say that Smith knows that someone in the office owns a Ford. As long as the premise in question is not essential for the inferred belief, it is possible to base knowledge on a false premise; or so one may argue.

In $\boxed{d} \rightarrow$ Pollock goes on to discuss the defeasibility analysis of knowledge. The basic idea behind this position is that sometimes justified true belief is not knowledge because the justification is incomplete in certain crucial respects. Not all of the important evidence has been taken into consideration. There are some facts which, if the person were to know them, would seriously weaken his justification for believing. Consider Gettier's example. Smith thinks that either Jones owns a Ford or Brown is in Barcelona (which is true) because he justifiably thinks that Jones owns a Ford (which is false). If he learned that Jones did not own a Ford, though, this would defeat his justification for thinking that either Jones owns a Ford or Brown is in Barcelona. So Smith, though he has a justification for truly thinking what he does, does not have an *undefeated* justification. There are truths which, if Smith learned them, would undermine his justification for thinking that either Jones owns a Ford or Brown is in Barcelona. Requiring undefeated justification for knowledge avoids Gettier's examples.

> Explain why the library example discussed in the passage marked $\boxed{e} \rightarrow$ indicates that the defeasibility analysis of knowledge stated in $\boxed{d} \rightarrow$ is too strong.

On the defeasibility theory stated in $\boxed{d} \rightarrow$, what prevents a subject's having knowledge is that a defeating proposition q is present, whether or not the subject is aware of *q*. If the existence of defeaters alone could rob us of knowledge, then knowledge would become a rare commodity. Therefore, Lehrer and Paxson define knowledge as justified true belief that is undefeated by a proposition which the believer has a justification for believing false. Obviously you can only be justified in believing that a proposition is false if you are aware of this proposition.

And there is another reason for why the defeasibility analysis in $\boxed{d} \mapsto$ is too strong. As it stands, even *misleading* evidence can undermine justification. To see this, reconsider the library example in $\boxed{e} \mapsto$. The belief that

(*p*) Tom stole the book

appears to be defeated by the true proposition that

(*q*) Tom's mother testified that Tom was somewhere else at the time in question.

But does *q* really qualify as a defeater of *p*? The characterization in $\boxed{d} \mapsto$ seems to indicate that it does, for if *S* was made aware of *q*, he would no longer be justified in believing *p*. But once we learn the further fact that

(*r*) Tom's mother is a deranged liar and Tom was indeed at the scene of the crime

we see that we were right in our original inclination to regard *S*'s belief that *p* as knowledge. This suggests that a distinction must be drawn between genuine and misleading defeaters. Misleading defeaters such as *q* are defeaters that can themselves be defeated. Statement *r* is such a defeating defeater. The article ends with Pollock claiming that a distinction between genuine and misleading defeaters has a good chance of providing a solution to the Gettier problem. In the later sections of the appendix from which the article is taken, Pollock develops his own version of the indefeasibility theory.

Introduction to Nozick

Robert Nozick (1938–2002) was professor of philosophy at Harvard University. He is probably best known for his defence of individualism and free-market libertarianism. His most influential contributions to philosophy outside of political theory have been in epistemology and metaphysics. In *Philosophical Explanations* (1981) – from which the extract is taken – Nozick ranges over a host of fundamental issues, such as the analysis of knowledge, scepticism, free will, the identity of the self, the foundations of ethics and the meaning of life. In dealing with these topics, he rejects the idea of strict philosophical proof and instead adopts a notion of philosophical pluralism. He writes: 'There are various philosophical views, mutually incompatible, which cannot be dismissed or simply rejected. Philosophy's output is the basketful of these admissible views, all together' (p. 21). Nozick thinks that this basketful of views can be ordered according to criteria of coherence and adequacy and that even low-ranked views can offer important insights.

The most famous piece in *Philosophical Explanations* is the 'truth-tracking' account of knowledge: one knows a truth if one believes it, would not believe it were it false, but would believe it were it true. This account is said to solve the Gettier problem and avoid scepticism. *The Possibility of Knowledge: Nozick and his Critics* (1987), edited by S. Luper-Foy, contains 12 essays assessing Nozick's analysis of knowledge and evidence and his approach to scepticism.

Apart from *Philosophical Explanations*, Nozick wrote *Anarchy, State, and Utopia* (1974), *The Examined Life: Philosophical Meditations* (1989), *The Nature of Rationality* (1993), *Socratic Puzzles* (1997), and *Invariances: The Structure of the Objective World* (2001).

Robert Nozick, 'Conditions for Knowledge'

Our task is to formulate further conditions to go alongside

(1)   *p* is true
(2)   S believes that *p*.

We would like each condition to be necessary for knowledge, so any case that fails to satisfy it will not be an instance of knowledge. Furthermore, we would like the conditions to be jointly sufficient for knowledge, so any case that satisfies all of them will be an instance of knowledge. We first shall formulate conditions that seem to handle ordinary cases correctly, classifying as knowledge cases which are knowledge, and as nonknowledge cases which are not; then we shall check to see how these conditions handle some difficult cases discussed in the literature.*

The causal condition on knowledge, previously mentioned, provides an inhospitable environment for mathematical and ethical knowledge; also there are well-known difficulties in specifying the type of causal connection. $\boxed{a} \mapsto$ If someone floating in a tank oblivious to everything around him is given (by direct electrical and chemical stimulation of the brain) the belief that he is floating in a tank with his brain being stimulated, then even though that fact is part of the cause of his belief, still he does not know that it is true.

Let us consider a different third condition:

(3)   If *p* weren't true, S wouldn't believe that *p*.

Throughout this work, let us write the subjunctive 'if-then' by an arrow, and the negation of a sentence by prefacing "not-" to it. The above condition thus is rewritten as:

(3)   not-*p* → not-(S believes that *p*).

This subjunctive condition is not unrelated to the causal condition. Often when the fact that *p* (partially) causes someone to believe that *p*, the fact also will be causally necessary for his having the belief – without the cause, the effect would not occur. In that case, the subjunctive condition 3 also will be satisfied. Yet this condition is not equivalent to the causal condition. For the causal condition will be satisfied in cases of causal overdetermination, where either two sufficient causes of the effect actually operate, or a back-up cause (of the same effect) would operate if the first one didn't; whereas the subjunctive condition need not hold for these cases.[1] When the two conditions do agree, causality indicates knowledge because it acts in a manner that makes the subjunctive 3 true.

The subjunctive condition 3 serves to exclude cases of the sort first described by Edward Gettier, such as the following. Two other people are in my office and I am justified on the basis of much evidence in believing the first owns a Ford car; though he (now) does not, the second person (a stranger to me) owns one. I believe truly and justifiably that someone (or other) in my office owns a Ford car, but I do not know someone does. Concluded Gettier, knowledge is not simply justified true belief.

The following subjunctive, which specifies condition 3 for this Gettier case, is not satisfied: if no one in my office owned a Ford car, I wouldn't believe that someone did. The situation that would obtain if no one in my office owned a Ford is one where the stranger does not (or where he is not in the office); and in that situation I still would believe, as before, that someone in my office does own a Ford, namely, the first person. So the subjunctive condition 3 excludes this Gettier case as a case of knowledge.

The subjunctive condition is powerful and intuitive, not so easy to satisfy, yet not so powerful as to rule out everything as an instance of knowledge. A subjunctive conditional 'if *p* were true, *q* would be true', $p \rightarrow q$, does not say that *p* entails *q* or that it is logically impossible that *p* yet not-*q*. It says that in the situation that would obtain if *p* were true, *q* also would be true. This point is brought out especially clearly in recent 'possible-worlds' accounts of subjunctives: the subjunctive is true when (roughly) in all those worlds in which *p* holds true that are closest to the actual world, *q* also is true. (Examine those worlds in which *p* holds true closest to the actual world, and see if *q* holds true in all these.) Whether or not *q* is true in *p* worlds that are still farther away from the actual world is irrelevant to the truth of the subjunctive. I do not mean to endorse any particular possible-worlds account of subjunctives, nor am I committed to this type of account.[2]

---

[1]   . . . I should note here that I assume bivalence throughout this chapter, and consider only statements that are true if and only if their negations are false.

[2]   See Robert Stalnaker, "A Theory of Conditionals", in N. Rescher, ed., *Studies in Logical Theory* (Basil Blackwell, Oxford, 1968); David Lewis, *Counterfactuals* (Harvard University Press, Cambridge, 1973); and Jonathan Bennett's critical review of Lewis, "Counterfactuals and Possible Worlds", *Canadian Journal of Philosophy*, Vol. IV, no. 2, Dec. 1974, pp. 381–402. . . .

I sometimes shall use it, though, when it illustrates points in an especially clear way.*

d⟶   The subjunctive condition 3 also handles nicely cases that cause difficulties for the view that you know that p when you can rule out the relevant alternatives to p in the context. For, as Gail Stine writes, "what makes an alternative relevant in one context and not another?... if on the basis of visual appearances obtained under optimum conditions while driving through the countryside Henry identifies an object as a barn, normally we say that Henry knows that it is a barn. Let us suppose, however, that unknown to Henry, the region is full of expertly made papier-mâché facsimiles of barns. In that case, we would not say that Henry knows that the object is a barn, unless he has evidence against it being a papier-mâché facsimile, which is now a relevant alternative. So much is clear, but what if no such facsimiles exist in Henry's surroundings, although they once did? Are either of these circumstances sufficient to make the hypothesis (that it's a papier-mâché object) relevant? Probably not, but the situation is not so clear."[3] Let p be the statement that the object in the field is a (real) barn, and q the one that the object in the field is a papier-mâché barn. When papier-mâché barns are scattered through the area, if p were false, q would be true or might be. Since in this case (we are supposing) the person still would believe p, the subjunctive

   (3)   not-p → not-(S believes that p)

is not satisfied, and so he doesn't know that p. However, when papier-mâché barns are or were scattered around another country, even if p were false q wouldn't be true, and so (for all we have been told) the person may well know that p. A hypothesis q contrary to p clearly is relevant when if p weren't true, q would be true; when not-p → q. It clearly is irrelevant when if p weren't true, q also would not be true; when not-p → not-q. The remaining possibility is that neither of these opposed subjunctives holds; q might (or might not) be true if p weren't true. In this case, q also will be relevant, according to an account of knowledge incorporating condition 3 and treating subjunctives along the lines sketched above. Thus, condition 3 handles cases that befuddle the 'relevant alternatives' account; though that account can adopt the above subjunctive criterion for when an alternative is relevant, it then becomes merely an alternate and longer way of stating condition 3.[4]

[3]   9. G. C. Stine, "Skepticism, Relevant Alternatives and Deductive Closure", *Philosophical Studies*, Vol. 29 (1976) p. 252, who attributes the example to Carl Ginet.

[4]   This last remark is a bit too brisk, for that account might use a subjunctive criterion for when an alternative q to p is relevant (namely, when if p were not to hold, q would or might), and utilize some further notion of what it is to rule out relevant alternatives (for example, have evidence against them), so that it did not turn out to be equivalent to the account we offer.

e⟼   Despite the power and intuitive force of the condition that if p weren't true the person would not believe it, this condition does not (in conjunction with the first two conditions) rule out every problem case. There remains, for example, the case of the person in the tank who is brought to believe, by direct electrical and chemical stimulation of his brain, that he is in the tank and is being brought to believe things in this way; he does not know this is true. However, the subjunctive condition is satisfied: if he weren't floating in the tank, he wouldn't believe he was.

The person in the tank does not know he is there, because his belief is not sensitive to the truth. Although it is caused by the fact that is its content, it is not sensitive to that fact. The operators of the tank could have produced any belief, including the false belief that he wasn't in the tank; if they had, he would have believed that. Perfect sensitivity would involve beliefs and facts varying together. We already have one portion of that variation, subjunctively at least: if p were false he wouldn't believe it. This sensitivity as specified by a subjunctive does not have the belief vary with the truth or falsity of p in all possible situations, merely in the ones that would or might obtain if p were false.

The subjunctive condition

(3)   not-p → not-(S believes that p)

tells us only half the story about how his belief is sensitive to the truth-value of p. It tells us how his belief state is sensitive to p's falsity, but not how it is sensitive to p's truth; it tells us what his belief state would be if p were false, but not what it would be if p were true.

To be sure, conditions 1 and 2 tell us that p is true and he does believe it, but it does not follow that his believing p is sensitive to p's being true. This additional sensitivity is given to us by a further subjunctive: if p were true, he would believe it.

(4) p → S believes that p.

Not only is p true and S believes it, but if it were true he would believe it. Compare: not only was the photon emitted and did it go to the left, but (it was then true that): if it were emitted it would go to the left. The truth of antecedent and consequent is not alone sufficient for the truth of a subjunctive; 4 says more than 1 and 2.[5] Thus, we presuppose some (or another) suitable account of subjunctives. According to the suggestion tentatively made above, 4 holds true if not only does he actually truly believe p, but in the 'close' worlds where p is true, he also believes it. He believes

---

[5]   More accurately, since the truth of antecedent and consequent is not necessary for the truth of the subjunctive either, 4 says something different from 1 and 2.

that p for some distance out in the p neighborhood of the actual world; similarly, condition 3 speaks not of the whole not-p neighborhood of the actual world, but only of the first portion of it. (If, as is likely, these explanations do not help, please use your own intuitive understanding of the subjunctives 3 and 4.)

The person in the tank does not satisfy the subjunctive condition 4. Imagine as actual a world in which he is in the tank and is stimulated to believe he is, and consider what subjunctives are true in that world. It is not true of him there that if he were in the tank he would believe it; for in the close world (or situation) to his own where he is in the tank but they don't give him the belief that he is (much less instill the belief that he isn't) he doesn't believe he is in the tank. Of the person actually in the tank and believing it, it is not true to make the further statement that if he were in the tank he would believe it – so he does not know he is in the tank.*

The subjunctive condition 4 also handles a case presented by Gilbert Harman.[6] The dictator of a country is killed; in their first edition, newspapers print the story, but later all the country's newspapers and other media deny the story, falsely. Everyone who encounters the denial believes it (or does not know what to believe and so suspends judgment). Only one person in the country fails to hear any denial and he continues to believe the truth. He satisfies conditions 1 through 3 (and the causal condition about belief) yet we are reluctant to say he knows the truth. The reason is that if he had heard the denials, he too would have believed them, just like everyone else. His belief is not sensitively tuned to the truth, he doesn't satisfy the condition that if it were true he would believe it. Condition 4 is not satisfied.[7]

There is a pleasing symmetry about how this account of knowledge relates conditions 3 and 4, and connects them to the first two conditions. The account has the following form.

(1)
(2)
(3) not-1 → not-2
(4) 1 → 2

I am not inclined, however, to make too much of this symmetry, for I found also that with other conditions experimented with as a possible fourth condition there was some way to construe the resulting third and fourth

[6] Gilbert Harman, *Thought* (Princeton University Press, Princeton, 1973), ch. 9, pp. 142–54.
[7] What if the situation or world where he too hears the later false denials is not so close, so easily occurring? Should we say that everything that prevents his hearing the denial easily could have not happened, and does not in some close world?

conditions as symmetrical answers to some symmetrical looking questions, so that they appeared to arise in parallel fashion from similar questions about the components of true belief.

. . .

A person knows that p when he not only does truly believe it, but also would truly believe it and wouldn't falsely believe it. He not only actually has a true belief, he subjunctively has one. It is true that p and he believes it; if it weren't true he wouldn't believe it, and if it were true he would believe it. To know that p is to be someone who would believe it if it were true, and who wouldn't believe it if it were false.

It will be useful to have a term for this situation when a person's belief is thus subjunctively connected to the fact. Let us say of a person who believes that p, which is true, that when 3 and 4 hold, his belief *tracks* the truth that p. To know is to have a belief that tracks the truth. Knowledge is a particular way of being connected to the world, having a specific real factual connection to the world: tracking it.

One refinement is needed in condition 4. It may be possible for someone to have contradictory beliefs, to believe p and also believe not-p. We do not mean such a person to easily satisfy 4, and in any case we want his belief-state, sensitive to the truth of p, to focus upon p. So let us rewrite our fourth condition as:

(4) $p \rightarrow$ S believes that p and not-(S believes that not-p).*

As you might have expected, this account of knowledge as tracking requires some refinements and epicycles.

. . .

f ⊢→   The fourth condition says that if p were true the person would believe it. Suppose the person only happened to see a certain event or simply chanced on a book describing it. He knows it occurred. Yet if he did not happen to glance that way or encounter the book, he would not believe it, even though it occurred. As written, the fourth condition would exclude this case as one where he actually knows the event occurred. It also would exclude the following case. Suppose some person who truly believes that p would or might arrive at a belief about it in some other close situation where it holds true, in a way or by a method different from the one he (actually) used in arriving at his belief that p, and so thereby come to believe that not-p. In that (close) situation, he would believe not-p even though p still holds true. Yet, all this does not show he actually doesn't know that p, for actually he has not used this alternative method in arriving at his belief. Surely he can know that *p*, even though condition 4, as written, is not satisfied.

Similarly, suppose he believes that *p* by one method or way of arriving at belief, yet if *p* were false he wouldn't use this method but would use another one instead, whose application would lead him mistakenly to believe *p* (even though it is false). This person does not satisfy condition 3 as written; it is not true of him that if *p* were false he wouldn't believe it. Still, the fact that he would use another method of arriving at belief if *p* were false does not show he didn't know that *p* when he used this method. A grandmother sees her grandson is well when he comes to visit; but if he were sick or dead, others would tell her he was well to spare her upset. Yet this does not mean she doesn't know he is well (or at least ambulatory) when she sees him. Clearly, we must restate our conditions to take explicit account of the ways and methods of arriving at belief.

Let us define a technical locution, S knows, via method (or way of believing) M, that *p*:

(1) *p* is true.
(2) S believes, via method or way of coming to believe M, that *p*.
(3) If *p* weren't true and S were to use M to arrive at a belief whether (or not) *p*, then S wouldn't believe, via M, that *p*.
(4) If *p* were true and S were to use M to arrive at a belief whether (or not) *p*, then S would believe, via M, that *p*.

Commentary on Nozick

Gettier cases show that for a true belief to qualify as knowledge it must not be a lucky coincidence that the belief is true. The belief must be non-accidentally true. But what does it mean for a belief to not be accidentally true?

The key idea behind Nozick's solution to the Gettier problem is that, for a belief to qualify as knowledge or as justified, it has to stand in some *reliable* relationship to the facts that make the belief true. This raises the question of what constitutes reliability. Consider a petrol gauge in a car. The more reliable it is, the greater the probability that it will correctly indicate the amount of petrol in the tank at a particular time. But, despite its reliability, the petrol gauge may occasionally malfunction. Furthermore we could say of a brand-new petrol gauge that it is reliable even though it has never been used. This shows that the reliability of a mechanism or process is not just a property of its actual performances but also of its possible performances. Analogously, in determining the reliability of the relationship between believing that *p* and the truth of *p*, one must take into account, not only whether the relationship is in fact present, but also whether it would be present under other circumstances. For this reason Nozick expresses the reliable relationship in question by means of two subjunctive conditionals or counterfactuals:

> *Variation condition*: if p were not true, then S would not believe that p [not-$p \Box\!\!\rightarrow$ not-(S believes that p)]
> *Adherence condition*: if p were, contrary to fact, true, then S would believe that p [$p \Box\!\!\rightarrow S$ believes that p],

where '$\Box\!\!\rightarrow$ stands for the counterfactual 'if . . . then' connective.[1] (This is not Nozick's final theory but a first approximation.) In a slightly different formulation, a subject knows that p (i) if he believes that p, (ii) p is true, (iii) he wouldn't believe that p unless p was true, and (iv) he would believe that p if p were true. For example, S knows that the telephone is ringing if he would not believe that it was ringing unless it was ringing; and if it was ringing under slightly different conditions, he would still believe that it is ringing. The two counterfactual conditionals are meant to ensure that to know that p the belief is not accidentally true. A belief that fulfils these conditions is one that, in Nozick's expression, *tracks* the facts that make it true.

There is a subtle but important difference between subjunctive conditionals such as the variation condition and adherence condition and indicative conditionals. To see this difference compare: 'If Lee Harvey Oswald had not killed J. F. Kennedy, then someone else would have' with 'If Lee Harvey Oswald did not kill J. F. Kennedy, then someone else did'. It is not clear that if Oswald had not killed Kennedy, then someone else would have. But it is clear that if Oswald did not kill Kennedy, then someone else did.

Subjunctive conditionals make use of the idea of possible worlds. A possible world is a fictitious situation which differs from the actual world in a certain respect. To say that a belief would be true in a possible world is to say that even in a situation different from this one, the belief would be true. Possible worlds vary in their degree of resemblance to the actual world. Some are more similar to our world than others.

In paragraph $\boxed{c}\!\!\rightarrow$ Nozick explains that the variation condition and adherence condition do not need to hold in *all* possible worlds. 'If p were true, S would believe that p' does not mean that in *every* world in which p is the case, S believes that p. To see this, consider the following conditional: 'If kangaroos had no tails, they would topple over.'[2] The truth of this statement is compatible with a situation in which tailless kangaroos are provided with crutches to prevent them from toppling over. So it is not logically impossible that tailless kangaroos manage to stand on their legs. What the conditional statement really means is that, in worlds which are similar to ours, tailless kangaroos are not given crutches and do topple over. Analogously, the variation and adherence conditions are not supposed to hold in all possible worlds but only in those closest to the actual world. The relation symbolized by '$\Box\!\!\rightarrow$' is

---

[1] The subjunctive 'if . . . then' connective is usually symbolized by '$\Box\!\!\rightarrow$' and the indicative 'if . . . then' connective by '$\rightarrow$'. However, Nozick uses '$\rightarrow$' for both types of 'if . . . then' relations.

[2] This example is borrowed from D. Lewis, *Counterfactuals* (Blackwell, 1973), pp. 8–9.

considerably weaker than the relation of logical implication which is expressed by '→'. The notion of reliability explicated by the variation and adherence conditions does not *guarantee* truth; it does not imply infallibility.

Before setting forth his *reliabilist* analysis of knowledge, Nozick critically discusses the causal definition of knowledge. According to the causal analysis of knowledge, for *S* to know that *p*, the belief that *p* must be caused by the fact that *p*. To see how the causal condition helps with the Gettier problem, note that in each of Gettier's examples an appropriate causal relation is absent. For instance, what causes Smith to believe that Jones owns a Ford or Brown is in Barcelona is not the fact that makes his belief true (namely, that Brown is in Barcelona) but something else, namely the fact that causes him to falsely believe that Jones owns a Ford. So the causal condition is not satisfied. The facts that make Smith's belief true are not the facts that cause him to believe. That is why, despite having a justified true belief, Smith lacks knowledge.

A problem with the causal definition of knowledge is that it doesn't seem to work for mathematical knowledge or for knowledge of future events. It is not clear how the numbers 3 and 5 cause me to believe that they make 8, or how the future fact that the sun will rise tomorrow causes me to know this fact. Nozick's reliabilist account doesn't run into this kind of problem. I know that 3 plus 5 is 8 if this condition is met: if 3 plus 5 were not 8, then I would not believe that it was.

In the passage marked $\boxed{a}\!\mapsto$ Nozick provides a further argument against the causal analysis of knowledge. Suppose you are a brain suspended in a vat (or tank) full of liquid in a laboratory, and wired up to a computer which is feeding you your experiences and beliefs under the control of some ingenious scientist. The scientist can induce in you any belief and any experience that he chooses. Now suppose the scientist produces in you the true belief that you are a brain in a vat. In this case the causal condition is met: your belief that you are a brain in a vat is in part caused by the fact that you are a brain in a vat. Does this mean that the brain in a vat knows that it is a brain in a vat? Intuitively the answer is 'no'.

Why does Nozick claim in $\boxed{b}\!\mapsto$ that cases of causal overdetermination pose a problem for the causal analysis of knowledge but not for the variation condition?

Consider the following example of causal overdetermination: you are looking at a kangaroo and come to believe that there is a kangaroo. A hologram of a kangaroo is arranged to pop up if the kangaroo is not present, but you are looking at the real kangaroo. Since it is in fact the real kangaroo that is causing you to believe that there is a kangaroo, the causal theory of knowledge is committed to granting you knowledge. However, it is questionable whether you do really know, for the situation is such that you would believe that there is a kangaroo even if there were none. This suggests that the causal analysis of knowledge is too weak. In cases of causal overdetermination, we have causation but the variation conditional is false because another causal relation would sustain the belief if the proper cause did not.

In the passage marked $\boxed{d} \rightarrow$ Nozick discusses the *relevant alternative theory* of knowledge, which bears strong affinities to his own tracking account. According to the relevant alternative theory, a subject knows that p if he can distinguish or discriminate the truth of p from possible alternatives, i.e., states of affairs in which p is false. It is not enough, for example, to truly believe of the woman in front of you that she is Lilly to know it. If you cannot distinguish her from Milly (her twin sister), then despite the truth of your belief, and despite the justification for it (she looks exactly like Lilly), knowledge is absent. If knowledge required the discrimination of *all* possible alternatives, though, there would be little or no knowledge (must you be able to distinguish Lilly from cleverly disguised imposters?). In order to avoid this sceptical outcome, epistemologists restrict the scope of possible alternatives which a knower has to be able to discriminate among to *relevant* ones only. There are several possible views about what might be deemed 'relevant'.

> How does Nozick's variation condition help to determine which alternatives to p are relevant and thus need to be eliminated before S can know that p?

The variation condition may be viewed, Nozick claims, as fleshing out a criterion for when an alternative is relevant: the criterion is whether the alternative would have obtained were p false. (The philosopher who is largely responsible for the relevant alternative approach to knowledge is Dretske. In Chapter 6 we will discuss an essay in which Dretske employs the relevant alternative theory to refute scepticism.)

     Some claim that the variation condition is problematic because it doesn't permit us to admit that typically when S knows that p it will also be true that S knows that he doesn't falsely believe that p.[3] Even if S tracks the truth concerning the proposition p, the variation condition is not satisfied concerning the proposition 'S doesn't believe falsely that p'. S would still believe that he doesn't falsely believe that p even if it were the case that S was believing p falsely.

> Reread $\boxed{e} \rightarrow$ and the following paragraphs and explain in your own words why Nozick thinks that the variation condition, by itself, is too weak to give us an acceptable definition of knowledge.

There can be cases where the variation condition is met, and yet we would not have a case of knowledge. A case in point is the brain-in-a-vat scenario. Imagine, once again, that a brain in a vat is 'fed' the true belief that it is a brain in a vat. When applying the variation condition we get the following conditional: if (contrary to fact) S were not a brain in a vat, he wouldn't believe that he is a brain in a vat. This condition is indeed met. For if S had not been a brain in a vat, the scientist would not have been able to induce this belief in him via the electrodes to his brain, and hence he would not have

---

[3]   E. Sosa, 'Postscript to "Proper Functionalism and Virtue Epistemology" ', in J. L. Kvanvig (ed.), *Warrant in Contemporary Epistemology* (Rowman & Littlefield, 1996), p. 276.

believed that he was a brain in a vat. But although the variation condition is met, intuitively it seems wrong to say that *S* knows that he is a brain in a vat. The problem is, according to Nozick, that *S*'s belief that *p* is not 'sensitive to the truth' of *p*. It is nothing but a lucky coincidence that the brain in a vat's belief that it is a brain in a vat is true. If the scientist had stimulated a different part of *S*'s brain he would have had a different belief.

> Explain why a brain in a vat which believes that it is a brain in a vat meets the variation condition but not the adherence condition.

For the brain in a vat to meet the adherence condition, it must be the case that in close possible worlds the brain in a vat would believe that it is a brain in a vat. Yet it is possible that the scientist chooses to induce a different belief in the brain in a vat. The scientist could make the brain in a vat believe that it is a tailless kangaroo or that it is someone pretending to own a Ford. And because there are close possible worlds in which a brain in a vat does not believe that it is a brain in a vat, the adherence condition is not met.

While the variation condition demands sensitivity to the falsity of *p*, the adherence condition demands sensitivity to the truth of *p*. When combined, these conditions ensure that 'beliefs and facts vary together', that *S* believes that *p because p* is true. Nozick describes this situation as one in which the belief *tracks* the truth.

In $\boxed{f}$ ⊦→ Nozick realizes that, as it stands, the adherence condition is too demanding and rules out some obvious cases of knowledge. *S* can know that *p* without it being the case that whenever *p* is true, *S* believes that *p*. The variation condition is also too strict. Consider the following case. Suppose you acquire the true belief that Mr Havit owns a Ford and you do so because Mr Havit has shown you the registration papers. But suppose that if he did not own a Ford, you would still have believed that he did because Tom's mother (who, unbeknownst to you, is a notorious liar) would have told you that he did. Intuitively you do know that Mr Havit owns a Ford, even though the variation condition is not met.

In $\boxed{g}$ ⊦→ Nozick constructs another counterexample to the variation condition. A grandmother might know that her grandchild is well on the basis of good perceptual evidence, but she would still believe that he is well, even if he were sick, because other family members would tell her that he is well. So the adherence condition is not fulfilled even though intuitively the grandmother does know that her grandson is well, if he is well.

Nozick deals with these cases by relativizing the variation and adherence condition to a particular method. The method by which *S* acquires a belief must be held constant from the actual to the possible world. Concerning the first case, in the actual world you rely on perception to come to believe that Mr Havit owns a Ford, whereas in the counterfactual situation you rely on testimony of Tom's mother. Similarly in the second case, if the grandmother would rely only on her perception rather than on testimony of relatives, then she would not believe that her grandchild is well when in fact he is sick. Since in either of the counterexamples there is a shift in belief-formation method between the actual world and the counterfactual situation, relativizing the subjunctive conditionals to a particular method allows Nozick to rule out the counter-examples.

When evaluating Nozick's reliabilist analysis of knowledge, we have to examine two kinds of question. First, is the analysis demanding enough so as to ensure that a knower's belief be non-accidentally connected with the fact that makes it true? Second, is the analysis liberal enough so as to include all cases of knowledge?

Some critics think that the adherence condition is too strong. To understand their worry, consider a doorbell with a short circuit.[4] Whenever the doorbell rings inside the house, someone is outside pressing the bell-push. But sometimes pressing the bell-push does not result in the bell ringing. Given this scenario, whenever the bell rings, you know that someone is at the door. But when the bell does not ring you cannot be sure whether someone is at the door. Now the question is whether, by hearing the bell ring, you can come to know that there is someone at the door. Since the adherence condition is not fulfilled, Nozick seems to be committed to answer in the negative. Intuitively, however, you do know that someone is at the door when the bell rings.

Where does all this leave us? We seem to be caught in a dilemma: if we get rid of the adherence condition, we run into trouble with respect to the brain-in-a-vat scenario. And if we embrace the adherence condition we get counterintuitive results concerning the doorbell example. Some philosophers have taken this and similar problems to indicate that the search for a definition of the concept of knowledge is misguided. Maybe the concept of knowledge has vague boundaries and the only kind of conceptual analysis possible is one where the analysans is as vague as the analysandum. (The analysandum consists of the expression to be analysed and the analysans is the phrase by means of which it is analysed.)

[4]   This example was suggested to me by Fred Dretske.

2

Justification and Truth

Introduction to the Problem

When one is determining whether someone is justified in holding a certain belief or whether someone knows something, one must do so from some point of view. One can work from the point of view of the subject, or from the point of view of an external observer who knows all the relevant facts, some of which might not be available to the subject. Roughly speaking, those who adopt the subject's point of view for making these evaluations are *internalists*, and those who adopt a bird's-eye view are *externalists*. Internalists perform their epistemic evaluations from the first-person point of view, taking into account only that which is available to the subject at the given time, while externalists evaluate from the point of view of a fully informed spectator. The distinction between internalism and externalism is the most widely used distinction in contemporary epistemology, one that has been applied both to accounts of justification and to accounts of knowledge.

In its broadest formulation, *internalism about justification* is the view that all of the factors required for a belief to be justified must be cognitively accessible to the subject and thus internal to his mind. Something is internal to one's mind so long as one is aware of it or could be aware of it merely by reflecting. Beliefs are the sort of thing that are internal to the mind. Internalists therefore hold that it is the subject's other beliefs which are relevant to the question of whether he is justified in believing that *p*.

The chief motive for internalism is epistemic *deontology*, i.e., the idea that when one is justified in holding a belief, one has fulfilled one's epistemic duties and obligations in forming that belief. The epistemic duties arise from the goal of believing what is true and not believing what is false. The deontological notion of justification is normative; justification is not something that happens to a person; it is something one achieves by one's own efforts. If, therefore, justification is a function of meeting obligations, the factors that determine whether a belief is justified must be internal to the subject's mind. Deontology implies internalism.

Externalism about justification is simply the denial of internalism, holding that some of the justifying factors may be external to the subject's cognitive perspective. A belief is justified if it has the property of being truth-effective. This property of being truth-effective may, for example, consist in the belief being produced by a reliable method or process. No more than this is necessary for justification. So whether the subject takes his belief to be truth-effective doesn't add anything to the belief's epistemic status.

Internalism about knowledge maintains that, for a justified true belief to be knowledge, the subject must be able to know or at least (justifiably) believe that his belief is justified. According to *externalism about knowledge*, for a subject to have knowledge the justification condition must hold (in one form or another), but it is not necessary that he be able to know or justifiably believe that it holds. A subject can know without having any reason to think he knows.

The most prominent recent externalist theories have been versions of *reliabilism*. While externalism is only a negative thesis consisting in the denial that justification and knowledge are completely internal, reliabilism is a positive thesis maintaining that what qualifies a belief as knowledge or as justified is its reliable linkage to the facts that make the belief true. A belief amounts to knowledge if it is true and it is formed in a way that it leads to a high proportion of true beliefs. What makes this view externalist is the absence of any requirement that the knower have any sort of cognitive access to, any appreciation of, the relation of reliability that makes his true belief knowledge.

In the context of Nozick's tracking account of knowledge, we saw that the reliability of a belief-producing process is not just a property of its actual performance but also of its possible performances. If it is nothing but an odd coincidence that a belief-producing process generates truths, then we wouldn't call it a reliable process. To rule out accidentally truth-producing processes, we need to examine the performance of a belief-formation process in a possible world. For this reason philosophers use subjunctive conditionals such as 'if p were not true, then S would not believe that p' to determine whether the relation between a belief and the facts that make it true is or isn't reliable. The subjunctive conditional reveals whether the belief also would be true under other conditions. A method of belief acquisition is reliable if and only if it produces true beliefs in the actual world and would produce true beliefs in relevantly similar possible worlds.

Reliabilism comes in different flavours. The most popular version of reliabilism and the one discussed in this chapter is *process reliabilism*. Goldman's article, 'What is Justified Belief?', reprinted here, is a paradigmatic presentation of this position. Process reliabilism determines the justificatory status of a belief on the basis of the reliability of the process by which the belief is formed, revised, or maintained. A belief is justified if it is formed by a process whose operation generates a vast majority of true beliefs. Consider the belief-formation process of visual perception.

Suppose that S is endowed with 20–20 vision and a large proportion of his visually induced beliefs are true. Given process reliabilism, these beliefs are highly justified. S doesn't need to know or be aware that his visual apparatus is highly reliable; it is enough that his visual belief-formation process is in fact reliable. So S's visually induced beliefs would count as justified even if S were a young child or a higher animal such as a dog.

This is still only a rough sketch of process reliabilism. In order to make it more precise we would need to take into consideration the suitability of the belief-forming process. Just as there is no method which is useful for everything, the reliability of belief-formation processes is restricted to certain areas or subject matters. So, even though S's perceptual vision is highly reliable, it doesn't allow him to decide, say, whether the piano is playing in G major or G minor. And even when a reliable belief-forming process is used appropriately, it may fail to yield true beliefs because the circumstances are not right. For example, S's reliable faculty of vision will not generate true beliefs if S is placed in a pitch-dark room. To say that a belief-forming process is reliable is to say that it yields mostly true beliefs *in normal circumstances* (and in slightly altered circumstances).

There are three principal criticisms of process reliabilism. The first criticism (frequently referred to as the *meta-incoherence problem*) raises the issue of whether the reliability of a belief-formation process is sufficient for justification. The second criticism (called the *new evil-demon problem*[1]) concerns the necessity of reliability for justification. If all of our perceptual beliefs are unreliably produced because we live in an evil-demon world, wouldn't we still be justified in holding our perceptual beliefs true? According to the third objection (called the *generality problem*), it is not possible to define the belief-forming processes which count as reliable in a way that is neither too broad nor too narrow. Since Foley, in the article reprinted here, discusses the second and third but not the first objection, I will briefly explain it.

Is the fact that a belief has been reliably produced sufficient for its justification? The following example is intended to show that it is not.[2] Imagine someone who possesses a sixth sense of clairvoyance. Further suppose that this clairvoyant sense is remarkably reliable. Given externalist reliabilism, S might suddenly know that p, even though he has no evidence either way on whether p is true, on whether he possesses the power of clairvoyance, and on whether such a power is even possible. Internalists claim that the belief in question fails to be justified, despite the claim of reliabilism to the contrary. The belief fails to be justified because, from S's perspective, it is an accident that it is true. The upshot is supposed to be that epistemic justification requires that the acceptance of the belief in question be rational, which in turn requires that the believer be aware of a reason for thinking that the belief is true.

---

[1]   The *old* evil-demon problem is the demon hypothesis which Descartes uses to motivate external-world scepticism. See Chapter 6 on scepticism.
[2]   See L. BonJour, *The Structure of Empirical Knowledge* (Harvard University Press, 1985), ch. 3.

Every philosophical argument is open to legitimate objections. This also applies to the anti-reliabilist argument from clairvoyance. Some epistemologists deny that the clairvoyance case actually poses a threat to reliabilism.

Try to defend process reliabilism against the meta-incoherence problem.

The intuitive plausibility of the clairvoyance case hinges on the presumption that clairvoyance is *not* reliable. Yet if a clairvoyant faculty actually existed, then either it would prove itself reliable or not. If it proved itself reliable, then intuitively there would be no reason to deny clairvoyants justification and knowledge. The internalist interpretation of the thought experiment presupposes a bias against clairvoyance.

A reliabilist could also bite the bullet and insist that S the clairvoyant is in fact justified in believing that *p*. There is a difference between a person being justified in holding a belief and the belief itself being justified. S only lacks the former, but not the latter kind of justification. He has perfectly good reasons for knowing that *p*, but he lacks reasons for claiming that he knows this.

A more conciliatory response to the challenge to reliabilism posed by the clair-voyance case is to maintain that a justified belief resulting from a reliable belief-forming process must not be undermined by any other evidence the subject possesses. This thesis ensures that for a belief to become knowledge it must not be incoherent with the background information the subject possesses.

Introduction to Goldman

Alvin Ira Goldman is professor of philosophy at Rutgers University and works primarily in epistemology, philosophy of mind, and cognitive science. He is the most prominent proponent of externalist process reliabilism, which defines the justificatory status of a belief in terms of the reliability of the process that caused it.

Goldman's larger programme for reliabilist epistemology rests on two distinctions. First, he distinguishes between individual epistemology and social epistemology (or *epistemics*). Both branches identify and assess belief-formation processes in terms of their contribution to the production of true belief. While individual epistemology evaluates processes that occur with the epistemic subject, social epistemology evaluates social processes by which subjects exert influence on the beliefs of other subjects. Second, Goldman distinguishes between normative epistemology and descriptive epistemology. The latter branch aims to come up with psychologic-ally explanatory theories of how and why ordinary subjects form the beliefs that we do. Normative epistemology evaluates ordinary belief-forming processes and practices for their justification and reliability and formulates suggestions for improving them.

Goldman has developed all four branches of his reliabilist project. Apart from numerous articles, he has written five epistemological books: *Epistemology and Cognition* (1986), *Liaisons: Philosophy Meets the Cognitive and Social Sciences* (1992),

Philosophical Applications of Cognitive Science (1993), *Knowledge in a Social World* (1999), and *Pathways to Knowledge: Private and Public* (2002).

Alvin I. Goldman, 'What is Justified Belief?'

The aim of this paper is to sketch a theory of justified belief. What I have in mind is an explanatory theory, one that explains in a general way why certain beliefs are counted as justified and others as unjustified. Unlike some traditional approaches, I do not try to prescribe standards for justification that differ from, or improve upon, our ordinary standards. I merely try to explicate the ordinary standards, which are, I believe, quite different from those of many classical, e.g., 'Cartesian', accounts.

Many epistemologists have been interested in justification because of its presumed close relationship to knowledge. This relationship is intended to be preserved in the conception of justified belief presented here. In previous papers on knowledge,[1] I have denied that justification is necessary for knowing, but there I had in mind 'Cartesian' accounts of justification. On the account of justified belief suggested here, it *is* necessary for knowing, and closely related to it.

The term 'justified', I presume, is an evaluative term, a term of appraisal. Any correct definition or synonym of it would also feature evaluative terms. I assume that such definitions or synonyms might be given, but I am not interested in them. I want a set of *substantive* conditions that specify when a belief is justified. Compare the moral term 'right'. This might be defined in other ethical terms or phrases, a task appropriate to meta-ethics. The task of normative ethics, by contrast, is to state substantive conditions for the rightness of actions. Normative ethics tries to specify non-ethical conditions that determine when an action is right. A familiar example is act-utilitarianism, which says an action is right if and only if it produces, or would produce, at least as much net happiness as any alternative open to the agent. These necessary and sufficient conditions clearly involve no ethical notions. Analogously, I want a theory of justified belief to specify in non-epistemic terms when a belief is justified. This is not the only kind of theory of justifiedness one might seek, but it is one important kind of theory and the kind sought here.

In order to avoid epistemic terms in our theory, we must know which terms are epistemic. Obviously, an exhaustive list cannot be given, but here

---

[1] 'A Causal Theory of Knowing,' *The Journal of Philosophy* 64, 12 (June 22, 1967): 357–372; 'Innate Knowledge,' in S. P. Stich, ed., *Innate Ideas* (Berkeley: University of California Press, 1975); and 'Discrimination and Perceptual Knowledge,' *The Journal of Philosophy* 73, 20 (November 18, 1976), 771–791.

are some examples: 'justified', 'warranted', 'has (good) grounds', 'has reason
(to believe)', 'knows that', 'sees that', 'apprehends that', 'is probable' (in an
epistemic or inductive sense), 'shows that', 'establishes that', and 'ascertains
that'. By contrast, here are some sample non-epistemic expressions: 'believes
that', 'is true', 'causes', 'it is necessary that', 'implies', 'is deducible from',
and 'is probable' (either in the frequency sense or the propensity sense). In
general, (purely) doxastic, metaphysical, modal, semantic, or syntactic expressions are not epistemic.

There is another constraint I wish to place on a theory of justified belief, in
addition to the constraint that it be couched in non-epistemic language. Since
I seek an explanatory theory, i.e., one that clarifies the underlying source of
justificational status, it is not enough for a theory to state 'correct' necessary
and sufficient conditions. Its conditions must also be appropriately deep or
revelatory. Suppose, for example, that the following sufficient condition of
justified belief is offered: 'If S senses redly at t and S believes at t that he is sensing
redly, then S's belief at t that he is sensing redly is justified.' This is not the kind
of principle I seek; for, even if it is correct, it leaves unexplained *why* a person
who senses redly and believes that he does, believes this justifiably. Not every
state is such that if one is in it and believes one is in it, this belief is justified.
What is distinctive about the state of sensing redly, or 'phenomenal' states in
general? A theory of justified belief of the kind I seek must answer this question,
and hence it must be couched at a suitably deep, general, or abstract level.

A few introductory words about my *explicandum* are appropriate at this
juncture. It is often assumed that whenever a person has a justified belief, he
knows that it is justified and knows what the justification is. It is further
assumed that the person can state or explain what his justification is. On this
view, a justification is an argument, defense, or set of reasons that can be
given in support of a belief. Thus, one studies the nature of justified belief by
considering what a person might *say* if asked to defend, or justify, his belief. I
make none of these sorts of assumptions here. I leave it an open question
whether, when a belief *is* justified, the believer *knows* it is justified. I also
leave it an open question whether, when a belief is justified, the believer can
state or *give* a justification for it. I do not even assume that when a belief is
justified there is something 'possessed' by the believer which can be called a
'justification'. I do assume that a justified belief gets its status of being
justified from some processes or properties that make it justified. In short,
there must be some justification-conferring processes or properties. But this
does not imply that there must be an argument, or reason, or anything else,
'possessed' at the time of belief by the believer.

. . .

A theory of justified belief will be a set of principles that specify truth-
conditions for the schema ⌜S's belief in p at time t is justified,⌝ i.e., conditions
for the satisfaction of this schema in all possible cases. It will be convenient
to formulate candidate theories in a recursive or inductive format, which

would include (A) one or more base clauses, (B) a set of recursive clauses (possibly null), and (C) a closure clause. In such a format, it is permissible for the predicate 'is a justified belief' to appear in recursive clauses. But neither this predicate, nor any other epistemic predicate, may appear in (the antecedent of) any base clause.*

. . .

Correct principles of justified belief must be principles that make causal requirements, where 'cause' is construed broadly to include sustainers as well as initiators of belief (i.e., processes that determine, or help to overdetermine, a belief's continuing to be held.)*

The need for causal requirements is not restricted to base-clause principles. Recursive principles will also need a causal component. One might initially suppose that the following is a good recursive principle: 'If S justifiably believes q at t, and q entails p, and S believes p at t, then S's belief in p at t is justified'. But this principle is unacceptable. S's belief in p doesn't receive justificational status simply from the fact that p is entailed by q and S justifiably believes q. If what causes S to believe p at t is entirely different, S's belief in p may well not be justified. Nor can the situation be remedied by adding to the antecedent the condition that S justifiably believes that q entails p. Even if he believes this, and believes q as well, he might not put these beliefs together. He might believe p as a result of some other wholly extraneous, considerations. So . . . , conditions that fail to require appropriate causes of a belief don't guarantee justifiedness.

Granted that principles of justified belief must make reference to causes of belief, what kinds of causes confer justifiedness? We can gain insight into this problem by reviewing some faulty processes of belief-formation, i.e., processes whose belief-outputs would be classed as unjustified. Here are some examples: confused reasoning, wishful thinking, reliance on emotional attachment, mere hunch or guesswork, and hasty generalization. What do these faulty processes have in common? They share the feature of *unreliability*: they tend to produce *error* a large proportion of the time. By contrast, which species of belief-forming (or belief-sustaining) processes are intuitively justification-conferring? They include standard perceptual processes, remembering, good reasoning, and introspection. What these processes seem to have in common is *reliability*: the beliefs they produce are generally true. My positive proposal, then, is this. The justificational status of a belief is a function of the reliability of the process or processes that cause it, where (as a first approximation) reliability consists in the tendency of a process to produce beliefs that are true rather than false.

To test this thesis further, notice that justifiedness is not a purely categorical concept, although I treat it here as categorical in the interest of simplicity. We can and do regard certain beliefs as more justified than others. Furthermore, our intuitions of comparative justifiedness go along with our beliefs about the comparative reliability of the belief-causing processes.

Consider perceptual beliefs. Suppose Jones believes he has just seen a mountain-goat. Our assessment of the belief's justifiedness is determined by whether he caught a brief glimpse of the creature at a great distance, or whether he had a good look at the thing only 30 yards away. His belief in the latter sort of case is (*ceteris paribus*) more justified than in the former sort of case. And, if his belief is true, we are more prepared to say he *knows* in the latter case than in the former. The difference between the two cases seems to be this. Visual beliefs formed from brief and hasty scanning, or where the perceptual object is a long distance off, tend to be wrong more often than visual beliefs formed from detailed and leisurely scanning, or where the object is in reasonable proximity. In short, the visual processes in the former category are less reliable than those in the latter category. A similar point holds for memory beliefs. A belief that results from a hazy and indistinct memory impression is counted as less justified than a belief that arises from a distinct memory impression, and our inclination to classify those beliefs as '*knowledge*' varies in the same way. Again, the reason is associated with the comparative reliability of the processes. Hazy and indistinct memory impressions are generally less reliable indicators of what actually happened; so beliefs formed from such impressions are less likely to be true than beliefs formed from distinct impressions. Further, consider beliefs based on inference from observed samples. A belief about a population that is based on random sampling, or on instances that exhibit great variety, is intuitively more justified than a belief based on biased sampling, or on instances from a narrow sector of the population. Again, the degree of justifiedness seems to be a function of reliability. Inferences based on random or varied samples will tend to produce less error or inaccuracy than inferences based on non-random or non-varied samples.

Returning to a categorical concept of justifiedness, we might ask just *how* reliable a belief-forming process must be in order that its resultant beliefs be justified. A precise answer to this question should not be expected. Our conception of justification is *vague* in this respect. It does seem clear, however, that *perfect* reliability isn't required. Belief-forming processes that *sometimes* produce error still confer justification. It follows that there can be justified beliefs that are false.

d⟶   I have characterized justification-conferring processes as ones that have a 'tendency' to produce beliefs that are true rather than false. The term 'tendency' could refer either to *actual* long-run frequency, or to a 'propensity', i.e., outcomes that would occur in merely *possible* realizations of the process. Which of these is intended? Unfortunately, I think our ordinary conception of justifiedness is vague on this dimension too. For the most part, we simply assume that the 'observed' frequency of truth versus error would be approximately replicated in the actual long-run, and also in relevant counterfactual situations, i.e., ones that are highly 'realistic', or conform closely to the circumstances of the actual world. Since we ordinarily assume these frequencies to be roughly the same, we make no concerted effort to distinguish them. Since the purpose of my present theorizing is to capture our ordinary conception of justifiedness, and since our ordinary conception is vague on this matter, it is appropriate to leave the theory vague in the same respect.

e ↦ We need to say more about the notion of a belief-forming *process*. Let us mean by a 'process' a *functional operation* or procedure, i.e., something that generates a *mapping* from certain states – 'inputs' – into other states – 'outputs'. The outputs in the present case are states of believing this or that proposition at a given moment. On this interpretation, a process is a *type* as opposed to a *token*. This is fully appropriate, since it is only types that have statistical properties such as producing truth 80% of the time; and it is precisely such statistical properties that determine the reliability of a process. Of course, we also want to speak of a process as *causing* a belief, and it looks as if types are incapable of being causes. But when we say that a belief is caused by a given process, understood as a functional procedure, we may interpret this to mean that it is caused by the particular *inputs* to the process (and by the intervening events 'through which' the functional procedure carries the inputs into the output) on the occasion in question.

What are some examples of belief-forming 'processes' construed as functional operations? One example is reasoning processes, where the inputs include antecedent beliefs and entertained hypotheses. Another example is functional procedures whose inputs include desires, hopes, or emotional states of various sorts (together with antecedent beliefs). A third example is a memory process, which takes as input beliefs or experiences at an earlier time and generates as output beliefs at a later time. For example, a memory process might take as input a belief *at* t_1 that Lincoln was born in 1809 and generate as output a belief *at* t_n that Lincoln was born in 1809. A fourth example is perceptual processes. Here it isn't clear whether inputs should include states of the environment, such as the distance of the stimulus from the cognizer, or only events within or on the surface of the organism, e.g., receptor stimulations. I shall return to this point in a moment.

f ↦ A critical problem concerning our analysis is the degree of generality of the process-types in question. Input–output relations can be specified very broadly or very narrowly, and the degree of generality will partly determine the degree of reliability. A process-type might be selected so narrowly that only one instance of it ever occurs, and hence the type is either completely reliable or completely unreliable. (This assumes that reliability is a function of *actual* frequency only.) If such narrow process-types were selected, beliefs that are intuitively unjustified might be said to result from perfectly reliable processes; and beliefs that are intuitively justified might be said to result from perfectly unreliable processes.

It is clear that our ordinary thought about process-types slices them broadly, but I cannot at present give a precise explication of our intuitive principles. One plausible suggestion, though, is that the relevant processes are *content-neutral*. It might be argued, for example, that the process of *inferring p whenever the Pope asserts p* could pose problems for our theory. If the Pope is infallible, this process will be perfectly reliable; yet we would not regard the belief-outputs of this process as justified. The content-neutral restriction would avert this difficulty. If relevant processes are required to admit as input beliefs (or other states) with *any* content, the aforementioned process will not count, for its input beliefs have a restricted propositional content, viz., '*the Pope* asserts *p*'.

In addition to the problem of 'generality' or 'abstractness' there is the previously mentioned problem of the '*extent*' of belief-forming processes. Clearly, the causal ancestry of beliefs often includes events outside the organism. Are such events to be included among the 'inputs' of belief-forming processes? Or should we restrict the extent of belief-forming processes to '*cognitive*' events, i.e., events within the organism's nervous system? I shall choose the latter course, though with some hesitation. My general grounds for this decision are roughly as follows. Justifiedness seems to be a function of how a cognizer deals with his environmental input, i.e., with the goodness or badness of the operations that register and transform the stimulation that reaches him. ('Deal with', of course, does not mean *purposeful* action; nor is it restricted to *conscious* activity.) A justified belief is, roughly speaking, one that results from cognitive operations that are, generally speaking, good or successful. But '*cognitive*' operations are most plausibly construed as operations of the cognitive faculties, i.e., 'information-processing' equipment *internal* to the organism.

With these points in mind, we may now advance the following base-clause principle for justified belief.

(1)   If S's believing p at t results from a reliable cognitive belief-forming process (or set of processes), then S's belief in p at t is justified.

Since 'reliable belief-forming process' has been defined in terms of such notions as belief, truth, statistical frequency, and the like, it is not an epistemic term. Hence, (1) is an admissible base-clause.

It might seem as if (1) promises to be not only a successful base clause, but the only principle needed whatever, apart from a closure clause. In other words, it might seem as if it is a necessary as well as a sufficient condition of justifiedness that a belief be produced by reliable cognitive belief-forming processes. But this is not quite correct, given our provisional definition of 'reliability'.

Our provisional definition implies that a reasoning process is reliable only if it generally produces beliefs that are true, and similarly, that a memory process is reliable only if it generally yields beliefs that are true. But these requirements are too strong. A reasoning procedure cannot be expected to produce true belief if it is applied to false premisses. And memory cannot be expected to yield a true belief if the original belief it attempts to retain is false. What we need for reasoning and memory, then, is a notion of 'conditional reliability'. A process is conditionally reliable when a sufficient proportion of its output-beliefs are true given that its input-beliefs are true.

With this point in mind, let us distinguish belief-dependent and belief-independent cognitive processes. The former are processes some of whose inputs are belief-states.* The latter are processes none of whose inputs are belief-states. We may then replace principle (1) with the following two principles, the first a base-clause principle and the second a recursive-clause principle.

(2_A) If S's belief in p at t results ('immediately') from a belief-independent process that is (unconditionally) reliable, then S's belief in p at t is justified.

(2_B) If S's belief in p at t results ("immediately") from a belief-dependent process that is (at least) conditionally reliable, and if the beliefs (if any) on which this process operates in producing S's belief in p at t are themselves justified, then S's belief in p at t is justified.*

If we add to (2_A) and (2_B) the standard closure clause, we have a complete theory of justified belief. The theory says, in effect, that a belief is justified if and only it is 'well-formed', i.e., it has an ancestry of reliable and/or conditionally reliable cognitive operations. (Since a dated belief may be over-determined, it may have a number of distinct ancestral trees. These need not all be full of reliable or conditionally reliable processes. But at least one ancestral tree must have reliable or conditionally reliable processes throughout.)

The theory of justified belief proposed here, then, is an Historical or Genetic theory. It contrasts with the dominant approach to justified belief, an approach that generates what we may call (borrowing a phrase from Robert Nozick) 'Current Time-Slice' theories. A Current Time-Slice theory makes the justificational status of a belief wholly a function of what is true of the cognizer at the time of belief. An Historical theory makes the justificational status of a belief depend on its prior history. Since my Historical theory emphasizes the reliability of the belief-generating processes, it may be called 'Historical Reliabilism.'

. . .

The theory articulated by (2_A) and (2_B) might be viewed as a kind of 'Foundationalism,' because of its recursive structure. I have no objection to this label, as long as one keeps in mind how different this 'diachronic' form of Foundationalism is from Cartesian, or other 'synchronic' varieties of, Foundationalism.

Current Time-Slice theories characteristically assume that the justificational status of a belief is something which the cognizer is able to know or determine at the time of belief. This is made explicit, for example, by Chisholm.[2] The Historical theory I endorse makes no such assumption. There are many facts about a cognizer to which he lacks 'privileged access', and I regard the justificational status of his beliefs as one of those things. This is not to say that a cognizer is necessarily ignorant, at any given moment, of the justificational status of his current beliefs. It is only to deny that he necessarily has, or can get, knowledge or true belief about this status. Just as a person can know without knowing that he knows, so he can have justified belief without knowing that it is justified (or believing justifiably that it is justified.)

A characteristic case in which a belief is justified though the cognizer doesn't know that it's justified is where the original evidence for the belief has long since been forgotten. If the original evidence was compelling, the cognizer's original belief may have been justified; and this justificational status may have been preserved through memory. But since the cognizer no longer remembers how or why he came to believe, he may not know that the belief is justified. If asked now to justify his belief, he may be at a loss. Still, the belief *is* justified, though the cognizer can't demonstrate or establish this.

. . .

[h]→ Let us return, however, to the standard format of conceptual analysis, and let us consider a new objection that will require some revisions in the theory advanced until now. According to our theory, a belief is justified in case it is caused by a process that is in fact reliable, or by one we generally believe to be reliable. But suppose that although one of S's beliefs satisfies this condition, S has no reason to believe that it does. Worse yet, suppose S has reason to believe that his belief is caused by an *un*reliable process (although *in fact* its causal ancestry is fully reliable). Wouldn't we deny in such circumstances that S's belief is justified? This seems to show that our analysis, as presently formulated, is mistaken.

Suppose that Jones is told on fully reliable authority that a certain class of his memory beliefs are almost all mistaken. His parents fabricate a wholly false story that Jones suffered from amnesia when he was seven but later developed *pseudo*-memories of that period. Though Jones listens to what his parents say and has excellent reason to trust them, he persists in believing the ostensible memories from his seven-year-old past. Are these memory beliefs justified? Intuitively, they are not justified. But since these beliefs result from genuine memory and original perceptions, which are adequately reliable processes, our theory says that these beliefs are justified.

---

[2]   Cf. R. M. Chisholm, *Theory of Knowledge*, Second Edition (Prentice-Hall, 1977), pp. 17, 114–116.

Can the theory be revised to meet this difficulty? One natural suggestion is that the actual reliability of a belief's ancestry is not enough for justified-ness; in addition, the cognizer must be *justified in believing* that the ancestry of his belief is reliable. Thus one might think of replacing (2_A), for example, with (3). (For simplicity, I neglect some of the details of the earlier analysis.)

(3)   If S's belief in p at t is caused by a reliable cognitive process, and S justifiably believes at t that his p-belief is so caused, then S's belief in p at t is justified.

It is evident, however, that (3) will not do as a base clause, for it contains the epistemic term 'justifiably' in its antecedent.

A slightly weaker revision, without this problematic feature, might next be suggested, viz.,

(4)   If S's belief in p at t is caused by a reliable cognitive process, and S believes at t that his p-belief is so caused, then S's belief in p at t is justified.

But this won't do the job. Suppose that Jones believes that his memory beliefs are reliably caused despite all the (trustworthy) contrary testimony of his parents. Principle (4) would be satisfied, yet we wouldn't say that these beliefs are justified.

Next, we might try (5), which is stronger than (4) and, unlike (3), formally admissible as a base clause.

(5)   If S's belief in p at t is caused by a reliable cognitive process, and S believes at t that his p-belief is so caused, and this meta-belief is caused by a reliable cognitive process, than S's belief in p at t is justified.

A first objection to (5) is that it wrongly precludes unreflective creatures – creatures like animals or young children, who have no beliefs about the genesis of their beliefs – from having justified beliefs. If one shares my view that justified belief is, at least roughly, *well-formed* belief, surely animals and young children can have justified beliefs.

A second problem with (5) concerns its underlying rationale. Since (5) is proposed as a substitute for (2_A), it is implied that the reliability of a belief's own cognitive ancestry does not make it justified. But, the suggestion seems to be, the reliability of a *meta-belief*'s ancestry confers justifiedness on the first-order belief. Why should that be so? Perhaps one is attracted by the idea of a 'trickle-down' effect: if an n+1-level belief is justified, its justification trickles down to an n-level belief. But even if the trickle-down theory is

correct, it doesn't help here. There is no assurance from the satisfaction of
(5)'s antecedent that the meta-belief itself is *justified*.

To obtain a better revision of our theory, let us re-examine the Jones case.
Jones has strong evidence against certain propositions concerning his past.
He doesn't *use* this evidence, but if he *were* to use it properly, he would stop
believing these propositions. Now the proper use of evidence would be an
instance of a (conditionally) reliable process. So what we can say about Jones
is that he *fails* to use a certain (conditionally) reliable process that he could
and should have used. Admittedly, had he used this process, he would have
'worsened' his doxastic states: he would have replaced some true beliefs with
suspension of judgment. Still, he couldn't have known this in the case in
question. So, he failed to do something which, epistemically, he should have
done. This diagnosis suggests a fundamental change in our theory. The
justificational status of a belief is not only a function of the cognitive
processes *actually* employed in producing it; it is also a function of processes
that could and should be employed.

With these points in mind, we may tentatively propose the following
revision of our theory, where we again focus on a base-clause principle but
omit certain details in the interest of clarity.

(6)   If S's belief in p at t results from a reliable cognitive process, and
there is no reliable or conditionally reliable process available to S
which, had it been used by S in addition to the process actually
used, would have resulted in S's not believing p at t, then S's
belief in p at t is justified.

There are several problems with this proposal. First, there is a technical
problem. One cannot use an additional belief-forming (or doxastic-state-
forming) process *as well as* the original process if the additional one would
result in a different doxastic state. One wouldn't be using the original
process at all. So we need a slightly different formulation of the relevant
counterfactual. Since the basic idea is reasonably clear, however, I won't try
to improve on the formulation here. A second problem concerns the notion
of '*available*' belief-forming (or doxastic-state-forming) processes. What is it
for a process to be 'available' to a cognizer? Were scientific procedures
'available' to people who lived in pre-scientific ages? Furthermore, it seems
implausible to say that all 'available' processes ought to be used, at least if we
include such processes as gathering *new* evidence. Surely a belief can sometimes be justified even if additional evidence-gathering would yield a different doxastic attitude. What I think we should have in mind here are such
additional processes as calling previously acquired evidence to mind, assessing the implications of that evidence, etc. This is admittedly somewhat
vague, but here again our ordinary notion of justifiedness is vague, so it is
appropriate for our analysans to display the same sort of vagueness.

Commentary on Goldman

In the paragraph marked $\boxed{a}\mapsto$ Goldman expresses his commitment to naturalism and in paragraph $\boxed{b}\mapsto$ to externalism. Goldman's theory of justification is naturalistic in that it is not the logical or probabilistic relation between the evidence and the target belief that fixes the justificatory status of the latter. Rather, justification is said to consist in the psychological processes causally responsible for a belief. A belief qualifies as justified if it is the product of a belief-formation process that has a high truth ratio. Even a belief in a tautology (e.g., A = A) is not justified if it is formed by blind trust in an unreliable informant or by confused reasoning. Goldman's theory of justification is externalist because he endorses the thesis that the factors responsible for epistemic justification may be external to the subject's cognitive perspective.

In paragraph $\boxed{c}\mapsto$ Goldman states the basic idea of process reliabilism: S's belief in p is justified if and only if S's believing p results from a reliable cognitive belief-forming process (or set of processes). To call a belief-formation process reliable means that such processes have a tendency to produce true beliefs rather than false ones. Thus, reliably formed beliefs are justified because they are likely to be true. As examples of reliable processes Goldman mentions perception, remembering, good reasoning, and introspection. Examples of unreliable processes are confused reasoning, wishful thinking, reliance on emotional attachment, mere hunch or guesswork, and hasty generalization.

In paragraphs $\boxed{d}\mapsto$ and $\boxed{e}\mapsto$ Goldman explicates two of the key concepts of process reliabilism: 'process' and 'probability'.

> Explain the notion of probability employed in Goldman's analysis of justification.

Goldman contrasts two interpretations of probability, both of which define probability in terms of the relative frequency of the occurrence of an attribute in a sequence over time. But while one interpretation refers only to the *actual* (or observed) long-run frequency, the other interpretation also refers to the *possible* long-run frequency. On the latter view, to say, for instance, that the probability of getting heads with a particular coin is one-half means that, in the potentially infinite sequence of tosses of the coin, the relative frequency with which heads occurs converges to the value one-half. Goldman intends to capture both notions of probability. For a belief-formation process to be reliable it must produce mostly true beliefs not only in the actual world but also in relevant (or 'close') counterfactual situations.

In paragraph $\boxed{e}\mapsto$ Goldman explains that the notion of a belief-forming *process* is a functional notion. Functional notions are defined in terms of input–output relations. Take, for example, the concept of a key. Keys are defined by what they allow us to do, namely to lock and unlock doors, rather than by the material they are made of or by their shape and size. Analogously, belief-formation processes are not defined in terms of, say, activity patterns in certain parts of the nervous system but rather in terms of their functional roles.

Belief-forming processes are to be understood as types rather than tokens. Tokens are concrete particulars while types are abstract universals. Fido, for example, is a token of the type dachshund. Since antiquity, philosophers have debated over whether types or universals exist or whether talk about types is nothing but short-hand for talk about tokens.

In the paragraph marked $\boxed{f} \mapsto$ Goldman explains that types of belief-forming processes can be specified more or less broadly. For example, when I look out my office window and see a dog, the cognitive process that produces the belief 'There is a dog over there' can be described as: (i) perception; (ii) vision during daylight; (iii) vision during daylight through a pair of correcting glasses; (iv) visual perception of a moving object during daylight and through a pair of correcting lenses at a distance of 20 metres, 45 minutes after the consumption of a glass of chilled 1999 Franconian Riesling wine, etc. Whether or not a type of belief-forming process is reliable depends in part on how broadly or narrowly it is individuated. If types of belief-formation processes are identified too narrowly, they only have very few tokens. If this one token leads to a true belief, the process type is completely reliable. If this one token leads to a false belief, the process is completely unreliable. On the other hand, if belief-formation processes are identified too broadly, reliabilism will be unable to distinguish between justified and unjustified beliefs. This is the so-called *generality problem*, which will be discussed in connection with Foley's article.

> Why does Goldman introduce in paragraph $\boxed{g} \mapsto$ the distinction between belief-dependent processes such as reasoning and memory that take beliefs as inputs, and belief-independent processes such as perception that do not?

We saw that a belief-forming process type is reliable if it tends to produce true beliefs. In the case of belief-forming processes which take beliefs as inputs, the output belief may be false not because the process is unreliable but because the input belief is false. There are four distinct ways in which beliefs resulting from a belief-dependent process such as memory may be false. To drive this point home, consider the ubiquitous S claiming to remember having seen a dog. First, S may incorrectly remember having thought he saw a dog; but what he really thought he saw, at that time, was a cat, and there was in fact a cat. In this case the fault lies with the memory and not the past perception. Second, S may correctly remember having thought he saw a dog; but what he saw was, say, a cat. In this case it is the past perception and not the memory which is to blame. Third, both kinds of mistakes can be combined: suppose S incorrectly remembers having seen a dog; but what he thought he saw, at that time, was a cat, and the perception was false for there was no cat but, say, a squirrel. Fourth, the perceptual mistake and the memory mistake may balance each other out. Suppose S claims to remember having seen a dog; but what he thought he saw, at that time, was a cat, and the perception was false for it was in fact a dog he saw. In this case, though the memory claim is veridical, it doesn't qualify as a justified belief, for it is nothing but a lucky coincidence that the memory claim is true.

Belief-independent processes are reliable if they bring about mostly true beliefs. Belief-dependent processes are conditionally reliable if and only if they tend to produce true beliefs when the input beliefs are true. Goldman calls this theory of epistemic justification *historical reliabilism* because 'it makes the justificational status of a belief depend on its prior history'. Historical reliabilism is a version of externalism since the agent need not have access to the facts that determine whether a belief is justified – the reliability of the source of the belief.

In paragraph $\boxed{h}\!\!\rightarrow$ Goldman goes on to recognize that, as it stands, historical reliabilism is vulnerable to objections from what Pollock and others call *defeasibility*. Such objections involve beliefs that are reliably produced but fail to be justified because the agent has misleading evidence for thinking that they are caused by an unreliable process. A case in point is the following variation of the clairvoyance example discussed in the introduction to this chapter. Suppose that S enjoys the power of perfectly reliable clairvoyance with respect to the truth of p. At any given moment, he can tell whether p is currently true. Suppose that S has convincing but misleading evidence to the effect that he does not possess the power and that such a power is impossible. When S comes to believe that p, on the basis of his clairvoyance, intuitively he is not justified in believing p. The reason is that the misleading evidence defeats the reliability of S's clairvoyance as a source of justification. According to Goldman's initial version of historical reliabilism, however, S's belief that p would be justified because it is reliably produced.

Goldman takes examples of this kind to indicate that actual reliability of belief production is not sufficient for justification. After considering three unsuccessful proposals to amend his initial statement of reliabilist justification, Goldman adds in paragraph $\boxed{j}\!\!\rightarrow$ the following clause: a belief that p is justified if and only if (i) it is reliably formed and (ii) there is no other reliable process available to S that, had it been used by S in addition to the process actually used, would have resulted in S's not forming the belief that p.

To see how this additional condition works, reconsider the above variation of the clairvoyance example. Because S ignores the evidence that undermines his clairvoyant belief that p, we may say that he uses the evidence available to him improperly. '[The] proper use of evidence would be an instance of a (conditionally) reliable process' (passage $\boxed{i}\!\!\rightarrow$). Even though this process was available to S, he does not make use of it. And since, if he used this process, he would not believe that p, condition (ii) is not satisfied and we can conclude that S's belief that p is not justified.

How does (what I have called) condition (ii) fit together with the externalist thesis expressed in paragraph $\boxed{b}\!\!\rightarrow$?

Condition (ii) – commonly called a *negative coherence condition* – is a concession to internalism. Goldman is an externalist in maintaining that a belief can be justified without the believer knowing or thinking that it is justified; yet Goldman agrees with internalists that the bearer of a justified belief may not have reasons for thinking that the belief is not justified. A justified belief resulting from a reliable belief-formation process must not be undermined by any other evidence that the subject possesses.

It is important to see that condition (ii) only applies in cases where the bearer of a reliably formed belief has reasons to think that the belief is not reliably formed. Condition (ii) does not get a foothold if the bearer of a reliably formed belief has no belief or opinion at all about the cognitive process involved or its reliability. If, instead of disregarding defeating evidence, S the clairvoyant possesses no evidence or reasons of any kind for or against the general possibility of the power of clairvoyance or for or against the thesis that he possesses it, then Goldman's historical reliabilism is committed to regard S's belief that p as being justified. (In Chapter 5 the negative coherence condition is set apart against the positive coherence condition.)

Introduction to Foley

Richard Foley is professor of philosophy at New York University and works primarily in epistemology. His first book, *The Theory of Epistemic Rationality* (1987), attempts to answer the question, 'Under what conditions is it rational for someone to believe a claim?' He proposes a subjectivist (or internalist) and foundationalist account of epistemic rationality according to which the persuasiveness of a proposition in relation to a person's perspective is what makes the proposition basic. His second book, *Working Without a Net* (1993), also defends a kind of subjectivism. Foley argues that having rational opinions is a matter of meeting our own internal standards rather than standards that are somehow imposed upon us from the outside. It is a matter of making ourselves invulnerable to intellectual self-criticism. In his most recent book, *Intellectual Trust in Oneself and Others* (2001), Foley expands the subjectivist position. The leitmotif of the book is the question to what degree we should rely on our own resources and methods to form judgements and to what extent we should defer to various authorities. Foley argues that it can be reasonable to have intellectual trust in oneself although it isn't possible to defend the reliability of one's resources, methods, and judgements without begging the question.

Richard Foley, 'What's Wrong with Reliabilism?'

I

An increasing number of epistemologists claim that having beliefs which are reliable is a prerequisite of having epistemically rational beliefs. Alvin Goldman, for instance, defends a view he calls "historical reliabilism." According to Goldman, a person S rationally believes a proposition p only if his belief is caused by a reliable cognitive process. Goldman adds that a proposition p is epistemically rational for S, whether or not it is believed by him, only if there is available to S a reliable cognitive process which if used would result in S's believing p.[1] Likewise, Marshall Swain, Ernest Sosa, and William Alston all claim that reliability is a prerequisite of epistemic rationality. Swain claims that S rationally believes p only if he has reasons for p which are reliable indicators that p is true.[2] Sosa says S rationally believes p only if the belief is the product of an intellectual virtue, where intellectual virtues are stable dispositions to acquire truths.[3] And, Alston says that S rationally believes p only if the belief is acquired or held in such a way that beliefs held in that way are reliable, i.e., mostly true.[4]

b→   Each of these philosophers is suggesting that there is some sort of logical, or conceptual, tie between epistemic rationality and truth. The exact nature of this tie depends on what it means for a cognitive process, or a reason, or an intellectual virtue, to be reliable. But, at least for the moment, let us set aside this question. I will return to it shortly. In particular, let us simply assume that each of the above positions suggests (even if each doesn't strictly imply) the thesis that if one gathered into a set all the propositions it is epistemically rational for a person S to believe it would be impossible for the set to contain more falsehoods than truths. Or short of this, let us assume that each suggests the thesis that if one gathered into a set all the propositions which *both are epistemically rational for S and are believed by him*, it would be impossible for the set to contain more falsehoods than truths.

Since this amounts to saying that what a person rationally believes, or what it is rational for him to believe, must be a reliable indicator of what is true, any position which implies such a thesis can be regarded as a version of reliabilism.

This is somewhat broader than the usual use of the term "reliabilism". With respect to accounts of rational belief (I will discuss reliabilist accounts of knowledge later), the term often is reserved for accounts which require that a belief be *caused*, or *causally sustained*, by a reliable cognitive process. But, for purposes here I want to distinguish between the causal component of such accounts and the reliability component. The causal component requires a belief to have an appropriate causal ancestry in

[1]   Alvin Goldman, "What Is Justified Belief?" in *Justification and Knowledge*, ed. G. Pappas (Dordrecht: D. Reidel, 1979), pp. 1–23.

[2]   Marshall Swain, "Justification and the Basis of Belief," in *Justification and Knowledge*, ed. Pappas, pp. 25–49.

[3]   Ernest Sosa, "The Raft and the Pyramid," in *Midwest Studies in Philosophy*, vol. V, eds. French, Uehling, and Wettstein (Minneapolis: University of Minnesota Press, 1980), pp. 3–25.

[4]   William Alston, "Self-Warrant: A Neglected Form of Privileged Access," *American Philosophical Quarterly*, 13 (1976), pp. 257–72, especially p. 268.

order to be rational. The reliability component requires a belief to have an appropriate relation to truth in order to be rational; in particular, on the present interpretation of reliability, it requires that more of a person's rational beliefs be true than false.

The advantage of isolating these components is that it makes obvious the possibility of endorsing a reliability requirement for rationality without endorsing a causal requirement, and vice-versa. It is possible, for example, to endorse noncausal versions of reliabilism. Consider a foundationalist position which implies that S rationally believes p only if either his belief p is incorrigible for him or propositions which are incorrigibly believed by him support p in a way which guarantees that most propositions so supported are true. A position of this sort is plausibly regarded as a reliabilist position, since it implies that a person's rational beliefs must be mostly true. It implies, in other words, that the set of such beliefs is a reliable indicator of what is true. Yet, it is not a causal position. It does not insist that S's belief p be caused or causally sustained in an appropriate way in order to be rational.[5]

So, in my broad sense of "reliabilism" both causal and noncausal accounts of rational belief can be versions of reliabilism. Indeed in my broad sense, Hume and Descartes might be plausibly interpreted as reliabilists.

My use of "reliabilism" is weak in one other way. It requires only that there be a very loose connection between epistemic rationality and truth. In order for an account to be a version of reliabilism, it need not guarantee that a huge percentage of the propositions a person S rationally believes are true. It need only guarantee that one more such proposition is true than is false.

Unfortunately, even when reliabilism is understood in this very weak way, it is too strong; it is possible for more propositions which S rationally believes to be false than true. Consider how this might be so. Consider a world in which S believes, seems to remember, experiences, etc., just what he in this world believes, seems to remember, experiences, etc., but in which his beliefs are often false. Suppose further that in this other world the confidence with which he believes, and the clarity with which he seems to remember, and the intensity with which he experiences is identical with the actual world. Suppose even that what he would believe on reflection (about, e.g., what arguments are likely to be truth preserving) is identical with what he would believe on reflection in this world. So, if S somehow were to be switched instantaneously from his actual situation to the corresponding situation in this other world, he would not distinguish any difference, regardless of how hard he tried. To use the familiar example, suppose that a demon insures that this is the case. Call such a demon world "w" and then consider this question: Could some of the propositions which a person S

[5]   I discuss causal, reliabilist accounts of knowledge in Section II. The arguments there also will apply to causal, reliabilist accounts of rational belief. See especially footnote 7.

believes in *w* be epistemically rational for him? For example, could some of the propositions which *S* perceptually believes be epistemically rational? The answer is "yes". If we are willing to grant that in our world some of the propositions *S* perceptually believes are epistemically rational, then these same propositions would be epistemically rational for *S* in *w* as well. After all, world *w* by hypothesis is one which from *S's* viewpoint is indistinguishable from this world. So, if given *S's* situation in this world his perceptual belief *p* is rational, his belief *p* would be rational in *w* as well.

In one sense this is not a particularly surprising result, but in another sense it can seem somewhat surprising. Notice that the possibility of there being such a world *w* follows from the fact that our being in the epistemic situation we are is compatible with our world being *w*. This in no way shows that it is not epistemically rational for us to believe what we do. But, and this is what might seem somewhat surprising, if the mere possibility of our world being a demon world is not sufficient to defeat the epistemic rationality of our believing what we do, then neither should the actuality. Even if, contrary to what we believe, our world is world *w*, it still can be epistemically rational for us to believe many of the propositions we do, since the epistemic situation in world *w* is indistinguishable from the epistemic situation in a world which has the characteristics we take our world to have.

The point here is a simple one. In effect, I am asking you: aren't some of the propositions you believe epistemically rational for you to believe? And wouldn't whatever it is that make those propositions epistemically rational for you also be present in a world where these propositions are regularly false, but where a demon hid this from you by making the world from your viewpoint indistinguishable from this world (so that what you believed, and what you would believe on reflection, and what you seemed to remember, and what you experienced were identical to this world)?

I think that the answer to each of these questions is "yes" and I think you do too. But, a "yes" answer to these questions suggests that the real lesson illustrated by the possibility of demon worlds is not a skeptical lesson as is sometimes thought, but rather an anti-reliabilist lesson. It suggests, in other words, that the demon by his deceits may cause us to have false beliefs, but he does not thereby automatically cause us to be irrational. And so, the possibility of such demon worlds illustrates that it is possible for more of what we rationally believe to be false than to be true, and it also illustrates that it is possible for more of what it is epistemically rational for us to believe (regardless of what we do in fact believe) to be false than to be true. Correspondingly, it illustrates that any version of reliabilism which implies that these are not genuine possibilities ought to be rejected.

Indeed, in one sense the claim that it is possible for more of what we rationally believe to be false than to be true is not even very controversial. It is but an extension of the claim that it is possible to rationally believe a falsehood. For if we admit that there are situations in which the conditions making a proposition epistemically rational are present but the conditions making it true are not, we will be hard-pressed to avoid the conclusion that it is possible for this to happen frequently. To put the matter metaphorically, if we allow the possibility of a crack developing between epistemic rationality and truth, such that some of what is epistemically rational can be false, we will be hard-pressed to avoid at least the possibility of a chasm developing, such that more of what is epistemically rational can be false than true. This is the lesson of demon examples, brain-in-the-vat examples, etc.

. . .

[c]→ The problem with all these versions of reliabilism is essentially the same. They all assume that in the demon worlds described it would be impossible for us to have rational beliefs. The assumption, in other words, is that the deceiving activities of the demon *no matter how cleverly* they are carried out – even if we have no indication that we are (or have been, or will be, or would be) so deceived – preclude even the *possibility* of our beliefs being epistemically rational. So, the mere fact that we do have, or have had, or will have, or would have false beliefs, implies that we cannot be epistemically rational.

But, to make such an assumption is counterintuitive. In everyday situations we do not regard deception as precluding rationality. Likewise, we do not regard the fact that we have been deceived, or will be deceived, or would be deceived, as precluding rationality. Suppose I play an elaborate practical joke on you in order to get you to believe that I have left town. I tell you I am leaving town, I leave my car with you, I have someone send you a postcard signed by me, etc. My deceits may get you to believe the false proposition that I have left town, but from this it does not follow that the proposition is not rational for you to believe. And one way to emphasize this point is to imagine (as I have done with the demon cases) a situation in which you have not been deceived and which in addition from your viewpoint is indistinguishable from the situation in which you have been deceived. In other words, imagine an ordinary situation. If in this ordinary situation it is possible for you to rationally believe that I have left town, it also is possible for you to rationally believe this in the situation in which I have deceived you. Everyone who allows rational beliefs to be false should agree to this. But then, it is natural to wonder why, if relatively modest deceits of this sort need not preclude the possibility of you having rational beliefs, more elaborate deceits of the sort a demon engages in should preclude you from having rational beliefs?

[d]→ The intuitive answer is that they should not. The demon by his deceits may get you to have mostly false beliefs but this need not indicate that these beliefs also are irrational. This answer, moreover, illustrates something about the way we think of rationality. Namely, we think that what it is rational for a person to believe is a function of what it is appropriate for him to believe given his perspective. More exactly, it is a function of what it is

appropriate for him to believe given his perspective *and* insofar as his goal is to believe truths and not to believe falsehoods.[6]

Precisely what makes reliabilist accounts of rational belief unacceptable is that they underemphasize this perspectival element. They imply that it is impossible for our beliefs to be rational if they are not in an appropriate sense reliable indicators of truths. And they imply that this is so regardless of what our perspective might be – even if, for example, it is indistinguishable from current perspective.

. . .

Reliability is not in any plausible sense a necessary condition of epistemic rationality. In order for S's belief p to be rational, it neither is necessary for most rational beliefs of all people everywhere to be true, nor for most of S's current rational beliefs to be true, nor for most of S's rational beliefs over his lifetime to be true, nor for most of the rational beliefs S would have in close counterfactual situations to be true.

II

I would guess that for many philosophers (but certainly not all) the remarks I have been making about the relationship between rationality and reliability will not seem surprising. The remarks might even strike them as obvious albeit unimportant. For, they would claim that the epistemic significance of reliability has to do not with beliefs which are merely rational but rather with beliefs which are instances of knowledge. So, they would argue that even if reliability is not a prerequisite of rationality, it is a prerequisite of knowledge. Thus, Goldman, Sosa, Alston, Swain, and others with reliabilist sympathies might be willing to agree with me that there is a sense of rationality for which reliability is not a prerequisite. But, they would go on to insist either that rationality is not a prerequisite of knowledge (i.e., it is possible to know p without rationally believing it) or that the kind of rational belief needed for knowledge is more restrictive than the kind with which I have been concerned. Both of these options leave room for the claim that reliability is a prerequisite of knowledge even if it is not a prerequisite of mere rational belief (or of a certain kind of rational belief).

Even so, reliabilist theses about knowledge in the end fare no better than reliabilist theses about rational belief. More exactly, significant, or nontrivial, reliabilist theses about knowledge fare no better. A reliabilist thesis is not significant if it is a thesis which almost any kind of account of knowledge would imply. Thus, suppose it is claimed that reliability is a

---

[6] This, of course, leaves open the question of what exactly makes it appropriate for a person S to believe a proposition given his perspective and given his goal of believing truths and not believing falsehoods.

prerequisite of knowledge in the following sense: Most beliefs which are instances of knowledge have to be true. This thesis about knowledge is true but insignificant; any account of knowledge which requires a belief to be true if it is to be an instance of knowledge implies it.

The problem, then, is to find a *true and significant* reliabilist account of knowledge. I claim it cannot be done; there is no such reliabilist account of knowledge.

To see this, consider how one might try to formulate a reliabilist account of knowledge. . . .

Suppose, then, that a reliable cognitive process is one which is relativized to persons. Suppose it is understood to be one which *has produced* mostly true beliefs for person S. But then, it is possible for S to *know* that a demon has been deceiving him perceptually but no longer is. And if S does know this, he might very well now know *p* perceptually even though he also knows that the perceptual process which causes him to believe *p* is unreliable. The fact that a demon has deceived him perceptually need not make it impossible for him now to have perceptual knowledge. Or, suppose a reliable cognitive process is thought to be one which will in the long-run produce mostly true beliefs for S. But, it is possible for S to *know* that although he is not now under the control of a deceiving demon, he shortly will be. And if he does know this, he might now perceptually know *p* even though he also knows that the process which causes him to believe *p* is unreliable in this sense. For, the fact that a demon will deceive him perceptually need not make it impossible for him now to have perceptual knowledge. Or, suppose a reliable cognitive process is one which would produce mostly true beliefs in appropriately close counterfactual situations. But then, S might *know* that there is an anti-reliabilist demon who is not now deceiving him but is (and was) prepared to do so had the situation been even a little different. And, knowing that there is such a demon who is poised to act but who does not is compatible with now knowing *p*. The fact that a demon is prepared to deceive him perceptually does not make it impossible for him to have perceptual knowledge.

The same general lesson even applies to a demon who is now deceiving S perceptually. But there is a wrinkle here, since it may be impossible for S to believe (and hence to know) that due to the actions of a deceiving demon more of his current perceptual beliefs are false than are true. This may be impossible because it may be impossible for S to believe a proposition *p* if he also genuinely believes that *p* is more likely to be false than true. But even if this is impossible, it nonetheless is possible for S to have adequate evidence for the claim that more of his current perceptual beliefs are false than are true (even if he does not believe it to be true) and yet for him to have perceptual knowledge *p*. Suppose, for example, he has adequate evidence for the truth that a demon is deceiving him with respect to most objects in his visual field but not those directly in front of him and within two feet of him.

If proposition p concerns an object of this latter sort, S might very well know p even though he may have adequate reasons for believing the true proposition that the visual process which causes him to believe p is unreliable – i.e., even though more of the S's current visual beliefs are false than true. The fact that a demon is deceiving him perceptually about objects not directly in front of him or not within two feet of him does not make it impossible for him to have perceptual knowledge about objects which are in front of him and within two feet of him.[7]

It may be tempting in this last case to insist that S's belief p is the product of a reliable cognitive process – namely, *a process as it operates on objects within two feet of him and directly in front of him*. In other words, it may be tempting to insist that this last case only illustrates that we must allow the notion of a reliable cognitive process to be narrowly specified. In the case here, for example, once we specify the process which causes S to believe p as a visual process as operating on objects directly in front of S and within two feet of him, it by hypothesis is true that his belief p is caused by a reliable process. Indeed, in the case here, perhaps the only beliefs produced by this narrowly specified process are the belief that p and beliefs in other propositions implied by p. And of course, by hypothesis all these propositions are true.

However, any attempt to save a reliabilist account of knowledge by this kind of maneuver is an attempt to save it by destroying it. For any reliabilist account which results from such a rescue maneuver will be an account which is insignificant. Indeed, it will be as insignificant as a reliabilist account which insists that most beliefs which are instances of knowledge must be true, and it will be insignificant for the same reason. Namely, *any* proponent of *any* kind of account of knowledge can endorse a reliabilism of this sort. Or, at least anyone who thinks knowledge requires true belief can endorse a reliabilism of this sort. After all, on any occasion where a person S has a true belief p, there will be *some* narrowly specified cognitive process which causes S to believe p and which in addition is reliable, if only because it is so narrowly specified that it produces only belief p and beliefs in propositions implied by p. So, insofar as a reliabilist resorts to such maneuvers to defend his account, his account will lose whatever distinctive character it was intended to have.

Reliabilist accounts of knowledge, then, face a dilemma. One horn of the dilemma is to allow the notion of a reliable cognitive process to be specified so narrowly that reliabilism is no longer an interesting thesis. It becomes true but trivial, since any true belief can be construed as being the product of

---

[7]   Since in all of the preceding examples S can be assumed to rationally believe p (as well as to know p), the examples also can be used to illustrate the inadequacy of various theses about rational belief. For example, they illustrate that S's believing or having adequate reason to believe that his belief p is caused by a reliable process is not a prerequisite of S's rationally believing p. Likewise, they illustrate that S's belief actually having been caused by a reliable process is not a prerequisite of S's rationally believing p.

a reliable cognitive process. The other horn is not to allow the notion of a reliable cognitive process to be so narrowly specified, in which case it becomes susceptible to demon counterexamples and the like. In other words, it becomes an interesting but false thesis.

III

I have not discussed every possible reliabilist thesis concerning rational belief and knowledge. But, I have discussed a number of representative theses, and neither they nor any other reliabilist thesis I can think of can avoid the difficulties raised for them by demon situations and the like. And so, I conclude that reliability is neither a necessary condition of rational belief (i.e., it is not necessary for more of a person's rational beliefs to be true than false) nor a necessary condition of knowledge (i.e., a belief in order to be an instance of knowledge need not be the product of a reliable cognitive process – provided "reliable" is used in a nontrivial way).

. . .

[f]→   All this, however, is not to say that considerations of reliability are altogether unimportant epistemically. As I suggested earlier, epistemic rationality is best understood to be a function of what it is appropriate for a person to believe given his perspective and given the goal of his having true beliefs and not having false beliefs. So, the goal in terms of which epistemic rationality can be understood is the goal of having reliable beliefs – i.e., mostly true beliefs. But, to say that reliability is the goal in terms of which epistemic rationality is to be understood is not to say that achieving that goal is a prerequisite of being epistemically rational. If a person, given his situation, believes what it is appropriate for him to believe with respect to the goal of his having true beliefs and not having false beliefs, then his beliefs can be epistemically rational even if they are mostly false. This is the lesson of demon examples and the like.

Likewise, nothing I have said implies that reliability is not an important consideration in understanding knowledge. Indeed, I think that reliability can be a crucial part of a set of conditions *sufficient* for knowledge. Recall D. H. Lawrence's story of the boy who when he rides his rocking horse is able unfailingly to pick the winners at a local race track. It is plausible to think that such a boy *somehow* knows who the winners will be,[8] and it is plausible to suppose this even if we also suppose that the boy has not been told that his picks are always correct. In other words, it is plausible to suppose that the

[8]   The story is cited by Roderick Firth, "Are Epistemic Concepts Reducible to Ethical Ones," in *Values and Morals*, eds. A. Goldman and J. Kim (Dordrecht, Holland: D. Reidel, 1978), pp. 215–29.

boy somehow knows who the winners will be even if he lacks adequate evidence for his picks. Two lessons are suggested by such cases. First, in order to have knowledge it is not necessary to have a rational belief as has been traditionally claimed. At the very least, this is not necessary in one important sense of rational belief – viz. one which makes rational belief a function of having adequate evidence. Second, having a true belief which is caused by a highly reliable cognitive process can be *sufficient* for knowledge. Or at least, it can be sufficient with the addition of a few other relatively minor conditions.[9] The mistake reliabilists tend to make is to try to draw a third lesson from such cases. Namely, they try to conclude that a *necessary* condition of a person S's knowing p is that his belief p be reliably produced.

Commentary on Foley

The first thing to notice is that, instead of talking about justification and justified belief, Foley is talking about rationality and rational belief. 'Rationality' is many things to many people. In the passages marked $\boxed{d} \mapsto$ and $\boxed{f} \mapsto$ Foley defines a rational belief as a belief that is appropriate for a subject to have 'given his perspective' – appropriate relative to the subject's goal to believe truths and avoid falsehoods. In *The Theory of Epistemic Rationality* (1987, p. 66), he explains the notion of a perspective in terms of reflection: a rational belief is a belief such that, on sufficient reflection, S thinks that holding that belief is an effective means to his epistemic end of having true beliefs. Since rationality is said to depend on reflection and since one can only reflect on things one is aware of, Foley seems to presuppose, from the outset, internalism about justification. If this observation were correct, then Foley's critique of reliabilism would beg the question by assuming what is at issue. But for now let's apply the principle of charity and suppose that Foley's notion of rationality is the same as our commonsensical notion of justification.

> Do you agree with the characterization of Goldman's position of historical reliabilism in the paragraph marked $\boxed{a} \mapsto$?

Interestingly, Foley omits the internalist aspects of historical reliabilism. Goldman (in paragraph $\boxed{j} \mapsto$ in his section above) concedes to internalism that it may not be the case that the bearer of a justified belief has reasons for thinking that the belief is not justified – even if the belief is in fact caused by a reliable cognitive process. This

---

[9] Perhaps, for example, it would not be plausible to say that the boy on the rocking horse knows who the winners will be if he has adequate evidence for the (false) proposition that the process which causes him to think some horse will win is unreliable. Thus, perhaps something at last roughly resembling the following conditions are sufficient for S's knowing p: S belief p is true, it is caused by a highly reliable process R, and S does not have adequate evidence for believing R is not highly reliable.

concession leads Goldman to add a negative coherence condition to his reliabilist analysis of epistemic justification.

> Do you agree with the general characterization of reliabilism in the paragraph marked [b]→?

Foley defines reliabilism as 'the thesis that if one gathered into a set all the propositions which *both are epistemically rational for S and are believed by him*, it would be impossible for the set to contain more falsehoods than truths' (paragraph [b]→). We saw that Foley defines rationality in terms of the subject reflectively taking his belief to be true. Obviously, not everything a subject takes to be true is true. Thinking doesn't make it so. The above definition of reliabilism, however, seems to pass swiftly from the presumed truth of a proposition to its actually being true. Since this move is highly contentious, the question arises whether Foley's characterization of reliabilism is correct. Go back to the introduction to this chapter and compare the account of reliabilism given there with Foley's account of reliabilism.

Section I of the article is devoted to (what others call) the *new evil-demon problem*, section II concerns, among other things, the *generality problem* (again not Foley's term), and section III draws a conclusion.

The new evil-demon problem challenges the *necessity* of the reliabilist justification/rationality condition by constructing cases where this condition is not satisfied, but where the believer seems intuitively to be justified/rational. Suppose two people are psychologically and neurologically indistinguishable and they also possess the same beliefs. If it is rational for one of them to believe that p, so it is for the other. But now suppose that one of them lives in the normal world while the other one lives in a demon world, in which most of his beliefs are false. Foley is claiming that while most of the beliefs of the person in the demon world are false, it is equally rational for both agents to believe what they do believe. For the person in the demon world has exactly the same reasons for forming his beliefs. So if the beliefs of the person in the normal world are rational, so are the beliefs of the person in the demon world. But since the beliefs of the person in the demon world are not reliably formed – most of them are false – reliability is not a necessary condition for epistemic rationality.

In paragraph [c]→ and following, Foley formulates the lesson of the new evil-demon problem: reliabilism denies a victim of an evil demon rational beliefs and thereby contradicts the intuition according to which deception does not preclude rationality. Rationality isn't a matter, as the reliabilist insists, of the external relations that exist between the believer and his world. The mistake of reliabilism is to disregard the perspectival or reflective element of rationality.

> How could a proponent of externalist reliabilism reply to the new evil-demon problem?

The reliabilist could simply bite the bullet and deny the intuition according to which the victim of the evil demon is as justified as a subject who inhabits an epistemically friendly environment. If epistemic justification consists in beliefs being reliably formed, then dupes of demons do not have justified beliefs. The fact that, from their points of view, it is still rational to believe the things they do believe is irrelevant for the issue of justification. So the reliabilist will want to dissociate justification from rationality: evaluations regarding rationality are made from a first-person point of view; evaluations regarding justification are made from a third-person point of view. By identifying rationality and justification, Foley *presupposes* that our theory of justification has an internalist element.

In *Epistemology and Cognition* (1986, p. 113), Goldman offers a more conciliatory response to the evil-demon problem. He proposes modifications to historical relia-bilism that are aimed at granting inhabitants of the demon world justified beliefs. The idea is that the reliability of a belief-formation process is determined by the propor-tion of true beliefs it produces in *normal worlds*. 'Normal worlds' are defined as those that are consistent with our general beliefs about our actual world. So normal worlds are epistemically friendly worlds. Despite the victim of an evil demon routinely having false beliefs, those beliefs are nonetheless justified because his belief-formation processes would generally produce true beliefs in the normal world.

> Do you think the normal-worlds response to the new evil-demon problem is successful?

It is questionable whether the normal-world response to the new evil-demon prob-lem accounts for the internalist intuition it is meant to account for. The intuition driving the problem is that the demon victim's beliefs *are* justified in the very environment he inhabits, not merely that they *would be* justified if he lived in a quite different environment. Goldman himself became aware of this point and has since abandoned normal-worlds reliabilism.

While section I tries to establish that reliability isn't necessary for rationality/justification, section II attempts to show that reliability isn't necessary for knowledge. Foley argues that a reliability theory of knowledge has no way to specify the (reliable) process which is supposed to confer knowledge. Either the process is specified so narrowly (*this* kind of process, the one that produced *this* true belief) that every process turns out to be reliable, or demon-world counterexamples are easily multi-plied. The problem of providing an account of process types that are reliable is called the *generality problem*.

In the paragraph marked [e] $\mapsto$ Foley sets up the generality problem by imagining situations in which S *knows* something via process X but also *knows* that X is an unreliable belief-formation process. He imagines situations in which S knows that he has been deceived by a demon but no longer is, and a situation in which S knows that he shortly will be deceived by a demon but is not now, and a situation in which S knows that in close counterfactual situations he would be deceived by a demon even though he is not being deceived by the demon in the actual situation. These thought experiments raise the question of how we are to identify which types of cognitive processes count as reliable.

When types of cognitive processes are identified too broadly, no belief can count as justified. For there is no process type that reliably produces true beliefs no matter what the circumstances are. Take, for example, colour vision. Colour vision only gives us justified beliefs when the lighting conditions are standard. Yet in darkness and in illumination by coloured lights, colour vision is not a reliable process type. So for a process type to be reliable it needs to be identified at some level of specificity. But when process types are described too narrowly (e.g., 'a process as it operates on objects within two meters of S and directly in front of him'), then it may produce only a single token. If a process type only has one token and that token produces a true belief, then the process type is reliable and the belief qualifies as justified. But it conflicts with our most basic epistemic intuitions to claim that the truth of the belief is a sufficient condition for the belief being justified. For then accidentally true beliefs would have to count as justified and false beliefs would automatically be unjustified. So the generality problem calls for a way of identifying process types that is neither too broad nor too narrow. But how should we identify process types short of total specificity? Foley is sceptical that this can be done. This is still an open issue for process reliabilism.

> Is the generality problem a knock-down argument against reliabilism or are there ways for the reliabilist to circumvent this problem?

Process reliabilism is the most widespread form of reliabilism, but it is not the only one. While process reliabilism takes the epistemic status of a belief to depend on the reliability of the belief-formation process, indicator reliabilism takes this status to depend on the reliability of the reasons upon which the target belief is based. In this view, a belief is justified if it is based on a reliable indication or conclusive reason. A conclusive reason for p is defined as some condition or fact that would not be the case unless p were true. To know that p one must have reasons one would not have unless what one believes were true. This theory is externalist because a person, in order to know that p, need not know (or be justified in believing) that the reason for why he holds p is conclusive. Since indicator reliabilism manages without reference to belief-formation processes, it avoids the generality problem.

In his conclusion Foley emphasizes that, even though reliability is necessary for neither rationality/justification nor knowledge, reliability may be sufficient. Yet unless externalists can somehow take care of the meta-incoherence problem (discussed in 'Introduction to the Problem'), reliability is not even sufficient for justification.

3

Duties and Virtues

Introduction to the Problem

Up to now the selected texts have favoured externalism over internalism. Nozick defends a form of externalism about knowledge and Goldman develops an externalist account of justification. And even though Foley is an internalist in the article reprinted here, he criticizes reliabilism rather than presenting his internalist position. Thus it is high time to take a closer look at epistemic internalism. The article by Steup is a state-of-the-art presentation and defence of an internalist account of justification. The second text of this chapter is an article by Sosa in which he attempts to combine the best features of both the internalist and externalist views while avoiding their pitfalls.

As was explained in the previous chapter, the chief motivation for internalism about justification is *epistemic deontologism*. According to epistemic deontologism, the concept of justification is to be defined in deontic terms, terms such as 'duty', 'obligation', 'permission', and 'freedom from blame'. The deontological concept of justification has it that satisfying one's intellectual duty or responsibility in relation to the acceptance of a particular belief is a necessary condition for the belief to be epistemically justified. This notion of justification is normative: justification is not something that happens to a person; it is something one achieves by one's own efforts.

The exact nature of epistemic duties is a matter of controversy. The basic idea is that epistemic duties arise in connection with the goal of believing what is true and not believing what is false. This raises the question of *how* an agent is to responsibly pursue the truth. Epistemic deontologists tend to spell out epistemic responsibility in terms of the agent employing good evidence. S is justified in believing p if and only if S has the epistemic goal of believing truly and, because of this goal, holds the belief that p on the basis of good evidence which indicates the likely truth of p.

There is a natural connection between internalism about justification and epistemic deontologism. Internalism holds that all of the factors required for a belief to be justified must be cognitively accessible to the subject and thus internal to his mind. According to deontologism, a belief is epistemically responsible if the subject holds it on the basis of good evidence and with the goal of attaining the epistemic end of believing truly. Both the evidence and the goal must, of course, be within the subject's cognitive perspective. Even though internalism is not logically compelled to embrace deontologism, deontologism is the chief motivation for internalism. For if justification is not a matter of following epistemic rules, why should we even care whether we have cognitive access to our justificatory factors? Having awareness of one's evidence only seems to matter if subjects are being praised or blamed for what they believe.

The notion of epistemic responsibility presupposes not only awareness of one's beliefs but also voluntary control over them. If one is epistemically responsible for a belief, then it must be within one's power to hold or not to hold that belief. Critics of deontologism argue that because most of our beliefs are involuntary, our beliefs can't be subject to epistemic duty. Prime examples of involuntary beliefs are perceptual and introspective beliefs. Take, for example, your belief that you are seeing a book in front of you. Can you help believing that you are seeing a book? If the answer is 'no', then it seems that the belief can't be subject to epistemic duty. Steup defends epistemic deontologism against objections from involuntariness.

Steup also defends deontological internalism against two further externalist charges: first, whether a belief is justified or not is frequently not recognizable on reflection and, second, deontological justification doesn't amount to genuine justification because it is not truth-conducive. Even if Steup were successful in fending off externalist criticisms, it doesn't necessarily follow that internalism is true, for there are also some positive lines of argument in favour of externalism.

Some pursue externalism because they think it important to ascribe knowledge to higher animals, small children, unsophisticated adults, and certain artificial cognitive devices. Such ascriptions seem incompatible with internalism, since the beliefs and inferences required by internalism about justification are too complicated to be plausibly ascribed to such subjects. Others pursue externalism because they think it is a good way to naturalize epistemology. Naturalized epistemology doesn't concern itself with how we *should* form beliefs but with how we *do* in fact form them. Externalism promises to be a way of eliminating deontological language in epistemology – the language of praise and blame – and substituting natural relations (causal and counterfactual) between beliefs and the environment in our understanding of knowledge and justification. Others embrace externalism because internalism has conspicuously failed to provide defensible, non-sceptical solutions to the classical problems of epistemology, while externalism makes these problems easily solvable. Internalists, of course, think the externalist solution is much *too* easy. Still others pursue externalism because it yields answers to questions that otherwise remain puzzling. Why, for instance, can one know that *p* without knowing (or being justified in believing) that one knows it? Because, the externalist replies, knowledge has little or nothing to do with subjective justification; it is a matter of standing in the right relations to the facts. Needless to say, there is an internalist reply for each of these arguments for externalism.

It is unlikely that there will ever be a conclusive argument in favour of either internalism or externalism. In light of the apparent tie between the two positions, a number of philosophers have thought that we should end the bickering over the 'correct' account of knowledge and justification. Internalism and externalism shouldn't be played off against each other but should somehow be reconciled. What seems to be needed is an intermediate position which admits the truth-conducive character of justification while accepting the transparency of evidence.

Some epistemologists combine internalism and externalism by distinguishing between knowledge and justification. The idea is simply that internalism is right about justification while externalism is correct about knowledge.[1] The problem with this proposal is that it stands no chance of convincing either party. For both internalists and externalists claim to account for *both* justification and knowledge. So the real challenge is to come up with parallel internalist and externalist views both for justification alone and for knowledge alone.

Another attempt to bridge the gulf between internalism and externalism employs a distinction between conditions for knowing and conditions for saying that someone knows. The idea is that externalism concerns conditions for knowledge, while internalism concerns conditions for the attribution of knowledge.[2] A person may be justified in knowing while not being justified in claiming that he knows, and vice versa. But internalists will, of course, not be happy to be told that their account doesn't concern conditions for knowing but merely conditions for the attribution of knowledge and justification.

Yet another strategy is to double the requirements for justification: a person is justified in believing a proposition only if the belief is produced by reliable cognitive faculties *and* if he has good reasons of which he is aware.[3] Apart from making justified belief a very rare commodity, this proposal is unlikely to convince either internalists or externalists. Internalists will not see the relevance of requiring that beliefs must be caused by reliable processes, and externalists will not see that the transparency condition adds anything to the justificatory status of a belief.

Yet another strategy to render internalism and externalism compatible is to claim that externalism provides a convincing account of non-inferential (e.g., perceptual) knowledge, while internalism is appropriate for inferential knowledge. There are at least two problems with this solution. First, since the distinction between inferential and non-inferential knowledge is far from sharp, the proposed marriage between internalism and externalism is bound to lead to contention. (Is inferring a self-conscious affair or could it be automatic? Is any instance of one belief causing another a case of inferring? Does seeing that there is a dachshund before one's eyes involve inference?)

---

[1]   E.g. R. Audi, *Belief, Justification, and Knowledge* (Wadsworth, 1988), p. 114.
[2]   E.g. K. Bach, 'A Rationale for Reliabilism', *Monist* 68 (1985), pp. 246–63.
[3]   E.g. W. Alston, 'An Internalist Externalism', *Synthese* 74 (1988), pp. 265–83.

Second, because inferential knowledge is frequently based on non-inferential knowledge, it is implausible to suppose that the conditions for inferential knowledge differ in kind from those for non-inferential knowledge.

Now, Sosa attempts to combine internalism and externalism by drawing a distinction not between *kinds* of knowledge but between *levels* of knowledge. (First-order knowledge is, for example, knowing that there is a dachshund before one's eyes; second-order knowledge is knowing that one knows that there is a dachshund before one's eyes.) Roughly, Sosa's idea is that genuine knowledge – or *reflective knowledge*, as he calls it – is a combination of first-order knowledge and second-order knowledge, where first-order knowledge is externalist and second-order knowledge is internalist. Reflective knowledge, according to Sosa, consists in a true first-order belief which is reliably produced as well as in a meta-belief which establishes that the first-order belief is reliably produced and which meets certain internalist, namely coherentist, demands.

Introduction to Steup

Matthias Steup is professor of philosophy at St Cloud State University. His main research interest is epistemology. He is the author of *An Introduction to Contemporary Epistemology* (1996), editor of *Knowledge, Truth and Duty* (2001), and co-editor (with E. Sosa) of *Contemporary Debates in Epistemology* (2004).

Steup's essay, 'A Defense of Internalism', grew out of a commentary on Goldman's paper, 'Internalism Exposed' (*Journal of Philosophy* 96 (1999), pp. 271–93). As the title suggests, Goldman's paper rejects the internalist conception of justification. Steup develops answers to the various problems identified by Goldman. Since Steup explains the (alleged) problems of internalism before attempting to dispel them, his essay can be understood even if one hasn't first read the essay by Goldman.

Matthias Steup, 'A Defense of Internalism'
Internalism and Direct Recognizability

In this paper I shall set forth what I take to be a plausible version of internalism and defend it against objections. According to internalism, the things that make beliefs justified or unjustified – "J-factors," as we may call them – must, in some sense, be internal to the subject. The perhaps strictest way to internalize J-factors is to limit them to beliefs. My own view is that the constraint internalists place on J-factors is more plausibly construed in terms of cognitive accessibility. What qualifies as a J-factor must be something that is cognitively accessible to us in such a way that we can always tell whether what we believe is justified or not. Following Chisholm, then, I take internalism to be the view that J-factors must be *directly* recognizable, that is, recognizable *on reflection*.[1]

I begin by trying to explain what I mean by the phrase "recognizable on reflection." When we recognize something on reflection, the knowledge we obtain in this way is neither exclusively a priori nor exclusively introspective. Rather, typically it will be both a priori and introspective. Consider an example. Suppose you are asking yourself whether you're justified in believing that you had corn flakes for breakfast. It's important not to misunderstand this question. The question is not whether you *could* acquire the information needed to believe justifiably that you had corn flakes for breakfast. If you're not sure, perhaps you could call somebody with whom you had breakfast and acquire relevant information this way. Perhaps you could find out some other way. But that's not what you are interested in when you ask yourself that question. Rather, what you're interested in is this: Am I *now, given the knowledge and justified background beliefs I have in this situation*, justified in believing that I had corn flakes for breakfast? To answer this question, you may make use of everything you can know and justifiably believe at the time denoted by "now."

You might make use of what you now remember about today's morning, of the visual images you can recall from when you were having breakfast, and of bits of conversation you may have had during breakfast. If you thus appeal to your memories, the knowledge you obtain through reflection will be, at least in part, introspective. But reflection is likely to involve an a priori element as well. You might consider what logical and epistemic connections obtain between what you can now remember about this morning and the belief in question, and appeal to general principles about these connections. And if we assume that epistemic principles, if known, are known a priori, it follows that reflection involves an a priori element whenever an appeal to epistemic principles is involved. Reflection, then, is a process that is typically both introspective and a priori: introspective because access to J-factors such as memorial and perceptual states is introspective and a priori because, as internalists assume, epistemic principles are knowable only a priori.

The question "Am I now justified in believing that *p*?" is relative, then, to a certain body of information, the content of which is fixed by the temporal indexical "now." Once the relevant body of information changes, the reference of "now" changes, and the question becomes a different one. It follows from this that the question can indeed be answered *only* through reflection. Suppose you do call somebody up who had breakfast with you and ask

[1] For passages in which Chisholm expresses his internalist point of view, see Roderick Chisholm, *Theory of Knowledge*, 2d edn (Englewood Cliffs, NJ: Prentice Hall, 1977), p. 17; and *Theory of Knowledge*, 3d edn (Englewood Cliffs, NJ: Prentice Hall, 1989), pp. 62, 76.

that person what you were having this morning when you had breakfast together. Obviously, whether you are justified in believing "I had corn flakes for breakfast" *after* that phone call is a different question than the question of whether you were justified in believing this *before* the phone call. Thus, if you ask the question before the phone call, and then try to answer it by making the phone call, you are really confusing two different questions:

1. Am I now justified in believing I had corn flakes for breakfast?
2. Did I have corn flakes for breakfast?

Though these two questions are quite similar, they differ in one important respect: You can answer (2), but not (1), by acquiring further relevant information. You can answer (2) by asking somebody else and receiving information you did not have before you asked. But you cannot answer (1) by receiving information you do not have at the time you're asking the question. Rather, (1) can only be answered on the basis of what you can know and justifiably believe at the time denoted by "now."

According to the kind of internalism I shall defend, then, the things that render beliefs justified or unjustified must be recognizable on reflection. They must be such that you do not need to gather further information, let alone launch an empirical research program, to become aware of them. According to this view, *wishful thinking* is among the things that qualify as J-factors. When a belief of yours is rendered unjustified because it's grounded in wishful thinking, you can tell this because there are two things you can recognize on reflection: (1) My belief is grounded in wishful thinking; (2) beliefs grounded in wishful thinking are unjustified. A second example: *Perceptual experiences* are among the things that qualify as J-factors. When a belief of yours is justified by an undefeated perceptual experience, you can tell that it is justified because there are, once again, two things you can recognize on reflection: (1) My belief is supported by an undefeated perceptual experience; (2) beliefs that are supported in this way are justified. A third example: According to internalism, the *reliability* of cognitive processes does not qualify as a J-factor. Whether your beliefs are produced by reliable cognitive processes is not always recognizable on reflection, for you might need further information to determine whether they are thus produced.

So internalism, as I understand it, is a view about the nature of justification: J-factors must be recognizable on reflection. When evaluating a belief's epistemic credentials at a certain time, what makes this belief either justified or unjustified must be *recognizable at that time*, that is, must be recognizable without having to rely on any information not available at that time. If J-factors are thus constrained, epistemic justification becomes transparent: Its presence or absence can nearly always be determined. Consequently, in advocating internalism, I take it that the following is true: For any proposition p, a rational person can nearly always recognize, on reflection, whether she is, or would be, justified in believing that p.*

Internalism and Deontology

My reason for placing a direct recognizability constraint on J-factors is that I take the concept of epistemic justification to be a *deontological* one. I believe that epistemic justification is analogous to moral justification in the following sense: Both kinds of justification belong to the family of deontological concepts, concepts such as permission, prohibition, obligation, blame, and responsibility. An act that is morally justified is an act that is morally permissible, an act for which one cannot be justly blamed, or an act the agent was not obliged to refrain from performing. I conceive of epistemic justification in an analogous way. A belief that is epistemically justified is a belief that is epistemically permissible, a belief for which the subject cannot justly be blamed, or a belief the subject is not obliged to drop.[2]

If one takes the concept of epistemic justification to be a deontological one and thus takes epistemic justification to be a matter of individual responsibility, the internalist constraint that J-factors must be recognizable on reflection is pretty much an unavoidable consequence. In ethics, it is particularly clear, and, as Linda Zagzebski has pointed out, nearly unquestioned, that responsibility and duty fulfillment demand direct recognizability.[3] Thus, among ethical theories we do not find a straightforward analog to externalism in epistemology. No one defends the view that what makes an *action* morally justified or unjustified is something the agent cannot directly recognize.* Rather, what makes actions justified or unjustified must be, at least ordinarily, directly recognizable. Likewise, if epistemic justification is analogous to the justification of actions in being deontological, then what makes beliefs epistemically justified or unjustified must be, at least ordinarily, directly recognizable.

Even though there is then an undeniably close link between justification, duty fulfillment, and the recognizability of justification, I do not think the link is tight enough to warrant, in any obvious way, the conclusion that justification, moral or epistemic, is *always* directly recognizable. There are at least three types of cases in which, one could plausibly argue, justification, or

---

[2] For statements of the deontological view of epistemic justification, see Chisholm, *Theory of Knowledge*, 2nd edn, p. 14; Carl Ginet, *Knowledge, Perception, and Memory* (Dordrecht: Reidel, 1975) p. 28, and Laurence BonJour, *The Structure of Empirical Knowledge* (Cambridge, MA: Harvard University Press, 1985), p. 8.

[3] See Linda Zagzebski, *Virtues of the Mind: An Inquiry into the Nature of Virtue and the Ethical Foundations of Knowledge* (Cambridge: Cambridge University Press, 1996), pp. 41ff.

the lack of it, cannot be recognized on reflection. First, there are cases of culpable ignorance. If there are certain things I ought to know but have either forgotten or never bothered to learn, then, so it might be argued, it is possible that, as a result of my ignorance, I do or believe certain things I am not justified in doing or believing – although, given my ignorance, this is not something I can recognize at the time in question. Second, it might be argued that, in both ethics and epistemology, there are certain cases of conflicting reasons where it is extremely hard to find out what one would be justified in doing or believing, cases in which one might not be able to recognize at all what one would be justified in doing or believing. Third, one could argue that there are agents whose character, through moral and epistemic neglect, is so deformed that they simply cannot see their moral or epistemic failings.*

Now, I'm not sure that any of these cases provides us with a compelling reason to deny that justification, moral or epistemic, can always be recognized. Nevertheless, I shall grant the point in question and define internalism as the view that J-factors are *nearly* always recognizable, where the difference between "nearly always" and an unqualified "always" is determined by the extent to which the three cases in question actually occur. Internalism, even if qualified in this way, still differs significantly from externalism with regard to the extent to which epistemic justification is directly recognizable. For if the reliability of cognitive processes is included among the things that are J-factors (or is perhaps even viewed as the only J-factor), then situations in which justification is not directly recognizable are much more widespread than under the kind of internalism I am defending here.

Internalism and the Analysis of Knowledge

C → To appreciate the strength of the internalist position, it is essential to understand how internalists approach – indeed, must approach – the analysis of knowledge. Now, the analysis of knowledge can be carried out in two different ways: Some philosophers analyze knowledge by incorporating a condition specifically designed to handle the Gettier problem; some do not. Few epistemologists would object to the following two necessary conditions: What is known must be (1) true and (2) something that is believed. Beyond that, however, there is a lot of disagreement. I believe that, in addition to the truth and belief conditions, two more conditions are required: What is known must be a true belief that is (3) justified and (4) lacks the features that are definitive of Gettier-type situations. I shall use the term "degettierized" to refer to this fourth condition of knowledge.

Those epistemologists who dispense with the degettierization condition would say that, in addition to (1) and (2), only *one* further condition is needed. This condition will have to specify what "epistemizes" true belief, that is, what carries a true belief all the way toward knowledge. It will have to accomplish both of the things the justification condition and the degettierization condition are supposed to accomplish. Alvin Plantinga is one of those who favor the latter of these approaches.[4] He defines *warrant* as that which epistemizes true belief, and he thus views internalism as the view that warrant is essentially a matter of justification – typically, deontologically conceived. His own view is that epistemization is an external affair. Consequently, warrant – the property that epistemizes true belief – has nothing to do with justification.

Now, I do not take justification to be that which epistemizes true belief, and I don't think other internalists do. Rather, I take justification in conjunction with degettierization to be what epistemizes true belief because, unlike Plantinga, I think that the analysis of knowledge must include a degettierization condition. I would, therefore, agree with Plantinga that epistemization – the process that turns true belief into knowledge – is an external affair. And I think most other internalists would, too. After all, internalism about justification is to be distinguished from internalism about knowledge. For two reasons, the latter kind of internalism must be rejected. First, taking the concept of justification to be deontological justifies placing a direct recognizability constraint on justification. It does not justify placing this constraint on knowledge. Second, internalism about knowledge is untenable because two necessary conditions of knowledge are clearly external: truth and degettierization. It is obviously false that, with regard to any proposition p, I can nearly always find out on reflection whether p is true or not.[5] And whether a belief is degettierized or not (whether I am in a Gettier-type situation or not) is not recognizable on reflection either.

To see why the fourth condition of knowledge is external, consider a Gettier case. Suppose I look out my office window and see a squirrel climbing up a tree. This is nothing extraordinary, and I spontaneously believe "There's a squirrel out there." My belief is justified, for it is based on undefeated perceptual evidence. Alas, what I take to be a squirrel is a hologram projected by a crazy professor from the Electrical Engineering Department. This hologram is so perfect that, without close examination, it would be impossible to tell that it's not a real squirrel but just a clever

---

[4]   See Alvin Plantinga, *Warrant and Proper Function* (Oxford: Oxford University Press, 1993).
[5]   This is so for two reasons. First, justification is fallible. Sometimes, I have perfectly good reasons to consider true what is in fact false. Under such circumstances, I cannot recognize on reflection that what I believe is not true but false. Second, there are numerous times when I just don't have enough evidence, or no evidence at all, to tell whether the proposition I'm considering is true. In such cases, I need more information, which is to say that I can't tell on reflection whether the proposition in question is true.

squirrel-like image. Suppose further there's actually a squirrel out there, but it is sitting quietly behind a large branch, and I can't see it from my current vantage point. My belief, then, is not only justified but also true, for there really is a squirrel out there. Yet it isn't knowledge. Now, can I tell on reflection that my present situation involves a factor that stands in the way of knowledge? Obviously not. If I were to reflect on whether or not I know there's a squirrel out there, I would have no reason at all to conclude that I do not know.*

This point will apply to all Gettier cases, irrespective of their specific features. For by definition, Gettier cases are cases in which there is an element hidden from me: My belief is true just because of some lucky accident. Suppose this element was not hidden from me. Suppose it was either known to me or recognizable on reflection. Well, this couldn't be reconciled with an essential feature of Gettier cases: What I believe must be justified. But if the justification condition is met, then that element – whatever it is – by virtue of which my belief is merely accidentally true must not be directly recognizable to me at the time in question. So if one is in a Gettier case, one can't tell on reflection that this is so. And since being in a Gettier case is something that can happen, it follows that whether the fourth condition – the degettierization condition – is met or not is not always directly recognizable.*

I take it, then, that knowledge involves two internal and two external conditions. The two internal conditions are belief and justification.[6] The two external conditions are truth and degettierization. Externalists take knowledge to be less internal than that. Extreme externalists might say that none of the necessary conditions of knowledge is internal. Moderate externalists might acknowledge the internal nature of belief but deny that epistemic justification is deontological and thus internal. Now, as I pointed out above, to justify this denial, Plantinga's point – turning true belief into knowledge is an external matter – will not suffice, for internalists do not contest this point. Rather, when externalists attempt to demonstrate that justification is not internal, they must try to show that turning a *true and degettierized* belief into knowledge is an external matter. And to show this, they would have to establish that deontological justification is not a necessary condition of knowledge. But if we take into account what, according to the kind of internalism I advocate, deontological justification amounts to, we will see that it is not easy to establish this.

 With regard to the content of our epistemic duties, internalists can take a variety of different positions. Since I cannot go into a discussion of their

---

[6] I'm inclined to say that we can nearly always tell, for a given proposition *p*, whether we believe *p* or not. Thus, I take belief to be an internalist concept. For doubts about the direct recognizability of belief, see Jaegwon Kim, *Philosophy of Mind* (Boulder, CO: Westview Press, 1996), p. 18.

respective merits, I shall merely indicate what I take to be the most plausible view. Our epistemic duty is to believe in accord with our evidence: believe p only if p is supported by our evidence, disbelieve p only if p is contradicted by our evidence, and suspend judgment about p if our evidence neither supports nor contradicts p. Now, does a person's evidence meet the internalist constraint that J-factors be recognizable on reflection? This depends on what we count as evidence. In my view, what qualifies as evidence is the following: perceptual, introspective, memorial states and states of rationally comprehending abstract matters, such as conceptual, arithmetical, or geometric connections, and of course beliefs. Items such as these qualify as J-factors, for whether or not they obtain is directly recognizable.

If we view internalism in this way, then the assertion that deontological justification is not a necessary condition of knowledge amounts to the following claim: It's possible to know something without directly recognizable supporting evidence. On the face of it, this seems to be an implausible view. Nevertheless, there is space for discussion here. After all, little children, cats, and dogs can plausibly be said to have knowledge of their environment. And if we study the behavior of rats, earthworms, and amoebas, it would appear that knowledge can be attributed even to rather primitive organisms. But surely, when we talk about rats, earthworms, and amoebas, the idea that such creatures can have directly recognizable evidence is rather far-fetched. And thus it would appear that knowledge without justification – that is, without the kind of justification that depends on having evidence – is possible after all.*

My reply to this objection is that, in my philosophical concern with knowledge, what I am interested in is not the kind of knowledge exemplified by higher and lower animals, but rather the kind of knowledge *humans* are capable of having. And that kind of knowledge is, I take it, qualitatively different from the kind of knowledge attainable by rats, earthworms, and amoebas. It is what Ernest Sosa calls "reflective" knowledge: the kind of knowledge that can itself become the object of knowledge. Humans can evaluate their evidence, assess whether or not what they believe is justified, and thus come to recognize when they know and when they do not. Little children and animals can't do that. Their response to their environment is, as Sosa would put it, "thermometer-like."[7] They can register features of their environment, but they do not have any capacity for discriminating between justified and unjustified beliefs and cases of knowledge and of ignorance. Reflective knowledge, then, is beyond their ken, for they can't attain knowledge of their epistemic states. But it is that kind of knowledge – knowledge

[7] See Ernest Sosa, *Knowledge in Perspective: Selected Essays in Epistemology* (Cambridge: Cambridge University Press, 1991), particularly "Reliabilism and Intellectual Virtue," pp. 131–145.

that can be recognized *as* knowledge – that, according to internalism, requires the kind of justification that involves both epistemic duty fulfill-ment and having evidence.*

The kind of internalism I am defending, then, can be summarized thus. Epistemic justification is the kind of justification that, when it comes in a sufficiently high degree, turns a true and degettierized belief into reflective knowledge. It is deontological and evidentialist in nature and nearly always directly recognizable. In the remainder of this paper, I shall address three objections to this account: (1) It is false that epistemic justification is nearly always directly recognizable; (2) epistemic justification is not deontological because belief is not under our voluntary control; and (3) epistemic justifi-cation is not deontological because it is not truth-conducive.

Evidentialism, Deontology, and Direct Recognizability

Let us compare internalism, as I conceive of it, with one version of extern-alism: reliabilism. First, reliabilism is not a deontological view. According to it, whether one's beliefs are justified does not depend on epistemic duty fulfillment but on whether one's beliefs are produced by reliable cognitive processes. Second, reliabilism is opposed to internalism with regard to the recognizability of epistemic justification: J-factors need not be directly rec-ognizable. Third, reliabilism is not evidentialist: If reliable belief production is both necessary and sufficient for justified belief, then having evidence is neither necessary nor sufficient for epistemic justification.

Reliabilists, then, reject my view that we can nearly always tell whether what we believe is justified or not. It seems to me, however, at bottom, our disagreement about the recognizability of justification is really indicative of another, more fundamental disagreement. I don't wish to dispute that, *if* we think about epistemic justification the way *reliabilists* do, there are plenty of cases in which it's not directly recognizable whether what one believes is justified or not. And that's because reliabilists reject deontology and eviden-tialism, which I endorse. Likewise, reliabilists should agree that, *if* we think about epistemic justification as being deontological and evidentialist, then there are much fewer cases in which it's not directly recognizable whether what one believes is justified or not. The recognizability of epistemic justification is a function of what makes beliefs justified or unjustified, and since internalists and externalists disagree about that, they of course disagree about the extent to which epistemic justification is directly recognizable.

Externalists might argue, however, that even granting deontology and evidentialism, internalists are too optimistic about direct recognizability. In other words, internalism suffers from incoherence: the internalist constraint that J-factors must nearly always be directly recognizable is inconsistent with deontology and evidentialism, since the latter two features allow in fact for massive failure of direct recognizability.

To substantiate this challenge, externalists would have to argue that at least one of the following two types of cases frequently occurs: (1) cases in which one has evidence *for p* without being able to recognize that one has evidence *for p*; (2) cases in which one has evidence *against p* without being able to recognize that one has evidence against *p*. Above, I indicated that internalists might be willing to concede the existence of certain cases in which justification is not directly recognizable. Externalists could try to show that there are even more such cases than one might think initially, thus bit by bit expanding the extent to which epistemic justification is not directly recognizable.

I don't think it likely this project will meet with success. Any such case must be, as I explained above, a case premised on deontology and evidentialism, or else the disagreement about it will merely be a reflection of an underlying, deeper disagreement about the nature of epistemic justification. But as long as externalist critics work within the constraints of deontology and evidentialism, I don't think it will be easy for them to succeed in producing cases in which a belief's justificational status is not directly recognizable. It won't be easy for them because direct recognizability is *built into* the concept of *having evidence*. Evidence that's not directly recognizable simply is not evidence a person has. It is not a person's epistemic duty to believe in accord with such evidence (evidence there is but which one does not have), and thus such evidence is irrelevant with regard to a belief's justificational status. In short, if we understand evidentialism to be the view that a belief is justified if and only if the subject meets her epistemic duty by *having* (undefeated) evidence for that belief and if we agree that evidence not directly recognizable is not evidence one has, then it will be difficult indeed to describe possible cases that are consistent with deontology and evidentialism but are cases in which epistemic justification or the lack of it is not directly recognizable.

Deontological Justification and Doxastic Involuntarism

According to William Alston, having justified beliefs cannot be a matter of epistemic duty fulfillment because beliefs are not under our voluntary control. His argument can be summed up thus:

1. If a belief is deontologically justified or unjustified, it is under the subject's voluntary control.
2. Beliefs are never under our voluntary control.
3. Therefore, beliefs are never deontologically justified or unjustified.

Let's begin with a preliminary point. I grant that beliefs are never under our *direct* voluntary control. Doing x is under my direct voluntary control when a mere act of will suffices to do x. For example, raising my arm is under my direct voluntary control; turning on the light is not. It is, however, indirectly under my voluntary control. I can get up and flip the switch, which I can bring about through a series of bodily motions each of which is under my direct voluntary control. Now, if the argument were concerned merely with direct voluntary control; it would have to be rejected immediately. Obviously, for an action to be deontologically justified or unjustified, it need not be under our direct voluntary control. Why, then, should we place a much stricter condition on deontological justification with regard to belief?

What is at issue, rather, is *indirect* voluntary control. But is it true that belief is never under our indirect voluntary control? More than just a few epistemologists think it is.[8] I must confess that I find this quite baffling, for I think there is no question at all that we do enjoy a great deal of indirect control over what we believe. Consider unjustified beliefs. To say that we don't have even indirect control over unjustified beliefs is to say that, at those times when we have an unjustified belief, there is nothing we can do to get rid of it. This, I think, is clearly false. We can assess the epistemic credentials of what we believe; we can weigh the evidence. Since this is something we can do, it is within our power, at least a good deal of the time, to recognize that what we believe is unjustified and, on the basis of such reflection, to quit believing what we unjustifiably believe.

Unfortunately, Alston's argument is not effectively rebutted by pointing this out. Opponents of deontology might as well grant that unjustified beliefs are frequently under our indirect voluntary control, for it seems fairly clear, at least initially, that most of our justified beliefs are *not* under our indirect voluntary control. Consider, for example, perceptual beliefs about our environment. If you see that it's raining and thus believe that it's raining, you're simply stuck with that belief. The same point can be made about the entire array of beliefs that are grounded in excellent sensory, memorial, introspective, or intuitional evidence. Such beliefs can quite plausibly be thought of as involuntary. And if they are indeed involuntary, it would then seem to follow that at best only *some* of our beliefs are deontologically justified or unjustified. But that's a disastrous consequence. It would mean that the type of theory I'm defending here is of very limited applicability and thus relevance.

h⟶   It seems to me there are two effective ways to rebut Alston's argument. To begin with, Richard Feldman challenges the first premise. Granting that

[8]   See, for example, Alston, *Epistemic Justification.* (Ithaca, NY: Cornell University Press, 1989) essays 4 and 5; Jonathan Bennett, "Why Is Belief Involuntary?" *Analysis 50* (1990), pp. 87–107; and Richard Feldman, "Epistemic Obligation," in *Philosophical Perspectives 2*, ed. James Tomberlin (Atascadero, CA: Ridgeview, 1988).

moral obligations require voluntary control, he points out that not all types of obligation are like moral obligations in this respect. For example, one can have a legal obligation to repay a debt even when one is unable to do this. Why, then, should we think that epistemic obligation is analogous to moral obligation? Given that there are many different types of obligation, and that not all of these require voluntary control, wouldn't it be more plausible to assume that, with regard to voluntary control, there is an important dis-analogy between moral and epistemic obligation?[9]

I agree with Feldman that the first premise ought to be challenged, but, unlike Feldman, I am inclined to argue that not even moral obligation demands voluntary control – at least if by voluntary control we mean what Alston means by that concept. According to Alston, I have voluntary control over doing x at t if and only if, at t, I can do x and refrain from doing x.[10] If this is what we mean by voluntary control, then I think it is not at all clear that we can have a moral obligation to do x only if we have voluntary control over doing x.

Consider an example: Picture yourself at your favorite restaurant having dinner. At the table next to you, there is somebody who bothers you by talking and laughing in an overly loud manner. Now, let's grant that you are morally obliged to refrain from sticking your knife into that person's hand. According to the thesis in question, for you to be under this obligation, it must be the case that you *can* stick a knife in his hand. But can you? I do not mean to deny that, under certain circumstances, you can. But can you in the situation I am asking you to consider? And in the situation I'm asking you to consider, although you clearly are bothered by the man, you do not harbor violent emotions toward him. You don't feel even the slightest impulse to get up, take your knife, and drive it into the man's hand. Let's say, then, that you have absolutely no reason *for* sticking a knife in the unpleasant guest's hand and indeed plenty of decisive moral and prudential reasons *against* it. Could you, notwithstanding these reasons, get up and do so anyhow? I do not think there is a coherent account of what would be going on if, *under exactly the circumstances we are imagining*, you got up and stuck a knife in the man's hand. Whatever that sort of behavior would be, it would not be an *action* of yours. And if it was an action, it would not take place exactly under the circumstances we are imagining.[11]

The significance of the knife example is this: You are morally obliged to refrain from sticking a knife in the man's hand although this is something you couldn't do anyhow in the situation in question. Examples like this one,

---

[9] See Feldman, "Epistemic Obligation."
[10] See Alston, *Epistemic Justification.* p. 123.
[11] For a position on this matter similar to the one I am suggesting here, see Peter Van Inwagen, "When is the Will Free?" in T. O'Connor, ed. *Agents, Causes, and Events* (Oxford: Oxford University Press, 1985).

as well as others, show that it's a mistake to assume that deontological status – an action or a belief's being permissible, forbidden, or obligatory – depends on voluntary control over it, where voluntary control over doing x at t requires of the subject that she can, at t, do x and refrain from doing x.★ Yet I do not wish to dismiss the intuition that deontological status and voluntary control are conceptually linked. Let us therefore explore whether we can conceive of voluntary control in some other way.

It seems to me that, when we use the concept of voluntary control in its ordinary sense, sticking a knife in a person's hand is just the sort of thing over which we do take ourselves to have voluntary control. So what we really mean by "voluntary control" is perhaps not the ability to act in a certain way and refrain from acting in that way *at one and the same time*, but rather the ability to act in a certain way, or to refrain from acting in that way, depending on which way of acting is supported by our reasons. On this view, voluntary action is action that is responsive to our reasons.★

To make sense of this, consider again the situation in the restaurant. According to our ordinary view of things, it's unproblematic to say you are obliged to refrain from sticking a knife in the man's hand because we assume that it's under your voluntary control to do that sort of thing or not. And by that latter claim, we mean that you can stick a knife in the man's hand in response to a reason to do so and that you can refrain from sticking a knife in the man's hand in response to a reason to refrain from doing so. On this account, sticking a knife in somebody's hand is an action that's under my voluntary control if I can perform it, or refrain from performing it, in response to reasons for or against performing it.

I am sympathetic toward this concept of voluntary control.★ However, if this is what we mean by that concept, the second premise of the argument displayed above must be rejected. If voluntariness does indeed consist in responsiveness to reasons, then it would be rather odd to maintain that, while what we *do* is under our voluntary control, what we *believe* is not. Consider again what we mean when we identify voluntariness with responsiveness to reasons and take sticking a knife in somebody's hand to be under our voluntary control. What we mean is this: Should I have a suitable reason, it is the sort of thing I can do. Now, this might be otherwise. Perhaps my fear of blood or my inhibition to harm somebody is so great that I couldn't stick a knife in somebody's hand even if I had an extremely good reason to do so. In that case, sticking a knife in a person's hand is not the sort of thing over which I have voluntary control. But if I am not that kind of a person, if I can indeed respond to suitable reasons for sticking a knife in somebody's hand by going ahead and doing it, then it is something that is under my voluntary control.

Now consider a belief that is as good a candidate for the status of being involuntary as any: my belief that it's raining when I see that it's raining. When we consider this belief, it certainly looks as though we do not have voluntary control over it. It did not come about as the result of a decision, not could I effectively decide to drop this belief. The impression of involuntariness, however, arises only if we apply a different yardstick: if, now that we are considering *belief* instead of *action*, we switch from our current concept of voluntary control back to our previous one. Let us refer to voluntary control as defined by Alston as *narrow* and to the modified concept I subsequently introduced as *broad*. In the situation we are considering – I see and thus believe that it's raining – I do *not* enjoy narrow voluntary control over the belief that it's raining. But we agreed already that making deontological status dependent on narrow voluntary control is too restrictive, at least as far as action is concerned. Now, I do not think there is any justification for treating deontological status differently for actions and beliefs, to require merely broad voluntary control for deontological status of actions but narrow voluntary control for deontological status of belief. Let us therefore reconsider the voluntariness of my belief "It's raining," making sure that the concept of voluntary control we are working with is not narrow but broad.

The question, then, is the following: Can I, in response to suitable reasons, refrain from believing that it's raining when I take myself to see that it's raining? I don't see any reason to assume that I couldn't. For example, if I see that it's raining but then come to learn from a reliable source that under the present circumstances I am very likely to hallucinate that it's raining, I might drop this belief. My belief that it's raining, then, is a belief I can retain or drop in response to reasons for or against retaining it. Hence, it is a belief over which I have – in an indirect way – voluntary control. Of course, it could be otherwise. My ability to drop this belief in response to suitable reasons might be impeded by a funny drug, hypnosis, a brain lesion, and other bizarre phenomena. If this were the case, my belief that it's raining would be involuntary. Absent such bizarre phenomena, however, I am perfectly capable of responding to a suitable reason by dropping this belief. Thus, according to our revised concept of voluntariness, whether or not to believe it's raining is something that is indirectly under my voluntary control.

Note that treating the voluntariness of belief in this way is analogous to the way we treated the voluntariness of actions above. As long as you do not have any good reason for sticking a knife in somebody's hand, you can't do it. But suppose you are supplied with a pretty good reason to do that sort of thing. Well, if in *that* case you can do it, then you have voluntary control over whether or not to stick a knife in somebody's hand. Likewise, if you can stop believing that it's raining when supplied with a suitable reason, then you have voluntary control over whether or not to believe that it's raining.

If we conceive of voluntary belief as belief that is responsive to our reasons, the extent of involuntary belief will be rather small. What can prevent us from adjusting our beliefs to our reasons are things like the following: brain lesions, phobias, neurotic compulsions and inhibitions, various forms of paranoia, the effects of drugs, and other similar things. Things like that, when present and causally active in the right way, render beliefs as well as actions involuntary. But under normal circumstances, we act and form beliefs in response to the reasons we have and modify our behavior and change our beliefs when our reasons change. Under normal circumstances then, our beliefs are just as voluntary as our actions.[12]

The upshot of my discussion is that advocates of the involuntarism argument face a dilemma. They must base their argument either on Alston's narrow concept of voluntary control or on the broad conception I outlined above, or something similar to it. Depending on which alternative they prefer, either the argument's first or second premise must be considered dubious. I do not think, therefore, that the argument from doxastic involuntarism amounts to an obstacle to deontological accounts of epistemic justification.

Deontological Justification and Truth-Conduciveness

According to Alston, there is a second reason why epistemic justification is not deontological. Deontological justification is not truth-conducive. It does nothing toward turning true beliefs into knowledge and thus does not amount to epistemic justification.* This point, Alston argues, can be established by considering a case of cultural isolation. Here's an account of the kind of case Alston has in mind. Imagine a tribe whose members engage in doxastic habits that are not conducive to the acquisition of knowledge. Beliefs formed as the result of these habits have no tendency to be true. To the extent they are true, this is just a matter of luck. Consequently, the beliefs under consideration are not epistemically justified. They could never amount to knowledge. According to Alston, however, they are deontologically justified, for the tribe members cannot be blamed for they way they form their beliefs. This is so because in this tribe traditional intellectual practices are never critically questioned. Nor has the tribe, through contact with other cultures, ever been externally exposed to criticism of its intellectual procedures. Given these circumstances, the tribe members, according to Alston, are blame free.

How does Alston's cultural isolation objection raise a problem for internalism? Obviously, even if Alston were right about the type of case he has in mind, his objection would not establish that deontological justification is not necessary for knowledge. Even if it were true that deontologically justified beliefs fall sometimes short of being knowledge, it wouldn't follow that there are cases of knowledge without deontological justification. . . .

---

[12]   A solution along these lines is set forth in Matthias Steup, *An Introduction to Epistemology* (Upper Saddle River, NJ: Prentice Hall, 1996), pp. 77ff.

Reliabilists will not accept my position on this matter. According to them, for a belief to be justified it must be based on a reliable ground.* And whether a belief is based on a reliable ground is something that is frequently not recognizable on reflection. Hence, from the reliabilist point of view, it can easily happen that a belief is deontologically but not epistemically justified. I think, however, that it is not only unnecessary but indeed counterintuitive to place a reliability constraint on justification. It seems to me that this constraint is motivated by the expectation that epistemic justification – when things go right – turns beliefs into knowledge. And since a belief based on an unreliable ground cannot amount to knowledge, justification must involve reliability.

This line of reasoning, however, is not compelling. Its intuitive appeal arises from the conceptual link between knowledge and reliability. I accept this link. Without reliability there can't be knowledge. But from this link, it doesn't follow that reliability has to enter into the analysis of knowledge via the justification condition. After all, there is an alternative. Reliability could – and I think should – enter the analysis of knowledge through the fourth condition, whose job is to degettierize justified true belief.* It is therefore possible to retain reliability within the analysis of knowledge without imposing it as a necessary condition on justification.

Conclusion

In this paper, I have tried to defend an approach to epistemology that is deontological, evidentialist, and internalist. This approach, it seems to me, successfully withstands the objections externalists have raised against it. Moreover, as I have indicated in the previous paragraph, it can be defended against externalist objections without dismissing the intuitive appeal behind these objections. The intuitive appeal of externalism lies in the fact that knowledge is to a large extent external. One way of doing justice to its externality is to make epistemic justification an external affair. This, I think, is preserving one important intuition by sacrificing another: the intuition that justification is, by its very nature, an internal matter.* It would be better to preserve both of these intuitions. And both of them are preserved when we combine an internalist justification condition with an externalist degettierization condition.* This is, in my opinion, the right approach to analyzing knowledge.*

Commentary on Steup

Internalism makes the possession of justification and knowledge a transparent affair. Steup begins by spelling out what the transparency of justification amounts to. Of what kind is the cognitive access that a justified believer is said to have of his justificatory factors (or J-factors)? Steup explicates this cognitive access in terms of the route by which one has access: whether one is justified in believing p is wholly determined by factors which one is in a position to know by reflection alone. This, of course, raises the question of what is involved in such 'reflection'. By 'reflection' Steup means a priori reasoning, introspective awareness of one's own mental states and experiences, and one's memory of knowledge acquired in those ways.

In the paragraph marked $\boxed{b}$→ Steup gives two examples of J-factors which are recognizable on reflection (or 'directly recognizable'): perceptual experiences and wishful thinking. When a belief of yours is based on wishful thinking, it is unjustified and you are in a position to tell that it is unjustified. Analogously, when a belief of yours is based on perceptual experiences, it is justified and you are in a position to tell that it is justified. Factors which are not recognizable on reflection, such as the reliability of the cognitive process causing one's beliefs, are unable to bestow on a belief the quality of being justified.

> Do you agree with the claim that perceptual experiences are transparent to their subject in the sense that he can discriminate them from other mental states such as hallucinations and memory experiences?

Some types of mental states obviously fail of transparency in this sense: knowledge is not transparent, for example, because the subject cannot discriminate knowledge from mere belief just on the basis of introspection. On the other hand, bodily sensations are plausibly regarded as transparent: I can, by introspection, tell the difference between pain and pleasure. Now which category do perceptual experiences belong to? There are actually two issues here. First, are perceptual contents subjectively transparent? Are differences of perceptual seeming seeming differences? Second, are perceptual experiences qua *perceptual* experiences transparent to the mind? Intuitively the answer to the latter question is 'no'.

(By and large, propositional attitudes that are factive [i.e., imply truth] are subjectively opaque and non-factive propositional attitudes are subjectively transparent. 'To know', 'to see', and 'to remember' are paradigm examples of factive verbs and 'to believe' is a paradigm example of a non-factive verb. A convenient grammatical mark of the factivity of propositional verbs is the possibility of co-occurrences with wh-clauses, i.e., clauses beginning with 'who', 'whom', 'what', 'where', 'when', and 'why'.[1] Both factive and non-factive propositional verbs can take that-clause complements [e.g., 'I remember that the book was stolen', 'I believe that the book was stolen'], but only the factive verbs can accept their wh-transformations: we can say 'I remember who stole the book', 'I remember why he did it', 'I remember how did it', and 'I remember what he did with it'. But we cannot say 'I believe who stole the book', 'I believe why he did it', 'I believe how he did it', and 'I believe what he did with it'.)

---

[1] See Z. Vendler, *Res Cogitans: An Essay in Rational Psychology* (Cornell University Press, 1972), ch. 5 and 'Telling the Facts', in J. R. Searle, F. Kiefer, and M. Bierwich (eds.), *Speech Act Theory and Pragmatics* (Reidel, 1980), pp. 273–90.

In the second section, Steup connects the internalist conception of justification with a deontological one. Deontology serves as the motivation of internalism. Just as moral responsibility requires that the agent be able to tell whether and when he is following or violating moral rules, epistemic responsibility usually demands that the subject be able to recognize by reflection whether or not he is conforming to epistemic rules.

What is one's epistemic duty?

In the paragraph marked $\boxed{e}\mapsto$ Steup explains that, provided my epistemic end is to believe what is true and not believe what is false, my epistemic duty is to believe what is supported by my evidence and to avoid believing what is not supported by my evidence.

This account of epistemic duty raises at least two issues. First, to answer the question 'What should I do in order to believe truly' by saying 'Believe in accord with your evidence' doesn't seem to do more than to offer a truism. The problem is that the duty to believe in accord with the evidence is too general to be of concrete help. What seems to be needed is a catalogue specifying which belief is supported by which piece of evidence. But Steup is prudent not to even try to develop such a catalogue, for there are no wholly general principles dictating what a piece of evidence supports. Whether a belief is supported by a piece of evidence crucially depends on the context. Steup emphasizes the context-dependency of the evidence – belief relation in the passage marked $\boxed{a}\mapsto$. Rather than simply asking whether I am justified in believing that I had cornflakes for breakfast, Steup asks whether, given the knowledge and justified background beliefs I have in this particular situation, I am justified in believing that I had cornflakes for breakfast.

Second, to be told that we have an epistemic duty to believe as the evidence directs us doesn't tell us very much unless we know what qualifies as evidence. In the paragraph marked $\boxed{e}\mapsto$ Steup defines evidence as consisting of both beliefs and experiential states such as sensory, introspective, memorial, and intuitional states. Given this definition, a person's evidence is directly recognizable to that person. Steup's evidentialism and his internalism are two sides of the same coin: because evidence is directly recognizable it is the kind of thing that makes beliefs justified or unjustified.

Let's summarize: Steup's conception of justification is internalist, deontological, and evidentialist. It is internalist because justification is said to be 'nearly always' directly recognizable. It is deontological because it takes justification to be a matter of epistemic duty fulfilment, and it is evidentialist because the content of our epistemic duties is to believe in accord with the evidence.

A notorious problem for any internalist account of justification is that it is unable to eliminate the possibility that one's belief is only accidentally true and therefore doesn't count as knowledge. An internalist conception of justification is always consistent with cases where the satisfaction of the justification condition is not related to the satisfaction of the truth condition. And because these are the very cases that Gettier-type counter-examples exploit, any internalist conception of justification is subject to the Gettier problem. The reason is that an internalist condition, no matter how it is spelled out, doesn't seem to entail the truth of the proposition believed.

Since Steup is aware of this shortcoming of internalism, he maintains, in paragraph
$\boxed{c}$→ and following, that in addition to the truth condition and the internalist
justification condition, knowledge demands an externalist 'degettierization condition'. The degettierization condition ensures that the satisfaction of the justification
condition entails the truth of what is believed. One possible candidate for such a
degettierization condition, mentioned in $\boxed{i}$→, is indicator reliabilism: the belief that
p is justified if it is based on a reliable ground, where a reliable ground for p is defined
as some condition or fact that would not be the case unless p were true.

Why can Steup still call himself an internalist given that he proposes to supplement the internalist justification condition with an externalist degettierization
condition?

Internalism about justification is defined as the view that all the factors required for a
belief to be justified must be recognizable on reflection. Because the externalist
degettierization condition doesn't contribute to the justification of a belief, Steup
can embrace the degettierization condition and still count as an internalist about
justification. The degettierization condition is a necessary component not of justification but of knowledge. Knowledge is external, justification internal. Note that, in
$\boxed{d}$→, Steup distances himself from internalism about knowledge.

How does Steup defend internalism against the charge that it is implausible to
deny knowledge to higher animals, small children, unsophisticated adults?

Small children and higher animals don't fulfil the conditions for justification. They
are not in a position to reflectively recognize their J-factors for the simple reason that
they (presumably) don't (yet) possess the concept of justification. But at the same
time we often say of children and animals that they know various things. Do we only
speak metaphorically when we attribute knowledge to these beings? In the paragraph
marked $\boxed{f}$→ Steup solves the issue by differentiating between different senses of the
word 'knowledge'. The kind of knowledge deontological internalism is about is not
animal knowledge but reflective knowledge. While animal knowledge is only a
matter of arriving at true and degettierized beliefs, reflective knowledge requires, in
addition, that the subject be reflectively aware of the evidence supporting his belief.
We will return to the distinction between animal knowledge and reflective knowledge in connection with Sosa.

Section IV discusses the anti-internalist claim that whether a belief is justified or
not is frequently not recognizable on reflection. At least since Sigmund Freud, it has
been widely accepted that much of our inner life is hidden from us and that the access
we have to our beliefs can be distorted by self-deception. Now, in light of the
undeniable fact that we often don't keep track of the evidence for our beliefs and
that we are sometimes mistaken about the grounds for why we hold the beliefs we do
hold, the cognitive accessibility requirement of internalism seems to be psychologically unrealistic.

The internalist might try to defend the accessibility assumption by arguing that what matters is whether the evidence is *in principle* accessible to the believer.[2] As long as the believer *can* directly recognize the evidence that supports his belief, he is justified in holding the belief. This is not the strategy Steup adopts. Instead Steup maintains in paragraph g→ that, by definition, evidence is directly accessible to the believer. This may be called an *analytic* solution to the accessibility problem, because it amounts to holding that the statement, 'Epistemic evidence is recognizable on reflection', is analytic: it is true solely by virtue of the ordinary meanings of the words in it. So, in the end, Steup defers the accessibility problem rather than solves it.

Section V discusses a criticism of epistemic deontologism. Deontologism has it that, for a subject to justifiably believe *p*, he should have the goal of believing what is true and he should follow the evidentialist rule, 'Believe in accord with your evidence'. But for the normative talk of rule following to make sense, subjects must have voluntary control over their beliefs. The reason is that 'ought' implies 'can'. To say of someone that he ought to do *X*, implies that he can do *X*. If he couldn't do *X*, it would be incoherent to demand of him that he do *X*. Thus deontologism seems to claim that, for you to justifiably believe *p*, it must be within your control to refrain from believing *p*. This claim is said to be psychologically implausible. Many of your beliefs are out of your control. You can *pretend* to believe all sorts of things, but you cannot simply take up any belief at will. This idea is called doxastic involuntarism. 'Doxa' is Greek for 'belief'.

> Explain, in your own words, how Steup answers the charge of doxastic involuntarism.

Steup develops a two-step response. First step: In the paragraph marked h→ he denies that we are epistemically responsible for our beliefs only if our beliefs are under our control. For example, a member of the Flat Earth Society may not be able to help believing that the world is not spherical. But this need not stop us from saying that in relation to the goal of believing truly, it is the person's duty to refrain from believing that the world is not spherical. Second step: In the remainder of section V Steup argues that the involuntarism objection is mistaken because there is a sense in which we *do* have voluntary control over our justified beliefs. The second step rests on a distinction between a soft and a hard notion of involuntariness. When a justified belief is softly involuntary, then, if one's evidence were to change, one could refrain from holding the belief. The belief is unavoidable only *vis-à-vis* the evidence one has. Hard involuntariness, however, means that one will hold on to a belief, no matter what, and that one is unable to react to a change in one's evidence. Steup defends deontologism by arguing that most of our beliefs are typically only softly involuntary and that deontologism is compatible with soft involuntariness.

[2] Chisholm, for example, takes this route in *Theory of Knowledge* (2nd edition, Prentice-Hall 1977), p. 17.

It is not clear that what Steup calls 'broad voluntary control' is genuine voluntary control. Even if my beliefs change according to the evidence, if I can't affect the evidence, I have no control over my beliefs. Of course, my beliefs could be otherwise, but there is nothing I can do to make them otherwise.

Introduction to Sosa

Ernest Sosa is professor of philosophy both at Brown University and at the State University of New Jersey at Rutgers. He works primarily in epistemology, metaphysics, and philosophy of mind. In epistemology, Sosa has developed a position called *virtue perspectivism*, which is a kind of middle ground between Goldman-type process reliabilism and internalism about justification. According to process reliabilism, the justificatory status of a belief depends on the reliability of the belief-formation process, while internalism claims that for a belief to qualify as justified the believer must have cognitive access to the justifying factors. Sosa combines both insights by claiming, roughly, that genuine or 'reflective' knowledge is true belief which is reliably produced and which the subject knows is reliably produced.

Sosa has written *Knowledge in Perspective: Selected Essays in Epistemology* (1991) and (together with L. BonJour) *Epistemic Justification: Internalism vs. Externalism, Foundationalism vs. Virtues* (2003). Among the numerous collections co-edited by Sosa are *A Companion to Epistemology* (1992, with J. Dancy), *The Blackwell Guide to Epistemology* (1999, with J. Greco), *Epistemology* (2000, with J. Kim), and *Contemporary Debates in Epistemology* (2004, with M. Steup). *Ernest Sosa and His Critics* (2004), edited by J. Greco, contains 22 critical essays on Sosa's epistemology and metaphysics, as well as Sosa's replies.

Ernest Sosa, 'Reliabilism and Intellectual Virtue'

A   Generic Reliabilism

Generic reliabilism might be put simply as follows:

> S's belief that *p* at t is justified iff it is the outcome of a process of belief acquisition or retention which is reliable, or leads to a sufficiently high preponderance of true beliefs over false beliefs.

That simple statement of the view is subject to three main problems: the generality problem, the new evil-demon problem, and the meta-incoherence problem (to give it a label). Let us consider these in turn.

The generality problem for such reliabilism is that of how to avoid processes which are too specific or too generic. Thus we must avoid a process with only one output ever, or one artificially selected so that if a belief were the output of such a process it would indeed be true; for every true belief is presumably the outcome of some such too-specific processes, so that if such processes are allowed, then every true belief would result from a reliable process and would be justified. But we must also avoid processes which are too generic, such as perception (period), which surely can produce not only justified beliefs but also unjustified ones, even if perception is on the whole a reliable process of belief acquisition for normally circumstanced humans.[1]

The evil-demon problem for reliabilism is not Descartes's problem, of course, but it is a relative. What if twins of ours in another possible world were given mental lives just like ours down to the most minute detail of experience or thought, etc., though they were also totally in error about the nature of their surroundings, and their perceptual and inferential processes of belief acquisition accomplished very little except to sink them more and more deeply and systematically into error? Shall we say that we are justified in our beliefs while our twins are not? They are quite wrong in their beliefs, of course, but it seems somehow very implausible to suppose that they are unjustified.[2]

The meta-incoherence problem is in a sense a mirror image of the new evil-demon problem, for it postulates not a situation where one is internally justified though externally unreliable, but a situation where one is internally unjustified though externally reliable. More specifically, it supposes that a belief (that the President is in New York) which derives from one's (reliable) clairvoyance is yet *not* justified if either (a) one has a lot of ordinary evidence against it, and none in its favor; or (b) one has a lot of evidence against one's possessing such a power of clairvoyance; or (c) one has good reason to believe that such a power could not be possessed (e.g., it might require the transmission of some influence at a speed greater than that of light); or (d) one has no evidence for or against the general possibility of the power, or of one's having it oneself, nor does one even have any evidence either for or against the proposition that one believes as a result of one's power (that the President is in New York).[3]

. . .

---

[1]   This problem is pointed out by Goldman himself ("What is justified Belief?" in George Pappas, ed., *Justification and knowledge*, Dordrecht: D. Reidel, 1979, p. 12), and is developed by Richard Feldman in "Reliability and Justification," *The Monist* 68 (1985): 159–74.

[2]   This problem is presented by Keith Lehrer and Stewart Cohen in "Justification, Truth, and Coherence," *Synthese* 55 (1983): 191–207.

[3]   This sort of problem is developed by Laurence Bonjour in "Externalist Theories of Empirical Knowledge," in *Midwest Studies in Philosophy*, vol. 5: *Studies in Epistemology*, ed. P. French et al. (Minneapolis: University of Minnesota Press, 1980).

D   A Stronger Notion of the
"Internally Justified": Intellectual Virtue

a ⊢→ Let us define an intellectual virtue or faculty as a competence in virtue of
which one would mostly attain the truth and avoid error in a certain field of
propositions F, when in certain conditions C. Subject S believes proposition
P at time t out of intellectual virtue only if there is a field of propositions F,
and there are conditions C, such that: (a) P is in F; (b) S is in C with respect
to P; and (c) S would most likely be right if S believed a proposition X in field

b ⊢→ F when in conditions C with respect to X. Unlike Historical Reliabilism, this
view does not require that there be a cognitive process leading to a belief in
order for that belief to enjoy the strong justification required for constituting
knowledge. Which is all to the good, since requiring such a process makes it
hard to explain the justification for that paradigm of knowledge, the Cartesian cogito. There is a truth-conducive "faculty" through which everyone
grasps their own existence at the moment of grasping. Indeed, what Descartes noticed about this faculty is its infallible reliability. But this requires
that the existence which is grasped at a time t be existence at that very
moment t. Grasp of earlier existence, no matter how near to the present,
requires not the infallible cogito faculty, but a fallible faculty of memory. If
we are to grant the cogito its due measure of justification, and to explain its
exceptional epistemic status, we must allow faculties which operate instantaneously in the sense that the outcome belief is about the very moment of
believing, and the conditions C are conditions about what obtains at that
very moment – where we need place no necessary and general requirements
about what went before.

By contrast with Historical Reliabilism, let us now work with intellectual
virtues or faculties, defining their presence in a subject S by requiring

that, concerning propositions X in field F, once S were in conditions C
with respect to X, S would most likely attain the truth and avoid error.

c ⊢→ In fact a faculty or virtue would normally be a fairly stable disposition on the
part of a subject *relative to an environment*. Being in conditions C with respect
to proposition X would range from just being conscious and entertaining X –
as in the case of "I think" or "I am" – to seeing an object O in good light at a
favorable angle and distance, and without obstruction, etc. – as in "This
before me is white and round." There is no restriction here to processes or
to the internal. The conditions C and the field F may have much to do with the
environment external to the subject: thus a moment ago we spoke of a C
that involved seeing an external object in good light at a certain distance, etc. –
all of which involves factors external to the subject.

Normally, we could hope to attain a conception of C and F which at best and at its most explicit will still have to rely heavily on the assumed nature of the subject and the assumed character of the environment. Thus it may appear to you that there is a round and white object before you and you may have reason to think that in conditions C (i.e., for middle-sized objects in daylight, at arm's length) you would likely be right concerning propositions in field F (about their shapes and colors). But of course there are underlying reasons why you would most likely be right about such questions concerning such objects so placed. And these underlying reasons have to do with yourself and your intrinsic properties, largely your eyes and brain and nervous system; and they have to do also with the medium and the environment more generally, and its contents and properties at the time. A fuller, more explicit account of what is involved, in having an intellectual virtue or faculty is therefore this:

> Because subject S has a certain inner nature (I) and is placed in a certain environment (E), S would most likely be right on any proposition X in field F relative to which S stood in conditions C. S might be a human; I might involve possession of good eyes and a good nervous system including a brain in good order; E might include the surface of the earth with its relevant properties, within the parameters of variation experienced by humans over the centuries, or anyhow by subject S within his or her lifetime or within a certain more recent stretch of it; F might be a field of propositions specifying the colors or shapes of an object before S up to a certain level of determination and complexity (say greenness and squareness, but not chartreuseness or chiliagonicity); and C might be the conditions of S's seeing such an object in good light at arm's length and without obstructions.

If S believes a proposition X in field F, about the shape of a facing surface before him, and X is false, things might have gone wrong at interestingly different points. Thus the medium might have gone wrong unknown to the subject, and perhaps even unknowably to the subject; or something within the subject might have changed significantly: thus the lenses in the eyes of the subject might have become distorted, or the optic nerve might have become defective in ways important to shape recognition. If what goes wrong lies in the environment, that might prevent the subject from knowing what he believes, even if his belief were true, but there is a sense in which the subject would remain subjectively justified or anyhow virtuous in so believing. It is this sense of internal virtue that seems most significant for dealing with the new evil-demon argument and with the meta-incoherence objection. . . . Can something more positive be said in explication of such internal intellectual virtue?

Intellectual virtue is something that resides in a subject, something relative to an environment – though in the limiting case, the environment may be null, as perhaps when one engages in armchair reflection and thus comes to justified belief.

> A subject S's intellectual virtue V relative to an "environment" E may be defined as S's disposition to believe correctly propositions in a field F relative to which S stands in conditions C, in "environment" E.

It bears emphasis first of all that to be in a certain "environment" is *not* just a matter of having a certain spatio-temporal location, but is more a matter of having a complex set of properties, only some of which will be spatial or temporal. Secondly, we are interested of course in non-vacuous virtues, virtues which are not possessed simply because the subject would never be in conditions C relative to the propositions in F, or the like, though there may be no harm in allowing vacuous virtues to stand as trivial, uninteresting special cases.

Notice now that, so defined, for S to have a virtue V relative to an environment E at a time t, S does not have to be *in* E at t (i.e., S does not need to have the properties required). Further, suppose that, while outside environment E and while not in conditions C with respect to a proposition X in F, S still retains the virtue involved, *relative to E*, because the following ECF conditional remains true of S:

e →   (ECF) that if in E and in C relative to X in F, then S would most likely be right in his belief or disbelief of X.

If S does so retain that virtue in that way, it can only be due to some components or aspects of S's intrinsic nature I, for it is S's possessing I together with being in E and in C with respect to X in F that fully explains and gives rise to the relevant disposition on the part of S, namely the disposition to believe correctly and avoid error regarding X in F, when so characterized and circumstanced.

We may now distinguish between (a) possession of the virtue (relative to E) in the sense of possession of the disposition, i.e., in the sense that the appropriate complex and general conditional (ECF) indicated above is true of the subject with the virtue, and (b) possession of a certain ground or basis of the virtue, in the sense of possessing an inner nature I from which the truth of the ECF conditional derives in turn. Of course one and the same virtue might have several different alternative possible grounds or bases. Thus the disposition to roll down an incline if free at its top with a certain orientation, in a certain environment (gravity, etc.), may be grounded in the sphericity and rigidity of an object, or alternatively it may be grounded in its cylindricality and rigidity. Either way, the conditional will obtain and the object will have the relevant disposition to roll. Similarly, Earthians and Martians may both be endowed with sight, in the sense of having the ability to tell colors and shapes, etc., though the principles of the operation of Earthian sight may differ widely from the principles that apply to Martians, which would or might presumably derive from a difference in the inner structure of the two species of being.

What now makes a disposition (and the underlying inner structure or nature that grounds it) an intellectual virtue? If we view such a disposition as defined by a C–F pair, then a being might have the disposition to be right with respect to propositions in field F when in conditions C with respect to them, relative to one environment E but not relative to another environment E'. Such virtues, then, i.e., such C–F dispositions, might be virtuous only relative to an environment E and not relative to a different environment E'. And what makes such a disposition a virtue relative to an environment E seems now as obvious as it is that having the truth is an epistemic desideratum, and that being so constituted that one would most likely attain the truth in a certain field in a certain environment, when in certain conditions *vis-à-vis* propositions in that field, is so far as it goes an epistemic desideratum, an intellectual virtue.

f→ What makes a subject intellectually virtuous? What makes her inner nature meritorious? Surely we can't require that a being have all merit and virtue before it can have any. Consider then a subject who has a minimal virtue of responding, thermometer-like, to environing food, and suppose him to have the minimal complexity and sophistication required for having beliefs at all – so that he is not literally just a thermometer or the like. Yet we suppose him further to have no way of relating what he senses, and his sensing of it, to a wider view of things that will explain it all, that will enable him perhaps to make related predictions and exercise related control. No, this ability is a relatively isolated phenomenon to which the subject yields with infant-like, unselfconscious simplicity. Suppose indeed the subject is just an infant or a higher animal. Can we allow that he knows of the presence of food when he has a correct belief to that effect? Well, the subject may of course have reliable belief that there is something edible there, without having a belief as reliable as that of a normal, well-informed adult, with some knowledge of food composition, basic nutrition, basic perception, etc., and who can at least implicitly interrelate these matters for a relatively much more coherent and complete view of the matter and related matters. Edibility can be a fairly complex matter, and how we have perceptual access to that property can also be rather involved, and the more one knows about the various factors whose interrelation yields the perceptible edibility of something before one, presumably the more reliable one's access to that all-important property.

Here then is one proposal on what makes one's belief that-*p* a result of enough virtue to make one internally justified in that belief. First of all we need to relativize to an assumed environment, which need not be the

environment that the believer actually is in. What is required for a subject S
to believe that-p out of sufficient virtue relative to environment E is that the
proposition that-p be in a field F and that S be in conditions C with respect to
that proposition, such that S would not be in C with respect to a proposition in
F while in environment E, without S being most likely to believe correctly
with regard to that proposition; and further that by comparison with epistemic group G, S is not grossly defective in ability to detect thus the truth in
field F; i.e., it cannot be that S would have, by comparison with G:

(a) only a relatively very low probability of success,
(b) in a relatively very restricted class F,
(c) in a very restricted environment E,
(d) in conditions C that are relatively infrequent,

where all this relativity holds with respect to fellow members of G and to
their normal environment and circumstances. (There is of course some
variation from context to context as to what the relevant group might be
when one engages in discussion of whether or not some subject knows
something or is at least justified in believing it. But normally a certain group
will stand out, with humanity being the default value.)

E   Intellectual Virtue Applied

 Consider now again the new evil-demon problem and the problem of meta-
incoherence. The crucial question in each case seems to be that of the
internal justification of the subject, and this in turn seems not a matter of
his superweak or weak or meta justification, so much as a matter of the
virtue and total internal justification of that subject relative to an assumed
group G and environment E, which absent any sign to the contrary one
would take to be the group of humans in a normal human environment for
the sort of question under consideration. Given these assumptions, the
victim of the evil demon is virtuous and internally justified in every relevant
respect, ... for the victim is supposed to be just like an arbitrarily selected
normal human in all cognitively relevant internal respects. Therefore, the
internal structure and goings on in the victim must be at least up to par, in
respect of how virtuous all of that internal nature makes the victim, relative
to a normal one of us in our usual environment for considering whether we
have a fire before us or the like. For those inclined towards mentalism or
towards some broadly Cartesian view of the self and her mental life, this
means at a minimum that the experience-belief mechanisms must not be
random, but must rather be systematically truth-conducive, and that the
subject must attain some minimum of coherent perspective on her own
situation in the relevant environment, and on her modes of reliable access to

information about that environment. Consider next those inclined towards naturalism, who hold the person to be either just a physical organism, or some physical part of an organism, or to be anyhow constituted essentially by some such physical entity; for these it would be required that the relevant physical being identical with or constitutive of the subject, in the situation in question, must not be defective in cognitively relevant internal respects; which would mean, among other things, that the subject would acquire beliefs about the colors or shapes of facing surfaces only under appropriate prompting at the relevant surfaces of the relevant visual organs (and not, e.g., through direct manipulation of the brain by some internal randomizing device).[4]

We have appealed to an intuitive distinction between what is intrinsic or internal to a subject or being, and what is extrinsic or external. Now when a subject receives certain inputs and emits as output a certain belief or a certain choice, that belief or choice can be defective either in virtue of an internal factor or in virtue of an external factor (or, of course, both). That is to say, it may be that everything inner, intrinsic, or internal to the subject operates flawlessly and indeed brilliantly, but that something goes awry – with the belief, which turns out to be false, or with the choice, which turns out to be disastrous – because of some factor that, with respect to that subject, is outer, extrinsic, or external.[5]

In terms of that distinction, the victim of the demon may be seen to be internally justified, just as internally justified as we are, whereas the meta-incoherent are internally unjustified, unlike us.

My proposal is that justification is relative to environment. Relative to our actual environment A, our automatic experience-belief mechanisms count as virtues that yield much truth and justification. Of course relative to the demonic environment D such mechanisms are not virtuous and yield neither truth nor justification. It follows that relative to D the demon's victims are not justified, and yet *relative to A their beliefs are justified*. Thus may we fit our surface intuitions about such victims: that they lack knowledge but not justification.

In fact, a fuller account should distinguish between "justification" and "aptness"[6] as follows:

---

[4]   As for the generality problem, my own proposed solution appears in my *Knowledge in Perspective* (Cambridge: Cambridge University Press, 1991), Chapter 16.

[5]   This sort of distinction between the internal virtue of a subject and his or her (favorable or unfavorable) circumstances is drawn in *Knowledge in Perspective*, Chapter 2. There knowledge is relativized to epistemic community, though not in a way that imports any subjectivism or conventionalism, and consequences are drawn for the circumstances within which praise or blame is appropriate (see especially the first part of Section II).

[6]   For this sort of distinction, see, e.g., *Knowledge in Perspective*, Chapter 14. The more generic distinction between external and internal justification may be found in Chapter 1 of *Knowledge in Perspective*.

(a) The "justification" of a belief B requires that B have a basis in its inference or coherence relations to other beliefs in the believer's mind – as in the "justification" of a belief derived from deeper principles, and thus "justified," or the "justification" of a belief adopted through cognizance of its according with the subject's principles, including principles as to what beliefs are permissible in the circumstances as viewed by that subject.

(b) The "aptness" of a belief B relative to an environment E requires that B derive from what relative to E is an intellectual virtue, i.e., a way of arriving at belief that yields an appropriate preponderance of truth over error (in the field of propositions in question, in the sort of context involved).

As far as I can see, however, the basic points would remain within the more complex picture as well. And note that "justification" itself would then amount to a sort of inner coherence, something that the demon's victims can obviously have despite their cognitively hostile environment, but also something that will earn them praise relative to that environment only if it is not just an inner drive for greater and greater explanatory comprehensiveness, a drive which leads nowhere but to a more and more complex tissue of falsehoods. If we believe our world not to be such a world, then we can say that, relative to our actual environment A, "justification" as inner coherence earns its honorific status, and is an intellectual virtue, dear to the scientist, the philosopher, and the detective. Relative to the demon's D, therefore, the victim's belief may be inapt and even unjustified – if "justification" is essentially honorific – or if "justified" simply because coherent then, relative to D, that justification may yet have little or no cognitive worth. Even so, relative to our environment A, the beliefs of the demon's victim may still be both apt and valuably justified through their inner coherence.

The epistemology defended in this paper – virtue perspectivism – is distinguished from generic reliabilism in three main respects:

(a) Virtue perspectivism requires not just any reliable mechanism of belief acquisition for belief that can qualify as knowledge; it requires the belief to derive from an intellectual virtue or faculty....

(b) Virtue perspectivism distinguishes between aptness and justification of belief, where a belief is apt if it derives from a faculty or virtue, but is justified only if it fits coherently within the epistemic perspective of the believer – perhaps by being connected to adequate reasons in the mind of the believer in such a way that the believer follows adequate or even impeccable intellectual procedure.... This distinction is used as one way to deal with the new evil-demon problem....

(c) Virtue perspectivism distinguishes between animal and reflective knowledge. For animal knowledge one needs only belief that is apt and derives
from an intellectual virtue or faculty. By contrast, reflective knowledge
always requires belief that not only is apt but also has a kind of justification, since it must be belief that fits coherently within the epistemic
perspective of the believer.... This distinction is used earlier in this
chapter to deal with the meta-incoherence problem, and it also opens
the way to a solution for the generality problem....

Commentary on Sosa

Since virtue perspectivism is a development and refinement of Goldman-type process
reliabilism ('generic reliabilism' or 'historical reliabilism'), Sosa begins by presenting
the three major objections to process reliabilism: the generality problem, the new
evil-demon problem, and the meta-incoherence problem. As was explained in
Chapter 2, there are reliabilist replies to each of these problems. But instead of
subjecting the reader to a lengthy and tedious investigation of how process reliabilism
can be defended against these objections, Sosa makes a fresh start and sets forth a
new epistemological approach on the basis of process reliabilism – virtue perspectivism. Virtue perspectivism promises to account for the intuitions and worries driving
the generality problem, the new evil-demon problem, and the meta-incoherence
problem. Yet in this essay Sosa concerns himself only with the second and third
problem.

At the centre of virtue reliabilism is the notion of an intellectual virtue. Intellectual
virtues are understood as (innate or acquired) epistemic abilities or dispositions of a
person such that, under the appropriate circumstances, he believes true propositions
and avoids believing false propositions within a field of propositions. A belief has
positive epistemic status if it is formed by virtuous dispositions and not by vicious
dispositions. Examples of intellectual virtues are vision, hearing, introspection, memory, logical intuition, deduction, and induction. Just as moral virtues are dispositions
that lead for the most part to morally valuable actions, intellectual virtues are
dispositions that, by and large, bring about true beliefs.[1]

Whereas process reliabilism claims that a belief is justified if it results from a
reliable cognitive process, virtue perspectivism restricts the types of processes that
can generate justified beliefs to those which have their basis in intellectual virtues.

In the passages marked a ⊢→ and c ⊢→ Sosa emphasizes the context-dependency
of intellectual virtues. Intellectual virtues are only appropriate with respect to certain
propositions and in certain circumstances. The circumstances include psychological
conditions (such as being awake) as well as environmental conditions (such as good

---

[1]   Other authors understand intellectual virtues quite differently. On their view, intellectual virtues are more like personality traits than cognitive abilities. See, for example,
J. Montmarquet, 'Epistemic Virtues', *Mind* 96 (1987), pp. 482–97.

lighting). Consider, for example, a virtuous faculty of vision. If the environment is epistemically unfriendly because, say, it is controlled by an evil demon, then the otherwise virtuous faculty of vision is going to produce mostly false beliefs. But that doesn't mean that the faculty is not virtuous relative to the normal world.

In the passages marked $\boxed{d} \mapsto$ and $\boxed{g} \mapsto$ Sosa uses the context-dependency of virtues to develop a response to the new evil-demon problem. Victims of an evil demon are virtuous relative to the normal world, but simply have the bad luck of being in an environment where their virtuous capacities are foiled. They are conditionally or 'internally' virtuous; that is, given a normal environment, their beliefs would be reliable. By filling in the variables of formula (ECF) in paragraph $\boxed{e} \mapsto$, we get the following conditional truth: if the victim of the evil demon lived in the normal world, then he would most likely be right in his belief or disbelief of X. In sum, the victim of an evil demon who falsely believes that he is seeing X is justified relative to normal worlds.

Sosa's solution to the new evil-demon problem is essentially the same as Goldman's normal-world response, which was explained in Chapter 2. Goldman also maintains that the reliability of a belief-formation process is determined by the proportion of true beliefs it produces in normal worlds.

> Why does Sosa claim in the paragraph marked $\boxed{b} \mapsto$ that process reliabilism has problems explaining the infallible knowledge I have of my present existence?

Assuming Descartes's 'cogito ergo sum' ('I am thinking, therefore I exist') is intended as an argument rather than just an appeal to intuition, it rests on the idea that beliefs about one's own present thoughts enjoy a special authority that make them immune to sceptical doubts. Not even an evil demon could trick me into thinking that I am thinking when I am not thinking, for to think that I am thinking *is* to be thinking. The first part of the cogito argument – 'I am thinking' – is therefore said to be indubitable. The premise 'I am thinking' in conjunction with the presupposition that it is impossible for that which is thinking not to exist yields the conclusion 'I exist'. Since the premise is indubitable and the conclusion follows from it by the light of nature, the conclusion too is indubitable.

The 'cogito ergo sum' argument shows that I can infallibly know that I exist *now*. The knowledge I have of my past existence does not have the same epistemic authority as the knowledge of my present existence. There are numerous scenarios which render the statement, 'I am thinking, therefore I existed', false. Now for the process reliabilist to account for the different epistemic status of 'cogito ergo sum' and 'cogito ergo eram', a distinction has to be drawn between the highly reliable cognitive faculty via which I know of my present existence and the less reliable cognitive faculty via which I know of my past existence. Yet Sosa seems to think that it is implausible to assume that the faculty through which I know that I exist now differs in kind from the faculty through which I know that I existed a split second ago.

Does someone whose belief results from an intellectual virtue need to know (or believe) that his belief is virtuously produced?

As is explained in the paragraph marked $\boxed{f}\!\mapsto$, virtue-based reliabilism is an externalist theory in that it doesn't require that the subject be aware of the fact that he is believing out of an intellectual virtue. A belief can have its source in a cognitive virtue without one being aware of it and hence without one having any reason for thinking that the belief is reliably formed.

Section III introduces a distinction between aptness and justification proper (paragraph $\boxed{j}\!\mapsto$) and between animal knowledge and reflective knowledge (paragraph $\boxed{k}\!\mapsto$). Aptness is the positive epistemic status that a belief has by virtue of being caused by an intellectual virtue. Aptness arises as a result of the proper functioning of one or more intellectual virtues. A belief is apt if it is produced by an intellectual virtue and not apt if it is produced by an intellectual vice. When an apt belief is true, it is a piece of animal knowledge. Animal knowledge is externalist in that it doesn't require subjects to know or believe that their beliefs are produced by intellectual virtues.

While animal knowledge is only a matter of arriving at true beliefs by the employment of virtuous faculties, reflective knowledge requires, in addition, that the believer grasps the fact that his belief is grounded in a reliable cognitive faculty. Justification proper consists in the subject attaining a 'coherent perspective on her own situation in the relevant environment, and on her modes of reliable access to information about that environment' (passage $\boxed{h}\!\mapsto$). In other words, a subject has reflective knowledge if his virtuously produced belief also fits into a coherent perspective which includes awareness of the fact that the belief is virtuously produced. So we end up with two tiers of positive epistemic status – first-order externalist aptness and second-order internalist justification. The kind of externalism used in the first order is reliabilism and the kind of internalism used in the second order is coherentism.

As will be explained in Chapter 5, coherentism claims that individual beliefs are justified by the entire system of beliefs in which they cohere. The items in coherent systems of beliefs must mutually support each other. A belief can only be justified 'from within', from the relations of mutual support that it bears to other beliefs. The aim of coherentism, therefore, is internalistic. A coherentist justification is accessible to the believer.

How does the distinction between animal and reflective knowledge help to solve the meta-incoherence problem?

The meta-incoherence problem relies on the internalist intuition that epistemic justification requires that the acceptance of the belief in question be rational, which in turn requires that the believer be aware of a reason for thinking that the belief is true. As was explained in Chapter 2, we are asked to imagine a person who possesses reliable clairvoyant powers, but who has no reason to think that he has such cognitive powers and perhaps even good reasons to the contrary. On the basis of these powers, he comes to believe p, which, in fact, is true. The claim, however, is that he is not justified in accepting the belief that p, despite the fact that the reliabilist condition is satisfied. Using the distinction between external aptness and internal justification, Sosa holds that the person's clairvoyant belief constitutes animal knowledge but doesn't amount to reflective knowledge. For reflective knowledge is a true first-order belief which is reliably produced *plus* a meta-belief which establishes that the first-order belief is reliably produced and which is justified in the coherentist sense. The clairvoyant lacks reflective knowledge because he is 'internally unjustified' (passage $\boxed{i}$$\mapsto$) in thinking that his first-order belief is reliably formed.

Finally consider whether Sosa's virtue epistemology satisfactorily combines internalist and externalist features in a single theory.

> Can internalism and externalism be combined by bifurcating the account of knowledge and justification into an object-level and a meta-level and assigning externalism and internalism to different levels?

It seems as if Sosa's epistemology creates a Gettier problem at the second level. To see this, compare the features that render meta-beliefs true with the features that render them justified. Meta-beliefs concerning the reliability of one's object-level beliefs are true by virtue of these object-level beliefs being reliably formed (or apt). Yet what justifies meta-beliefs is something quite different. In Sosa's view, meta-beliefs are justified in virtue of fitting together coherently with other beliefs and experiences. Thus there is a gap between the satisfaction of the justification condition and the satisfaction of the truth condition. And, as was explained in Chapter 1, it is this gap that lies at the heart of the Gettier problem.

Whether the notion of reflective knowledge is in fact vulnerable to Gettier cases depends, among other things, on whether internalist coherence in the second order increases reliability or aptness in the first order. Is the probability of an object-level belief being reliable higher given that one has a meta-belief which is justified in the coherentist sense? Sosa claims that 'broad coherence is valuable and admirable in a subject because it increases the likelihood that the subject will have true beliefs and avoid false beliefs'.[2] If it were in fact the case that internalist coherence at the second level increases reliability at the first level, then the threat of a Gettier problem would disappear. The satisfaction of the truth condition of meta-beliefs would indeed be linked with the satisfaction of the justification condition of meta-beliefs. In the context of BonJour's article (Chapter 5) we will return to the question of whether there is a relation between coherence and truth.

---

[2] 'Perspectives in Virtue Epistemology: A Response to Dancy and BonJour', *Philosophical Studies* 78 (1995), p. 232.

4

Knowledge by Hearsay

Introduction to the Problem

Testimony is often considered one of six basic sources of knowledge and justification. The other five sources are perception (including proprioception, i.e., awareness of the condition and activities of one's own body), introspection, memory, reason, and inference. This classification has been disputed. Some epistemologists regard introspection not as an independent source of knowledge but as a form of perception. Memory is sometimes considered not as a source of knowledge but merely as a retention of knowledge already obtained in some other way. Inference is arguably not an independent source of knowledge since the premises or facts from which one infers a conclusion must come from elsewhere. And some philosophers would dispute the power of pure reason as a source of a priori knowledge.

Knowledge through what others tell us forms a large part of the body of our knowledge. Small children depend almost entirely on what their parents tell them. And large portions of the body of knowledge adults possess are also gained second-hand – through books, the media, friends or teachers, and the internet. Most of us know about, say, quantum mechanics only on the say-so of others. Testimony allows knowledge to be spread throughout the community and to be passed on through generations; it is the foundation of culture and civilization. Without second-hand knowledge our lives would be epistemically impoverished.

There is no question that most of what we know we know because we accept the word of others. There is a question, however, over whether testimony belongs among the sources of knowledge. According to some philosophers, testimony is not a *source* of knowledge because you cannot know something on the basis of testimony unless the attester knows it. If the attester doesn't know that p, then his attesting to it cannot cause in you testimonially grounded knowledge that p. Rather than generating knowledge, testimony only transmits knowledge. The knowledge transmitted by testimony was generated by some source other than testimony, such as perception.

Some philosophers grant that testimony is a source of knowledge but they deny that it is a *basic* source. They take testimony to be a species of inferential knowledge. On this view, when one learns from S some fact, one always reasons (if only half-consciously) in something like the following way: S said that p; S is a fairly reliable fellow and he should know about p; so p is true. Since in this picture testimony is not an independent source of knowledge, but reduces to perception, memory, and inference, it is labelled the *reductionist* view of testimony. Reductionism is a kind of internalism about testimony and can be characterized by two claims:

(i) The mere fact that the speaker said that p, provides no reason to believe that p.
(ii) A testimonial belief is justified to the extent that one has reasons for acceptance.

Others grant that sometimes we accept second-hand information only when we have independent reasons for thinking that the inference from 'S said that p' to 'p is true' is justified, but they find it questionable whether we *always* reason in this way or whether such reasoning is even necessary. On an externalist or *anti-reductionist* view, we just believe what people tell us, and we believe it in a way that is very much like the way we believe our eyes and ears when they 'tell' us what is happening around us. Testimonial beliefs are non-inferentially justified and testimony is a basic source of knowledge. Anti-reductionism may be characterized by the following two theses:

(i) Other things being equal, we have a basic epistemic right to believe intelligible testimony.
(ii) Acceptance of testimony produces a justified belief (knowledge) if the attester's belief was justified (known).

This chapter applies the internalism/externalism debate to the topic of testimony. The two texts represent internalist reductionism and externalist anti-reductionism. According to Fricker, to acquire knowledge by hearsay one must ensure that the speaker is trustworthy. Burge, on the other hand, holds that we have a blanket presumptive right to trust others unless we have strong reasons not to do so.

Regardless of whether testimony belongs among the basic sources of knowledge, testimony differs from other sources in at least two respects. First, unlike with other sources of knowledge, (reductionists claim that) one can, in principle, check the reliability of testimony or confirm the deliverance of an attester without having to rely on testimony itself. Second-hand information can be checked by using other sources of knowledge. (See Fricker's refutation of the 'negative claim'.) However, to test the reliability of, say, my memory I must try harder to recall or consult the memory of others. And to verify the deliverances of my eyes I have to rely on other people's perception. Second, while other sources of knowledge usually don't involve other people, testimony always depends on someone else's will and action. The attester decides what to attest and thus can lie. Obviously, for a person to come to know that *p* on the basis of testimony, the attester must not lie.

Given that some attesters are *not* trustworthy and that it *is* possible to independently check the reliability of testimonially based beliefs, the reductionist seems to be right in demanding that we gather independent evidence for *S*'s trustworthiness and *p*'s truth before we can be said to justifiably infer '*p* is true' from '*S* said that *p*'. After all, how else should *justified* belief based on testimony be distinguished from merely lucky guesses? The anti-reductionist will object, however, that usually we 'just believe' what people tell us. Unless we have positive reasons to question the credibility and/or competence of the attester as well as the truth of the attested proposition, we unreservedly accept testimonial information. Given our credible-unless-otherwise-indicated attitude, if reductionism was right, the majority of our beliefs based on testimony would be unjustified. And surely this can't be right.

Introduction to Fricker

Elizabeth Fricker is lecturer in philosophy at Oxford University and tutorial fellow at Magdalen College. She works mainly in epistemology and philosophy of mind and language. Apart from numerous essays on testimony, she has written on self-knowledge, linguistic understanding, and the concept of knowledge. Fricker is the leading advocate of 'local reductionism', i.e., the doctrine that hearers need independent evidence that a particular piece of testimony is reliable if they are to be justified in believing it.

Some of Fricker's other papers on testimony are: 'The Epistemology of Testimony', *Aristotelian Society Supp.* 61 (1987), pp. 57–83, 'Telling and Trusting', *Mind* 104 (1995), pp. 393–411, and 'Testimony: Knowing through Being Told', in I. Niiniluoto, M. Sintonen, and J. Wolenski (eds.), *Handbook of Epistemology* (2004), pp. 109–30.

Elizabeth Fricker, 'Against Gullibility'

1

One main school in the Indian classical tradition of philosophy insists that testimony – 'learning from words' – is a source or type of knowledge *sui generis*, one which cannot be reduced to any other type – not to perception, memory, or inference nor, we may add, to combinations of these. Such an irreducibility thesis could take diverse specific forms. One form it may take is as the thesis that a hearer has a presumptive epistemic right to trust an arbitrary speaker. We may essay an initial formulation of this thesis thus:

PR thesis: On any occasion of testimony, the hearer has the epistemic right to assume, without evidence, that the speaker is trust worthy, i.e. that what she says will be true, unless there are special circumstances which defeat this presumption. (Thus she has the epistemic right to believe the speaker's assertion, unless such defeating conditions obtain.)

The claim that there is such a special presumptive right (PR) to trust associated with testimony constitutes a kind of irreducibility thesis, since the hearer's right to believe what she is told, on this view, stems from a special normative epistemic principle pertaining to testimony, and is not a piece of common-or-garden inductively based empirical inference.

Testimony's alleged status as a special source of knowledge is underlined if this PR thesis is conjoined with a negative claim, which we may formulate initially thus:

NC: It is not, generally speaking, possible for a hearer to obtain independent confirmation that a given speaker is trustworthy – that what she says will be true.

If this Negative Claim is true, then knowledge can regularly be gained through testimony only if there is no need for independent confirmation of the trustworthiness of speakers; that is, if the PR thesis holds. So the existence of this special normative epistemic principle is then essential to the gaining of knowledge through testimony. This pair of claims together is one apt explication of the irreducibility thesis of the Nyaya school of Indian philosophy.*

In this paper I shall give one half of a refutation of the PR thesis, by arguing against the Negative Claim, which features as a premise in one central argument for it. My discussion also shows the prima facie case against a PR. A fuller treatment would also consider, and reject, various positive arguments for a PR which may be made, which appeal to the essential nature of language, and of understanding, arguing that these imply that a general disposition to trust is essential to language, and thence to its epistemic legitimacy. Here I can only record my view that no such argument succeeds.

The Negative Claim that there can, generally speaking, be no non-circular confirmation that a given speaker is trustworthy, is false. And any fully competent participant in the social institution of a natural language simply knows too much about the characteristic role of the speaker, and the possible gaps which may open up between a speaker's making an assertion, and what she asserts being so, to want to form beliefs in accordance with the policy a PR allows. The PR thesis is an epistemic charter for the gullible and undiscriminating. This paper argues against gullibility.

2

. . .

The PR thesis is . . . a normative epistemic principle, amounting to the thesis that a hearer has the epistemic right to believe what she observes an arbitrary speaker to assert, just on the ground that it has been asserted: she need not attempt any assessment of the likelihood that this speaker's assertions about their subject matter will be true, nor modify her disposition to believe according to such an assessment. A corollary of the PR thesis is thus that a hearer gives a fully adequate justification of her belief just by citing the fact that "Someone told me so". This simple defence does not need supplementation with evidence for the trustworthiness of her informant. Nor, on this view, does an ordinary hearer need to supplement the simple defence by invoking the PR thesis itself. That thesis is formulated by the philosopher, as a theoretical registering of the fact that the simple defence is all that is needed.

a⊢→ The PR thesis is not to be confused with a descriptive premiss that 'speakers mainly tell the truth.' The view that belief in what is asserted is justified by reference to such a descriptive premiss, cited as part of the first-level justification of the belief, is a quite different view, one which would constitute a reduction of knowledge from testimony to an ordinary case of inductively based inferential knowledge. The alleged descriptive premiss (whether claimed to be empirically confirmed fact, or a priori conceptual truth about language) might be invoked in an attempted philosophical argument for the PR thesis. But this is entirely different from its featuring among the premisses which an ordinary hearer must know and be able to cite, to justify her belief.

Our target is the PR thesis. Arguments for it fall into two kinds: the positive arguments from the essential nature of language already mentioned,
b⊢→ and a negative argument. This last is a transcendental argument which runs thus:

(1) Knowledge can be and frequently is gained by means of testimony;
(2) [NC] It is not, generally speaking, possible for a hearer to obtain independent confirmation that a given speaker is trustworthy; therefore
(3) There is knowledge gained by testimony only if there is a presumptive right on the part of any hearer to trust an arbitrary speaker; therefore
(4) There is such a presumptive right to trust.[1]

[1] This argument seems to be implicit in C. A. J. Coady 'Testimony and Observation', *Amer. Phil. Quart.* 10, No. 2, April 1973, pp. 49–55.

One might reject this argument by rejecting its initial premiss. This is not my strategy. I agree with the proponent of the argument that it is a constraint on any epistemology of testimony, that it preserve our common-sense view that knowledge can be gained through testimony. This paper is devoted to stopping the transcendental argument by showing its second premise, the Negative Claim, to be false.

3

The epistemological 'problem of justifying belief through testimony' is the problem of showing how it can be the case that a hearer on a particular occasion has the epistemic right to believe what she is told – to believe a particular speaker's assertion. If an account showing that and how this is possible is given, then the epistemological problem of testimony has been solved.

The solution can take either of two routes. It may be shown that the required step – from 'S asserted that p'* to 'p' – can be made as a piece of inference involving only familiar deductive and inductive principles, applied to empirically established premises. Alternatively, it may be argued that the step is legitimised as the exercise of a special presumptive epistemic right to trust, not dependent on evidence.

The Negative Claim, when appropriately glossed, is equivalent to the thesis that the first, *reductionist*, route to justifying testimony is closed. The gloss in question is to fix the notion of a speaker's 'trustworthiness' pro-grammatically, as precisely that property of a speaker which would, if empirically established, allow the inference (using only standard principles) to the truth of what she has asserted. As we saw above, the *anti-reductionist* about testimony argues from the alleged closedness of the first route, to the conclusion that the second route *must* be open: to the existence of a special presumptive epistemic right to trust.

. . .

Before we can consider whether the 'trustworthiness' of particular speakers can be non-circularly confirmed, and so whether the reductive route to justifying testimony is open, we need to determine just what this property is best taken to be.

. . .

To find such a notion: which just suffices, together with 'S asserted that p on [occasion] O', to entail 'p'; which constitutes a genuine property of S, hence, flukes and special cases apart, is epistemically independent of 'p'; and which constitutes an explication of the intuitive notion of S's being trust-worthy on an occasion of testimony, is our aspiration. A first approximation is the property of S specified by the subjunctive conditional:

Trus 1: 'If S were to assert that p on O, then it would be the case that p.'

This bridges the gap and is, special subject matters apart, epistemically independent of 'p'.* Knowing it to hold of S will, generally speaking, require having knowledge about S herself – her character, circumstances, etc. . . . The best explication of S's trustworthiness makes it relative not just to an occasion and an assertion-content, but to a particular utterance U by S. I shall adopt this relativisation from now on, although it is only in our final explication that it is not idle. It is in any case apt, since it is only with respect to her actual utterance that [hearer] H *needs* to know that S is trustworthy.

4

. . . But we have enough, armed with the provisional suggestion Trus1, to make some initial points regarding our central concern: the question whether the trustworthiness of a speaker can sometimes be empirically confirmed, so that the reductionist route from 'S asserted that p' to 'p' is open. The reductionist must make good the following claim (of which, accordingly, the anti-reductionist's Negative Claim is to be construed as the denial):

Local Reductionist Claim: It can be the case that,* on a particular occasion O when a speaker S makes an utterance U and in doing so asserts that p to a hearer H, H has, or can gain, independent evidence sufficient to warrant her in taking S to be trustworthy with respect to U.

. . .

The reduction here claimed is only 'local'. That is to say, the claim is only that there can be occasions when a hearer has evidence that the *particular* speaker in question is to be trusted with respect to her *current* utterance, without assuming this very fact. I shall call the question whether this local reductionist claim is true the 'local question' about testimony. The conception of the epistemological problem of justifying testimony adopted in §3 implies that a local reduction is all we need aspire to, or hope for. A 'reductionist' account of knowledge through testimony, in the context of this approach, means such a local reduction of each instance of knowledge through testimony to broader categories of knowledge, and patterns of inference.

Thus on our conception of the problem, justifying testimony by the reductionist route does not, at least in the first instance, require showing that the blanket generalisation, 'Testimony is generally reliable', (or, more simply, 'Most assertions are true') can be non-circularly empirically established. Such globally independent confirmation of the veracity of testimony would require that a hearer have evidence that *most of what she has ever learned through testimony is true*, where this evidence does not in any way rest on knowledge acquired by her through testimony. The fact that such a *global reduction* is not required for it, is crucial to the local reductionist position I argue for in this paper. For, as I readily agree with the anti-reductionist, there are general reasons, stemming from the essential role of simply-trusted testimony in the causal process by which an infant develops into the possessor of a shared language and conception of the world, why the prospects for a global reduction seem hopeless. So *this* negative claim is correct; but beside the present point. Notice therefore how the plausibility of the transcendental argument evaporates, once we identify just what the relevant Negative Claim is. For then we see how modest are the possibilities of non-circular confirm-ation which it denies, but which are all that is required, for knowledge through testimony to be possible in the absence of a presumptive right to trust.

True, the local reductionist question would transform itself into the global one, if it were the case that the only way of showing that a given speaker was trustworthy with respect to an utterance, was via appeal to the blanket generalisation. But, I suggest, this is not so. The blanket generalisa-tion is actually neither sufficient nor necessary evidence to justify belief, on a particular occasion, that *this* speaker is trustworthy with respect to *this* utterance of hers, which is what it takes to justify belief in what she has thereby asserted.* Even if the generalisation were true, there could be circumstances surrounding particular utterances which rendered the speaker's trustworthiness with respect to them doubtful in spite of it. And typically the grounds, when there are such, for expecting a speaker to be trustworthy with respect to a particular utterance of hers, relate to the circumstances and character of the speaker, and the nature of her subject matter; they do not concern the generality of assertoric utterances at all.

. . .

Anti-reductionism about testimony looks plausible if reductionism is so construed as to involve commitment to the claim that the blanket general-isation can be non-circularly established.* But my 'local' reductionist can happily grant that this is impossible. There is no need to show that the blanket generalisation can be non-circularly established, in order to show that a hearer can earn herself the right to trust a speaker on an occasion, without needing the gift of a PR; thereby providing a reductionist solution to the only epistemological problem of testimony which needs to be solved, viz. the local problem.

There is no space in the present paper to consider the reasons why the project of non-circularly confirming the global generalisation is hopeless, nor to defend my view that this does not undermine the rationale for insisting on justification severally for beliefs acquired through testimony. So I shall simply state my views. My view of the global 'problem' about testimony is that it is not a problem. The project of trying simultaneously to justify all of our beliefs which rest in any way on testimony (or equally, to justify a single testimony-belief, but without appealing to any beliefs based on testimony) is not one that is properly embarked on, and we certainly do not need to seek to found these beliefs as a totality in something else. The desire to show that the blanket generalisation can be non-circularly established is an instance of the foundationalist yearning to provide credentials for our system of beliefs from outside that system, or from a privileged subset of it. In this instance this task would be to hive off the part of our belief-system which rests, inter alia, on testimony, and show that it can be 'founded' in the remainder which is not. My insistence that the local question is the only legitimate question about testimony is of a piece with a more general coherentist approach in epistemology. Insofar as the anti-reductionist about testimony is expressing an adherence to coherentism, in opposition to foundationalism, I am with her. But this issue of global reductionism, or foundationalism about testimony, comes apart from the issue I am concerned to address. My issue is the local reductionist question: whether, *within* a subject's coherent system of beliefs and inferential practices (in the gradual dawning of light over which testimony will have played an essential part), beliefs from testimony can be exhibited as justified in virtue of very general patterns of inference and justification; or if a normative epistemic principle special to testimony must be invoked to vindicate them and explain their status as knowledge. The issue whether there is a presumptive right to trust not based on evidence is this internal, coherentist issue.

5

Is knowledge through testimony a distinctive category of knowledge at all? First note that we may define as our epistemic category, and topic of investigation: coming to know that something is so, through knowing that a certain speaker has asserted it to be so.

Testimony, defined as just suggested, does indeed constitute a distinctive kind of *epistemic link*. There is a distinctive type of connection, characteristic of testimony, between a state of affairs, and a hearer's coming to believe in its obtaining. This connection runs through another *person*, a speaker – her own original acquisition of the same belief, her other mental states, her subsequent linguistic act, which transmits that belief to the hearer.* There being this distinctive type of link between a hearer, and what she comes to believe, in testimony, means that there is a distinctive type of justification associated with testimony, in the sense suggested earlier: we can identify a characteristic justificatory schema *I*. A hearer has knowledge through testimony just when she has knowledge whose content is given by appropriate instances of the elements of *I*, and can cite such knowledge, or evidence for it, in defence of her belief. But what there is not, this paper argues, is any new *principle of inference* or other normative epistemic principle involved, which is special to testimony.

. . .

7

The thesis I advocate in opposition to a PR thesis, is that a hearer should always engage in some assessment of the speaker for trustworthiness. To believe what is asserted without doing so is to believe blindly, uncritically. This is gullibility. (Though not the only kind. Believing in trustworthiness too easily, i.e. attempting assessment, but doing it badly, is also being gulled!)

So – to return to our central question – if indeed a properly discriminating hearer always assesses a speaker for trustworthiness, what precisely is this property, and how is an empirically-based estimate of it obtainable?

Our method is to develop an epistemology of testimony, including an account of what a speaker's trustworthiness with respect to an utterance consists in, by appeal to the relevant parts of our commonsense theory of the world. This stance is part of a coherentist approach in epistemology: we criticise our belief-forming methods, and standards of justification, from *within* our existing conceptual scheme, rather than attempting to find some mythical point outside it from which to do so.

Now, CSL [common-sense linguistics] tells us that, in the normal case,* a serious assertoric utterance by a speaker S is true just if S is sincere, i.e. believes what she knowingly* asserts, and the belief she thereby expresses is true. This breakdown is entailed by the commonsense conception of the nature of a speech act of assertion, and of the link between its occurrence, and the obtaining of the state of affairs asserted to obtain. And common-sense person-theory tells us that it is moreover contingent whether any particular utterance is both sincere, and expresses a true belief: it is inherent in the nature of the link, and the psychology of the human subjects who are speakers, that insincerity and honest error are both perfectly possible. Indeed, commonsense person theory tells us that false utterances are quite common, especially for some subject matters. (This, we may note, constitutes the prima facie case against a blanket PR to assume any assertoric utterance to be true, a fortiori against one to assume that the speaker is trustworthy. The case is an application of the epistemic precept: 'If a significant percentage of Fs are not G, one should not infer that X is G, merely from the fact that it is F.' A belief so formed is not epistemically rational, which is to say it is not justified.)

In §3 we gave Trus1 as a rough initial explication of a speaker's trustworthiness with respect to an utterance U made on an occasion O, by which she asserts that p. Trus1 is logically equivalent to the claim: 'If S were to assert that p on O, then her assertion would be true'. We have now seen that the truth of S's utterance breaks down (in the normal case to which we confine ourselves) into the utterance's being sincere, and S's expressed belief being true.

Thus, I suggest, our best and final definition of a speaker's trustworthiness with respect to an utterance U is as follows:

Trus(S, U): A speaker *S* is trustworthy with respect to an assertoric utterance by her *U*, which is made on an occasion *O*, and by which she asserts that *p*, if and only if
(i) *U* is sincere, and
(ii) *S* is *competent with respect to 'p' on O*, where this notion is defined as follows:
If *S* were sincerely to assert that *p* on *O*, then it would be the case that *p*. In this definition the relativisation to a particular utterance *U* by *S* is not idle.

. . .

Trus(*S, U*) is weaker than the everyday notion of someone's being a trustworthy or reliable informant, since the latter usually refers to a speaker's assertions more generally, implying that she is generally sincere, and is competent with respect to most of the things she makes claims about. But a person *S* who is untrustworthy, in this generalised sense, can still be Trus(*S, U*), and known by a hearer *H* to be so, with respect to a particular utterance *U*; in which case, *H* has grounds to believe what is asserted by that utterance. Trus(*S, U*) is the minimal gap-bridging property which we set out to find. As such, it captures the idea that *that utterance* of the speaker is to be trusted.

8

. . .

In recognising an utterance by a speaker as a speech act of serious assertion, with a certain content, a hearer is ipso facto engaging in a minimal piece of *interpretation* of the speaker – ascribing to her an intentional action of a certain kind, and hence at the very least supposing the existence of some configuration of beliefs and desires which explain that action. The theme of my account is: the epistemically responsible hearer will do a bit more of the same. She will assess the speaker for sincerity and competence, by engaging in at least a little more interpretation of her.

A speaker's sincerity and competence, or lack of them, are aspects of her psychology – in the case of competence, in a suitably 'broad' sense, which takes in relevant parts of her environment. Assessment of them is part of, or a prediction from, a more extended psychological theory of her. So, in order to assess a speaker's trustworthiness, a hearer needs to piece together at least a fragment of such a theory of the speaker – an ascription of beliefs, desires, and other mental states and character traits to her. Thus it is commonsense psychology or person-theory, and the related epistemic norms for attribution of these states, that we must look to, to see how trustworthiness can be evaluated.

. . .

Indeed the primary task for the hearer is to construct enough of a theory of the speaker, and relevant portions of her past and present environment, to *explain* her utterance: to render it comprehensible why she made that assertion, on that occasion. Whether the speaker's assertion is to be trusted will, generally speaking, be fall-out from this theory which explains why she made it; and it is difficult to see how sincerity and competence could be evaluated other than through the construction of such an explanation.

(The need to explain the utterance is sharply felt, when a hitherto reliable informant makes a wildly unlikely claim. – Has she gone crazy? Or been elaborately tricked? Is she kidding? – Or is the best explanation that her outrageous claim to have seen flying saucers is really *true*? We feel at a loss; but it is these alternative explanatory hypotheses that we dither between.)

. . .

In claiming that a hearer is required to assess a speaker for trustworthiness, I do not mean to insist, absurdly, that she is required to conduct an extensive piece of MI5-type 'vetting' of any speaker before she may accept anything he says as true (cf. the implausibly onerous requirement dismissed earlier). My insistence is much weaker: that the hearer should be discriminating in her attitude to the speaker, in that she should be continually evaluating him for trustworthiness throughout their exchange, in the light of the evidence, or cues, available to her. This will be partly a matter of her being disposed to deploy background knowledge which is relevant, partly a matter of her monitoring the speaker for any tell-tale signs revealing likely untrustworthiness. This latter consists in it being true throughout of the hearer that if there were signs of untrustworthiness, she would register them, and respond appropriately.

Such monitoring of speakers, and appropriate doxastic responses formed on its basis are, I suggest, usually found in ordinary hearers, at least to some extent. However, this sort of monitoring for signs of untrustworthiness in a speaker is typically conducted at a non-conscious level. And while its results can generally be fished up into consciousness and expressed, albeit roughly, in words ("I didn't like the look of him"; "Well, she seemed perfectly normal"), no doubt the specific cues in a speaker's behaviour which constitute the informational basis for this judgement will often be registered and processed at an irretrievably sub-personal level. Can a justificationist account of knowledge allow that this kind of process may be knowledge-yielding? Yes, it can: insisting that subjects be able to retail the details of the cues they have responded to is demanding the impossible; but we may insist, compatibly with the sub-personal character of these perceptual or quasi-perceptual capacities, that the subject's beliefs must not be opaque to her, in that she must be able to defend the judgement which is the upshot of this capacity with the knowledge precisely that she indeed has such a capacity – that 'she can tell' about that kind of thing; though she does not know how she does it.

Expert dissimulators amongst us being few, the insincerity of an utterance is very frequently betrayed in the speaker's manner, and so is susceptible of detection by such a quasi-perceptual capacity. But honestly expressed false belief is not so readily detectable, and an informed assessment of a speaker's competence about some subject will typically require that the hearer already know something of the speaker's cognitive talents and failings. How then is knowledge of the latter attainable by a hearer, without, if not an MI5-style vetting, then at least a lot more research than is feasible, when you just want to know the time and have forgotten your watch? As regards sincerity, I suggested that it was tell-tale signs of its absence that a hearer must be disposed to pick up. The flip-side of this coin is that, while there is no right to assume sincerity without monitoring the speaker for it, sincerity is the default position, in assessing a speaker, in the sense we identified earlier; one is justified in taking a speaker to be sincere, unless one observes (and one must be alert for them) symptoms of duplicity.

And, I suggest, the same is true regarding a speaker's competence, *with respect to a certain range of subject matters* – namely, all those for which commonsense person theory tells us that people are nearly always right about such things. Just which topics come within this range is a further question; but it certainly includes such matters as: everyday perceptions of familiar types of item in one's current environment; memories, not too finely specified, of very recent events in one's personal history – such as what one had for breakfast; and a whole range of basic facts about oneself and one's life – one's name, where one works, one's tastes, etc. On such matters, I suggest, competence is the default position – that is to say, one may justifiedly assume a sincere assertion by a person of whom one has no previous knowledge to be true, when its subject matter comes within this range, just so long as one remains alert for any sign in their circumstances, or manner, to suggest otherwise, and there are no such signs.

. . .

10

The skeptical reader may want to ask at this point: – Just how different is the proposed account from a PR thesis? And can knowledge of trustworthiness obtained in the manner described really be called empirically based?

For assertions whose subject matter is outside the range for which there is a default position in favour of competence, the contrast between my account and a PR thesis is obvious. But a clear difference remains too in cases in which there is a default position in favour of both components of trustworthiness. My account requires a hearer always to take a critical stance to the speaker, to assess her for trustworthiness; while a true PR thesis, as we have seen, does not. The nub of this distinction is a clear and sharp difference: on my account, but not on a PR thesis, the hearer must always be monitoring the speaker critically. This is a matter of the actual engagement of a counterfactual sensitivity: it is true throughout of the hearer that if there were any signs of untrustworthiness, she would pick them up.

Moreover, as we have seen, the limited default positions in favour of the components of trustworthiness which my account posits, are precepts within the task of constructing a psychological theory of the speaker, not a dispensation from engaging in this task. There is no recognising their defeating conditions except through a general grasp of commonsense psychological concepts, and so the precepts can be conformed to (a fortiori appropriate defence of belief can be given), only by one who is a master of the latter. Thus, on my account, a person may gain knowledge from others only when she has the needed conceptual framework to conceive and understand them as persons and agents; and moreover engages, at least to some extent, in that interpretative task. The strongest PR thesis we identified earlier does not require this at all; our best formulation, while it required that the utterance is conceived as the speech act it is, did not require any interpretation of the speaker beyond what this itself involves.

Ascribing trustworthiness to a speaker is positing part of a larger psychological theory of her. Such a theory is empirically constrained by, and explanatory of, the speaker's behaviour. The fact that there are certain default settings regarding its construction does not detract from this. In any case the default position precepts do not allow ascription of trustworthiness on no evidence at all: even when trustworthiness is ascribed just on the strength of them, empirical warrant for this is needed, in the sense that the absence of defeaters must have been checked for – as, I have suggested, the hearer will show with such defence as "Well, she seemed perfectly normal".

But it is important to remember that, as we saw above, while our default position precepts represent what is, given the facts of commonsense psychology, sufficient ground for ascribing trustworthiness to an unknown person, what that person's indeed being trustworthy with respect to her assertion consists in is far from reducing to the obtaining of these limited-evidence ascription conditions. Consequently, while undefeated presumption gives a reasonable basis to believe a speaker to be right about, say, where she lives, one gains stronger confirmation (or disconfirmation!) of her trustworthiness about this and other matters, as one gets to know more about her – acquires more specific knowledge of her relevant cognitive talents and circumstances. A fuller treatment would refine the account offered here by introducing degrees of confirmation, and would introduce into the account of when it is rational (justified) to believe the costs of error: When it matters very much whether what someone says is true, we are less ready to accept what she says without checking her credentials.

. . .

Commentary on Fricker

As already mentioned in the introduction, Fricker is one of the leading advocates of reductionism. In her view, one cannot be said to derive knowledge (properly so called) from S's utterance that p unless one is aware of the possible gap between 'p is true' and 'S said that p'. If, as anti-reductionism maintains, one does not need any reasons or arguments to earn the right to believe that p from merely perceiving that p has been asserted, one wouldn't be aware of the possible gap. Therefore, the anti-reductionist conditions fail to generate genuine knowledge.

The paragraph marked $\boxed{a} \rightarrow$ draws a distinction between the psychology and the epistemology of testimony. Normative epistemology is concerned with the conditions under which a belief acquired through testimony could and would be justified, and whether and how a belief system with extensive dependence on testimony can be justified. Descriptive psychology, on the other hand, uncovers our actual practice of belief acquisition through testimony and the extent to which our belief system depends on testimony. Obviously Fricker is more interested in the epistemology of testimony. Specifically she addresses the question: under what conditions, and with what controls, should a mature adult believe what he is told, on some particular occasion?

Sections 1 to 3 set apart the two rival views: reductionism and anti-reductionism. Anti-reductionism consists in the presumptive epistemic right thesis, PR: a listener is entitled to presume a speaker to be sincere and competent regarding his subject matter, unless he has grounds to doubt this. Paragraph $\boxed{b} \rightarrow$ presents the reasoning behind anti-reductionism as a 'transcendental argument'. Generally speaking, a transcendental argument proves a conclusion by showing that, unless it were true, some fundamental phenomenon whose existence is unchallenged and uncontroversial would be impossible. In this context, the thesis PR is concluded from three premises, one of which is the negative claim NC: it is not possible for a listener to obtain independent confirmation that a given speaker is trustworthy. Given NC, unless PR was true, it wouldn't be possible that we gain knowledge by means of testimony. But since undoubtedly we do gain knowledge through testimony, PR must be true.

Rather than attacking the thesis PR head-on, Fricker attempts to undermine NC. She challenges NC by showing that it is indeed possible for a recipient of testimony to obtain independent confirmation that utterance U of speaker S at occasion O is trustworthy. If her arguments can be believed, the anti-reductionist is wrong in claiming that it is impossible to infer 'p is true' from 'S said that p'.

In section 4, Fricker sets her local reductionism apart from global reductionism. Local reductionism maintains that there can be occasions where a listener has independent reasons for thinking that a particular proposition asserted by a particular speaker at a particular occasion is trustworthy. Global reductionism, on the other hand, states that it is possible to justify the trustworthiness of testimony in general, without having to appeal to testimony.

> Why does Fricker think it is impossible non-circularly to establish the global thesis that testimony is generally reliable?

First, one cannot appeal to one's sense of the average attester's track record, for this sense often depends on what one believes on the basis of written or oral testimony. Second, paragraph $\boxed{c}\mapsto$ suggests that because language acquisition depends on testimony, we cannot say anything – let alone justify testimony – without already relying on testimony. Third, the paragraph marked $\boxed{d}\mapsto$ pairs global reductionism with foundationalism and local reductionism with coherentism. Anticipating the topic of Chapter 5, foundationalism is the view that justification has a two-tier structure: most beliefs are justified by reference to a few basic beliefs which are non-inferentially justified, i.e., their justification does not depend on any further justified belief. Coherentism, on the other hand, states that individual beliefs are justified by the entire system of beliefs in which they cohere. All justification is inferential. According to Fricker, the global reductionist project of non-circularly justifying testimony in general is motivated by the foundationalist ideal of justifying inferential beliefs by tracing them back to basic beliefs. Her rejection of global reductionism is an instance of her rejection of foundationalism. Yet Fricker doesn't explain why she prefers coherentism over foundationalism.

> After having worked through Chapter 5 you should go back to paragraph $\boxed{d}\mapsto$ and examine the connection between foundationalism and global reductionism.

The upshot of section 4 is that there is no global justification for the thesis that the whole set of a person's testimonially grounded beliefs is justified. But Fricker's point is that no such global justification is needed to disprove anti-reductionism. To undermine NC it suffices to establish that some testimonially grounded beliefs are locally justifiable.

> How does local reductionism differ from anti-reductionism?

The difference between anti-reductionism and local reductionism comes down to the difference between a negative and a positive coherence condition. (See the commentary on Goldman and the introduction to Chapter 5.) According to anti-reductionism, one is entitled to simply believe what one is told, unless one has reason to not trust the speaker. Local reductionism, on the other hand, demands that the recipient of testimony take a more active role. He has to be able to cite positive evidence in favour of the trustworthiness of the speaker (see paragraph $\boxed{e}\mapsto$), for it is the critical assessment of the speaker's trustworthiness that distinguishes justification from gullibility.

Notice that, like Foley and Steup, Fricker identifies epistemic justification with rationality and epistemic responsibility (see paragraphs $\boxed{f}\mapsto$ and $\boxed{g}\mapsto$). To blindly or uncritically believe the word of others is not only irrational and irresponsible but it is deemed epistemically unjustified. An externalist will, of course, object that justification and rationality are quite different things; the former has to do with truth-conduciveness while the latter is a matter of epistemic responsibility.

The beliefs we form on the basis of testimony are typically not held by way of inductive inference from other things we believe, say, about the credibility of the speaker. This being so, isn't it psychologically implausible to demand that the listener must continually evaluate the speaker's trustworthiness?

Is local reductionism psychologically plausible?

In the paragraph marked $\boxed{h} \mapsto$, Fricker weakens her internalist account of testimonial justification so as to render it psychologically more realistic. The weakening takes place in two respects. First, rather than requiring the listener to have positive evidence for the trustworthiness of the speaker, it suffices that the listener ensure that there are no signs revealing likely untrustworthiness. Second, the monitoring for signs of untrustworthiness doesn't have to take place at a conscious level. The recipient of testimony must only be disposed to become aware of the outcome of his subconscious evaluation of the speaker's trustworthiness.

In light of these modifications, the difference between anti-reductionism and local reductionism becomes rather fine. According to anti-reductionism, the listener is entitled to assume sincerity and competence on the part of the speaker, unless counter-evidence presents itself to him. Local reductionism, on the other hand, claims that the listener must 'remain alert' for signs of insincerity and incompetence. In the absence of detectable signs of untrustworthiness, the listener still doesn't have a right to assume that the speaker is trustworthy. The assumption of trustworthiness is simply the default position; it is what we do, rather than what we have a right to do.

In the end Fricker's local reductionism suggests a default-trigger picture of testimony: the default situation is simply to accept what we are told, but this may be overridden by a trigger that switches us into reductionist mode. Beliefs about the credibility of the speaker play a kind of filtering role by preventing our believing testimony that does not 'pass'. The laxity of filtering beliefs yields gullibility.[1]

Introduction to Burge

Tyler Burge is professor of philosophy at the University of California at Los Angeles and works mainly in philosophy of language and mind, epistemology, and history of philosophy. Burge is probably best known for his anti-individualism (also known as 'content externalism' and 'semantic externalism'), that is, the view that the contents of an individual's thoughts and the meanings of his words depend on systematic relations that the individual bears to aspects of his environment. By contrast,

---

[1]   The notion of a default trigger is borrowed from P. Lipton, 'The Epistemology of Testimony', *Studies in History and Philosophy of Science* 29 (1998), pp. 1–31. R. Audi in *Epistemology* (Routledge, 1998, p. 132) speaks about the 'filtering role' of beliefs about the attester's credibility.

individualists deny this and argue that a subject's thought contents are wholly dependent on her 'internal' states, such as her psychological or neurological states.

As well as numerous articles, Burge has written *Truth, Thought, Reason* (2005), a collection of essays on Gottlob Frege. M. Hahn and B. Ramberg have edited *Reflections and Replies: Essays on the Philosophy of Tyler Burge* (2003), which contains critical essays on anti-individualism and Burge's replies.

Tyler Burge, 'Content Preservation'

. . .

[a]→   I understand *'apriori'* to apply to a person's knowledge when that knowledge is underwritten by an apriori justification or entitlement that needs no further justification or entitlement to make it knowledge. A justification or entitlement is *apriori* if its justificational force is in no way constituted or enhanced by reference to or reliance on the specifics of some range of sense experiences or perceptual beliefs.

. . .

The distinction between justification and entitlement is this: Although both have positive force in rationally supporting a propositional attitude or
[b]→ cognitive practice, and in constituting an epistemic right to it, entitlements are epistemic rights or warrants that need not be understood by or even accessible to the subject. We are entitled to rely, other things equal, on perception, memory, deductive and inductive reasoning, and on – I will claim – the word of others. The unsophisticated are entitled to rely on their perceptual beliefs. Philosophers may articulate these entitlements. But being entitled does not require being able to justify reliance on these resources, or even to conceive such a justification. Justifications, in the narrow sense, involve reasons that people have and have access to. These may include self-sufficient premises or more discursive justifications. But they must be available in the cognitive repertoire of the subject. The border between the notions of entitlement and justification may be fuzzy. I shall sometimes use 'justified' and 'justification' broadly, to cover both cases.

A person's knowledge of a proposition might be adequately supported both by an apriori body and by an empirical body of justification or entitlement. Then the person's knowledge would be heterogeneously over-determined. The person would have both apriori and empirical knowledge of the proposition. To be apriori, the knowledge must be underwritten by an apriori justification or entitlement that needs no further justificatory help, in order for the person to have that knowledge. To be apriori, a person's justification or entitlement must retain its justificational force even if whatever empirical justifications or entitlements the person also has to believe the relevant proposition are ignored.

. . .

An apriori justification (entitlement) cannot rely on the specifics of sense experiences or perceptual beliefs for its *justificational force*. An apriori justification will usually depend on sense experiences or perceptual beliefs in some way. They are typically necessary for the acquisition of understanding or belief. But such dependence is not relevant to apriority unless it is essential to justificational force. Distinguishing the genesis of understanding and belief from the rational or normative force behind beliefs is fundamental to any view that takes apriori justification seriously.*

No serious conception of apriority has held that all justifications held to be apriori are unrevisable or infallible. Traditionally, the deepest apriori justifications were seen to be hard to come by. Putative apriori justifications were traditionally held to be revisable because one could fail to understand in sufficient depth the relevant propositions, or make errors of reasoning or analysis.

. . .

Relying on others is perhaps not metaphysically necessary for any possible rational being. But it is cognitively fundamental to beings at all like us. Though ontogenetically later than perception and memory, reliance on others for learning language and acquiring beliefs is deeply ingrained in our evolutionary history. Acquiring beliefs from others seems not only psychologically fundamental, but epistemically justified. We do not as individuals justify this reliance empirically, any more than we justify our use of perception empirically. But we seem entitled to such reliance. Most of the information that we have, and many of the methods we have for evaluating it, depend on interlocution. If we did not acquire a massive number of beliefs from others, our cognitive lives would be little different from the animals'.

What is the epistemic status of beliefs based on interlocution? I will state my view broadly before qualifying and supporting it. The use of perception is a background condition necessary for the acquisition of belief from others. But in many instances, perception and perceptual belief are not indispensable elements in the justification of such beliefs, or in the justificational force of entitlements underwriting such beliefs. . . . Without perception, one could not acquire beliefs from others. But perception plays a triggering and preservative role, in many cases, not a justificatory one. Sometimes, the epistemic status of beliefs acquired from others *is not empirical*. In particular, it is not empirical just by virtue of the fact that the beliefs are acquired from others.[1] Such beliefs are sometimes apriori justified in the sense that they

[1]   Contrast Roderick M. Chisholm, "The Truths of Reason," in *Theory of Knowledge*, 2nd ed. (Englewood Cliffs, N.J.: Prentice Hall, (1977), sec. 5, and James F. Ross, "Testimonial Evidence," in *Analysis and Metaphysics*, ed. Keith Lehrer (Dordrecht: D. Reidel, 1975). They assume that belief based on testimony cannot be justified apriori and, if it is knowledge at all, must be empirical.

need not rely for justificational force on the specifics of some range of sense experiences or perceptual beliefs.

. . .

Justification in acquiring beliefs from others may be glossed, to a first approximation, by this principle: *A person is entitled to accept as true something that is presented as true and that is intelligible to him, unless there are stronger reasons not to do so.* Call this the *Acceptance Principle.* As children and often as adults, we lack reasons not to accept what we are told. We are entitled to acquire information according to the principle – without *using* it as justification – accepting the information instinctively. The justification I develop below is a reflective philosophical account of an epistemic entitlement that comes with being a rational agent.

Justified (entitled) acceptance is the epistemic "default" position. We can strengthen this position with empirical reasons: "she is a famous mathematician." We can acquire empirical reasons *not* to accept what we are told: "he has every reason to lie." But to be entitled, we do not have to have reasons that support the default position, if there is no reasonable ground for doubt. Truth telling is a norm that can be reasonably presumed in the absence of reasons to attribute violations.

It is usually said that to be justified in accepting information from someone else, one must be justified in believing that the source believes the information and is justified in believing it. I think this misleading. A presupposition of the Acceptance Principle is that one is entitled not to bring one's source's sincerity or justification into question, in the absence of reasons to the contrary. This too is an epistemic default position.

The Acceptance Principle is not a statistical point about people's tending to tell the truth more often than not. Falsehoods might conceivably outnumber truths in a society. The principle is also not a point about innateness, though Reid's claim that a disposition to acceptance is innate seems to me correct. The principle is about entitlement, not psychological origin.

The epistemic default position articulated by the Acceptance Principle applies at an extremely high level of idealization in most actual communication, especially between sophisticated interlocutors. Social, political, or intellectual context often provides "stronger reasons" that counsel against immediately accepting what one is told. Given life's complexities, this default position is often left far behind in reasoning about whether to rely on a source. One might wonder, with some hyperbole, whether it can ever be the last word in the epistemology of acceptance for anyone over the age of eleven. The primary point – that it is a starting point for reason – would not be undermined if its purest applications were relatively rare. But I think that it has broader application than the hyperbolic conjecture suggests.

Acceptance underlies language acquisition. Lacking language, one could not engage in rational, deliberative activity, much less the primary forms of human social cooperation. (Indeed, this point suggests the line of justification for the principle that I shall begin to develop below.) But unquestioned reliance is also common in adult life. When we ask someone on the street the time, or the direction of some landmark, or when we ask someone to do a simple sum, we rely on the answer. We make use of a presumption of credibility when we read books, signs, or newspapers, or talk to strangers on unloaded topics. We need not engage in reasoning about the person's qualifications to be rational in accepting what he or she says, in the absence of grounds for doubt. Grounds for doubt are absent a lot of the time.

The primary default position, the Acceptance Principle, is not an empirical principle. The general form of justification associated with the principle is: *A person is apriori entitled to accept a proposition that is presented as true and that is intelligible to him, unless there are stronger reasons not to do so, because it is prima facie preserved (received) from a rational source, or resource for reason; reliance on rational sources – or resources for reason – is, other things equal, necessary to the function of reason.* The justificational force of the entitlement described by this justification is not constituted or enhanced by sense experiences or perceptual beliefs.*

. . .

Now I turn to filling in the justification for the Acceptance Principle. First, if something is a rational source, it is a prima facie source of truth. For a condition on reasons, rationality, and reason is that they be guides to truth. Explicating this idea is notoriously difficult; but I do not apologize for it. An epistemic reason for believing something would not count as such if it did not provide some reasonable support for accepting it as *true*. The same point applies to rational entitlements for belief. The entitlements that I am discussing are epistemic, not matters of politesse. If one has a reason or entitlement to accept something because it is, prima facie, rationally supported, one has a reason or entitlement to accept it as true. A source is a guide to truth *in* being rational. Rational mistakes are possible. But if there is no reason to think that they are occurring, it is rational to accept the affirmed deliverances of a rational source. For other things equal, reason can be reasonably followed in seeking truth.

It is not just the rationality of a source that marks an apriori prima facie connection to truth. The very content of an intelligible message presented as true does so as well. For content is constitutively dependent, in the first instance, on patterned connections to a subject matter, connections that insure in normal circumstances a baseline of true thought presentations. So presentations' having content must have an origin in getting things right. The prima facie rationality of the source intensifies a prima facie connection to truth already present in the prima facie existence of presented content.

The remaining main step in justifying the Acceptance Principle lies in the presumption that the source of a message is a rational source, or a resource for reason. I think that one is apriori prima facie entitled to presume that the interlocutor is a rational source or resource for reason – simply by virtue of the prima facie intelligibility of the message conveyed. That is enough to presume that the interlocutor is rational, or at least a source of information that is rationally underwritten.

The idea is not that we reason thus: "If it looks like a human and makes sounds like a language, it is rational; on inspection it looks human and sounds linguistic; so it is rational." Rather, in understanding language we are entitled to presume what we instinctively do presume about our source's being a source of rationality or reason. We are so entitled because intelligibility is an apriori prima facie sign of rationality.

If something is prima facie intelligible, one is prima facie entitled to rely on one's understanding of it as intelligible. One is entitled to begin with what putative understanding one has. But anything that can intelligibly present something as true can be presumed, prima facie, to be either rational or made according to a rational plan to mimic aspects of rationality. Presentation of propositional content presupposes at least a derivative connection to a system of perceptual, cognitive, and practical interactions with a world, involving beliefs and intentional activity.[2] Belief and intention in turn presuppose operation under norms of reason or rationality – norms governing information acquisition, inference, and practical activity. For propositional attitudes, especially those complex enough to yield articulated presentations of content, are necessarily associated with certain cognitive and practical practices. To be what they are, such practices must – with allowances for some failures – accord with norms of reason or rationality.

To summarize: We are apriori prima facie entitled to accept something that is prima facie intelligible and presented as true. For prima facie intelligible propositional contents prima facie presented as true bear an apriori prima facie conceptual relation to a rational source of true presentations-as-true: Intelligible propositional expressions presuppose rational abilities and entitlements; so intelligible presentations-as-true come prima facie backed by a rational source or resource for reason; and both the content of intelligible propositional presentations-as-true and the prima facie rationality of their source indicate a prima facie source of truth.* Intelligible affirmation is the face of reason; reason is a guide to truth. We are apriori prima facie entitled to take intelligible affirmation at face value.

We could be apriori entitled to false beliefs. Sounds or shapes could have no source in rationality but seem intelligible. A quantum accidental sequence of sounds could correspond to those of Hamlet's most famous speech.* But the fact that we could be mistaken in thinking that something

---

[2] The expression may be derivative in that a nonrational machine might express linguistic content. But such machines are ultimately made by beings who have propositional attitudes.

is a message, or in understanding a message conveyed, is compatible with our having an apriori prima facie rational right to rely on our construal of an event as having a certain meaning or intentional content. And where a message has meaning or intentional content, we are entitled to presume apriori that it has a rational source, or is a resource for reason.

f →   Just as the Acceptance Principle does not assume that truth is in a statistical majority, the justification of the Principle does not assume that most people are rational. We could learn empirically that most people are crazy or that all people have deeply irrational tendencies – not just in their performance but in their basic capacities. Human beings clearly do have some rational entitlements and competencies, even though we have found that they are surprisingly irrational in certain tasks. The justification presupposes that there is a conceptual relation between intelligibility and rational entitlement or justification, between having and articulating propositional attitudes and having rational competencies.

Rational backing is, other things equal, a ground for acceptance of something as true. But in dealing with others, one must often take account of their lies. Why is one *apriori* entitled, except when reasonable doubt arises, to abstract from the possibility that it may be in the interlocutor's rational interest to lie?

. . .

Can one have apriori prima facie rational entitlement to accept what one is told, without considering whether the interlocutor is lying – lacking special reasons to think he is?

Apart from special information about the context or one's interlocutor, neutrality (as well as doubt) is, I think, a rationally unnatural attitude toward an interlocutor's presentation of something as true. (Compare: lying for the fun of it is a form of craziness.) Explaining why, in depth, would involve wrestling with some of the most difficult issues about the relation between "practical" reason and reason. I will broach one line of explanation.

g →   Reason necessarily has a teleological aspect, which can be understood through reflection on rational practice. Understanding the notion of reason in sufficient depth requires understanding its primary functions. One of reason's primary functions is that of presenting truth, independently of special personal interests. Lying is sometimes rational in the sense that it is in the liar's best interests. But lying occasions a disunity among functions of reason. It conflicts with one's reason's transpersonal function of presenting the truth, independently of special personal interests.*

The Humean reply that reason functions *only* to serve individual passions or interests is unconvincing. Reason has a function in providing guidance to truth, in presenting and promoting truth without regard to individual interest. This is why epistemic reasons are not relativized to a person or to a desire. It is why someone whose reasoning is distorted by self-deception is in a significant way irrational – even when the self-deception serves the individual's interests. It is why one is rationally entitled to rely on deductive reasoning or memory, in the absence of counter-reasons, even if it conflicts with one's interests. One can presume that a presentation of something as true by a rational being – whether in oneself or by another – has, prima facie, something rationally to be said for it. Unless there is reason to think that a rational source is rationally disunified – in the sense that individual interest is occasioning conflict with the transpersonal function of reason – one is rationally entitled to abstract from individual interest in receiving something presented as true by such a source.

Another consideration pointing in the same direction is this. A condition on an individual's having propositional attitudes is that the content of those attitudes be systematically associated with veridical perceptions and true beliefs:* true contents must be presented and accepted as true within some individual; indeed, the very practice of communication depends on preservation of truth. If a rational interlocutor presents intelligible contents as true, one can rationally presume that the contents are associated with a practice of successfully aiming at and presenting truth. Now an inertial principle appears applicable: since the intelligibility of a presentation-as-true indicates a source of both rational and true content presentations, one needs special reason to think there has been deviation from rationally based, true truth-presentation. Other things equal, one can rationally abstract from issues of sincerity or insincerity.

The apriori entitlement described by the Acceptance Principle is, of course, no guarantee of truth. It is often a much weaker sign of truth, from the point of view of certainty, than empirically justified beliefs about the interlocutor. The lines of reasoning I have proposed justify a prima facie rational presumption, a position of non-neutrality – not some source of certainty.

. . .

I turn now from our entitlement to applications of the Acceptance Principle to the role of interlocution in the acquisition of knowledge. In the absence of countervailing considerations, application of the Acceptance Principle often seems to provide sufficient entitlement for knowledge. Most of our knowledge relies essentially on acceptance of beliefs from others – either through talk or through reading. Not only most of our scientific beliefs, but most of our beliefs about history, ourselves, and much of the macro-world, would have insufficient justification to count as knowledge if we were somehow to abstract from all elements of their justification, or entitlement, that depended on communication.

Our entitlement to ordinary perceptual belief is usually sufficient for perceptual knowledge. It is usually sufficient even though we may be unable specifically to rule out various possible defeating conditions. If there is no reason to think that the defeating conditions threaten, one has knowledge despite ignoring them. Something similar holds for acquisition of belief from others. Other things equal, ordinary interlocution suffices for know-ledge.[3]

In knowing something through interlocution, the recipient has his own entitlement to accept the word of the interlocutor, together with any supplementary justification the recipient might have that bears on the plausibility of the information. Let this include all the reasons available to the recipient, together with all the entitlements deriving from his own cognitive resources. Call this body (i) the recipient's *own proprietary justification*.

If the recipient depends on interlocution for knowledge, the recipient's knowledge depends on the source's having knowledge as well. For if the source does not believe the proposition, or if the proposition is not true, or if the source is not justified, the recipient cannot know the proposition. The recipient's own proprietary entitlement to rely on interlocution is insufficient by itself to underwrite the knowledge.[4] In particular, the recipient depends on sources' proprietary justifications and entitlements (through a possible chain of sources). The recipient depends on at least some part of this body of justification and entitlement in the sense that without it, his belief would not be knowledge. The recipient's own justification is incomplete and implicitly refers back, anaphorically, to fuller justification or entitlement. Call the combination of the recipient's own proprietary justification with the proprietary justifications (including entitlements) in his sources on which the recipient's knowledge depends (ii) *the extended body of justification* that underwrites the recipient's knowledge.

At the outset, I explained apriori knowledge in terms of apriori justification or entitlement. The question arises whether apriori knowledge based on interlocution is underwritten by the individual's proprietary justification or

---

[3]   The fact that most of our knowledge is dependent on others and has distinctive epistemic status is increasingly widely recognized. See C. A. J. Coady, "Testimony and Observation" *American Philosophical Quarterly* 10 (1973): 149–55; John Hardwig, "Epistemic Dependence," *Journal of Philosophy* 82 (1985): 335–49; Michael Welbourne, *The Community of Knowledge* (Aberdeen: Aberdeen University Press, 1986). For a wildly implausible, individualistic view of the epistemic status of testimony, see John Locke, *An Essay Concerning Human Understanding* 1.3.24.

4   Because the interlocutor must have knowledge and because of Gettier cases, the interlocutor must have more than true, justified belief if the recipient is to have knowledge. The recipient's dependence for having knowledge on the interlocutor's having knowledge is itself an instance of the Gettier point. The recipient could have true justified belief, but lack knowledge because the interlocutor lacked knowledge.

In requiring that the source have knowledge if the recipient is to have knowledge based on interlocution, I oversimplify. Some chains with more than two links seem to violate this condition. But there must be knowledge in the chain if the recipient is to have knowledge based on interlocution.

by a justification that must include some nonproprietary part of the extended body of justification.

The extended body of justification – the one that reaches beyond the individual – is the relevant one. If I am apriori entitled to accept an interlocutor's word, but the interlocutor provides me with empirically justified information, it would be wrong to characterize my knowledge of the information as apriori. Similarly, if my source knows a proposition apriori, but I must rely on empirical knowledge to justify my acceptance of the source's word, it would be wrong to say that *I* know the proposition apriori – even though I have knowledge that is apriori known by someone. It seems most natural to think that a strand of justification that runs through the extended body into the individual's proprietary body of justification must be apriori for the recipient's knowledge to be apriori. People who depend on interlocution for knowledge of mathematical theorems but do not know the proofs can have apriori knowledge in this sense. The source mathematician knows the theorem apriori and the recipient is entitled apriori to accept the word of the source, in the absence of reasons to doubt. Most of us knew the Pythagorean theorem at some stage in this manner. When apriori knowledge is preserved through reports which the recipient is apriori justified in accepting, the receiver's knowledge is apriori.

. . .

The Acceptance Principle entails a presumption that others' beliefs are justified, that others are sources of rationality or reason. . . . The presumption that others are reliable indices of truth rests on a presumption that they are rational sources. Their reliability is not some brute correlation between belief and world. We are entitled to treat others as reliable partly *because* we are entitled to presume that they are rationally justified or rationally entitled to their beliefs. We are entitled, most fundamentally, to think of others as sources of rationality or reason not because we take them as objects of interpretation and explanation, but because prima facie intelligibility is an apriori prima facie sign of rationality.

This focus on others is articulated from a first-person point of view. Each of *us* is justified in presuming that others are justified. But we are possible interlocutors too. The idea that others are prima facie justified in their beliefs makes general sense only if we presume generally: people, including each of us, are reliable rational sources of true justified beliefs. Obviously the conclusion requires qualification and elaboration. But the route to it is, I think, of interest. I arrived at it by arguing that we have intellection grounded prima facie entitlements to applications of the Acceptance Principle, though they are empirically defeasible. I think that this approach to epistemology may help with some of the traditional problems of philosophy.

Commentary on Burge

Burge argues that we are a priori justified in relying on the word of others. We have an a priori entitlement to trust in testimony, although in each case the entitlement may be defeated by empirical circumstances. In paragraph $\boxed{c} \mapsto$ Burge formulates what he calls the *acceptance principle*: a person is entitled to accept as true something that is presented as true and that is intelligible to him, unless there are stronger reasons not to do so.

The discussion of testimonial justification is part of a larger project: a defence of a rationalist or a priorist account of justification and knowledge. In the parts of the essay omitted here Burge argues that an analogue of the acceptance principle holds for what we seem to remember: a person is a priori entitled to accept a proposition that he seems to remember, unless there are stronger reasons not to do so. Both remembering a belief and understanding an utterance preserves without any addition or transformation the content of the belief communicated, and this is what makes it unproblematically acceptable – hence the title of the essay, 'Content Preservation'.

Burge starts out by explaining his conception of a priori justification. The paragraph marked $\boxed{a} \mapsto$ provides a negative characterization: a priori justification is independent of sense experience. It is important to note that, unlike some philosophers, Burge's notion of a priori justification does not imply infallibility. Testimonial belief is not immune from error. One can be a priori entitled to a false belief.

Burge's notion of entitlement is externalist. For the listener to be entitled to accept a proposition presented in testimony, he does not need to realize that he is entitled to accept the proposition: 'entitlements are epistemic rights...that need not be understood or even accessible to the subject' (paragraph $\boxed{b} \mapsto$). While entitlements need not be transparent to the subject, the reasons that undermine a default entitlement do need to be transparent. In a different essay Burge writes that the acceptance principle 'says that the entitlement holds unless there are stronger reasons (available to the person) that override it...It is enough for the individual's being warranted that there *are* no defeaters; defeaters of the entitlement must be available to him.'[1]

Assuming Burge is right in claiming that we are a priori entitled to accept propositions presented in testimony, does this mean that everything we know by testimony we know a priori?

The answer is negative. For, in Burge's view, the function of testimony is not to *generate* but to *transfer* warrant (see paragraph $\boxed{h} \mapsto$). The recipient's warrant for a belief based on testimony is parasitic on the attester's warrant. If the attester's warrant for the belief is a posteriori, then the recipient knowledge is also a posteriori – despite the fact that the recipient is a priori entitled to accept the attester's words.

---

[1] 'Interlocution, Perception, and Memory', *Philosophical Studies* 86 (1997), p. 45, n. 4.

And for a belief acquired by testimony to qualify as a priori knowledge, the attester's warrant for the belief must be a priori. Only 'when a priori knowledge is preserved through reports which the recipient is a priori justified in accepting, the receiver's knowledge is a priori' (paragraph $\boxed{i}\mapsto$).

In paragraph $\boxed{e}\mapsto$ and the following five paragraphs Burge presents the acceptance principle as the conclusion from two premises. The first premise states that when a listener understands the attester's utterance, he is a priori entitled to presume that the attester is a 'rational source'. According to the second premise, rational sources are 'sources of truth'. When one has reasons to think that a speaker is rational, one has reasons to accept his intelligible utterances as true. Therefore, we are a priori entitled to accept an intelligible proposition acquired by testimony as true. In Burge's own words: 'We are a priori prima facie entitled to take intelligible affirmation at face value.'

The acceptance principle is a conceptual rather than an empirical thesis (see paragraphs $\boxed{d}\mapsto$ and $\boxed{f}\mapsto$). Even if most attesters would tend to tell lies, there is still a conceptual relation between the intelligibility of an utterance, the presumed rationality of the attester, and the acceptance of the attester's utterance as true. Nevertheless the worry remains that the acceptance principle is a licence to be gulled.

> Why is a recipient of testimony a priori entitled – except when manifest doubt arises – to abstract himself from the possibility that the speaker doesn't tell the truth?

According to the paragraph marked $\boxed{g}\mapsto$, there is a close connection between rationality, on the one hand, and truth and objectivity (i.e., independence of special person interests), on the other. To be rational usually implies that one abstracts oneself from one's self-interest so as to present the truth. Deceiving one's audience can serve one's personal interests, but it is irrational in that it misuses reason. 'Reason has a function . . . in presenting and promoting truth without regard to individual interest.' And insofar as there are grounds for regarding a speaker as reasonable and as a 'rational source', one is entitled to presume that he is not lying; or so Burge argues.

An immediate problem with the preceding argument seems to be that honesty does not imply truth. Just because a speaker tries to tell the truth doesn't mean that he does tell the truth. Veracity of speakers is not the same thing as speakers telling the truth.

In the Commentary on Fricker we discussed the worry that local reductionism is psychologically implausible because testimonial beliefs are typically not held by way of inductive inference from the trustworthiness of the speaker. Interestingly Burge's anti-reductionist position is also vulnerable to objections from psychological reality grounds. For Burge it is what he sees as the purely preservative character of successful communication that entitles us to rely on what we understand others to be saying. Yet some empirical studies of communication suggest that understanding what a speaker has said involves more than linguistic decoding of the meaning that the speaker has encoded. Comprehension is largely inferential.[2]

Among the proponents of an inferential view of communication and comprehension is Paul Grice.[3] In his view, successful communication depends upon co-operation between speakers and listeners towards a common goal. Speakers should conform to maxims of conversation that guide their co-operation. One of these maxims concerns truthfulness and says: 'Do not say what you believe to be false.' For the audience correctly to pick up the speaker's meaning, it must be presupposed that the speaker follows the conversational maxims. Taking a stance of trust in the truthfulness of the speaker is a condition for linguistic comprehension. This trust by default may or may not lead to acceptance of the contents of the utterance. The upshot of Grice's position is that the trust we place in the attester of testimony is neither passive nor blind; rather, trusting speakers is thought to be an essential component of the richly interpretative process that underlies linguistic understanding.

[2]   Cf. A. Bezuidenhout, 'Is Verbal Communication a Purely Preservative Process?', *Philosophical Review* 107 (1998), pp. 261–88; S. Sperber and D. Wilson, *Relevance: Communication and Cognition* (2nd edition, Blackwell, 1995); D. Sperber, 'Understanding Verbal Understanding', in J. Khalfa (ed.), *What is Intelligence?* (Cambridge University Press, 1994), pp. 179–98.
[3]   P. Grice, *Studies in the Ways of Words* (Harvard University Press, 1989).

5

Foundations or Coherence?

Introduction to the Problem

Until now we have been concentrating on the justification for individual beliefs. In this chapter we will be concerned with the justification of whole sets of beliefs. Most of the things we know are based on other things we know. For example, I know that I got a telephone call while I was out of the office because I see the blinking 'new message' light on my answering machine. Here, one belief – that the 'new message' light is blinking – is more basic than the other. One belief stands under or supports another. This naturally raises the question of whether there is a hierarchy of beliefs with a bottom level which is not itself based on any more basic beliefs. Are there, in other words, unjustified (by other beliefs) justifiers, unsupported supporters?

Foundationalism is the view that there is such an ultimate level of non-inferentially (immediately, directly) justified beliefs. All other beliefs are derived from them or are demonstrated by appeal to them. Foundationalism divides our beliefs into two classes: those which need support from others and those which do not. We thus get the picture of our beliefs forming a pyramid with non-basic beliefs being supported by reasoning that traces back ultimately to the basic beliefs. Perhaps an upside-down pyramid would be a more appropriate model, since there are few basic beliefs compared to the vast number of beliefs in common sense and in science that stand in need of justification.

The driving force behind foundationalism is the *infinite regress problem*: if every justified belief could be justified only by being inferred from some further justified belief, the justificational regress would go on forever. To avoid the regress, a foundationalist argues that we are forced to suppose that in tracing back the inferential chain we arrive at one or more immediately justified beliefs that stop the regress. These immediately justified beliefs are not based on other beliefs. They qualify as knowledge (or at least as justified) not because we have reasons to support them, but because they address a special realm of facts to which the mind has direct access. These facts constitute what some philosophers call 'the Given' or 'the Directly Evident'.

Prima facie it might seem that the only beliefs that are not held on the basis of reasoning are perceptual beliefs. I do not *infer* that the 'new message' light is blinking. I can *see* that it is blinking. But, as we all know, such beliefs can be mistaken. Given that perceptual beliefs are fallible, they stand as much in need of justification as any other belief and therefore cannot provide an ultimate stopping point. In response, foundationalism maintains that the basic beliefs are not ordinary perceptual beliefs about physical objects but beliefs about our own sensory states or immediate experiences – how things seem or appear to us. We can be wrong about whether the light is blinking, but not about the fact that it appears to be blinking. Beliefs about how the world appears to us thus seem to be a more basic level of belief than perceptual beliefs about the world. They seem to be self-justifying.

Foundationalism comes in various flavours. While strong foundationalism claims that basic beliefs are infallibly justified or known, weak foundationalism demands that basic belief be only fallibly justified. According to internalist foundationalism, for a belief to be immediately justified, the subject must justifiably believe that it is immediately justified. Externalist foundationalism, on the other hand, holds that a belief may be non-inferentially justified without the subject being aware of this fact. Alston argues for a version of weak externalist foundationalism, which he calls 'simple foundationalism'.

Foundationalism can be criticized both for its commitment to non-inferential justification and for its claim that inferentially justified beliefs depend on non-inferentially justified ones. Some critics deny that there is such a privileged class of self-justifying beliefs, others deny that even if there were such, it would be sufficient to support all other beliefs.

The rival theory to foundationalism is *coherentism*. Coherentists deny that there is a class of beliefs which justify other beliefs without standing in need of justification themselves. According to coherence theories, individual beliefs are justified by the entire system of beliefs in which they cohere. The idea is that the items in coherent systems of beliefs must mutually support each other. All justification is inferential. A belief can only be justified 'from within', from the relations of mutual support (logical, probabilistic, explanatory) that it bears to other beliefs. The spirit of coherentism, therefore, is typically internalistic. A coherentist justification – consisting, as it does, in the relations of beliefs to one another – is accessible to the believer.[1]

---

[1] In *Self-Trust: A Study of Reason, Knowledge, and Autonomy* (Oxford University Press, 1997) Lehrer defends a version of coherentism that combines internalist and externalist features. He distinguishes between objective (verific) and subjective justification, the latter consisting, for example, in the elimination of false beliefs from one's background belief system. Both kinds of justification are necessary for knowledge. In order to know you must be verifically justified and you must be subjectively justified in thinking that you are trustworthy.

The coherentist theory of justification, according to which a belief is justified only if it is supported by other beliefs, must not be mixed up with the 'negative coherence condition' mentioned in connection with Goldman's and Fricker's essays. The negative coherence condition invokes coherence only as a constraint or check on justified beliefs: a justified belief may not be inconsistent with the background information the subject possesses. While negative coherence consists in the absence of background beliefs providing reasons to question the truth of the target belief, positive coherence consists in the presence of positive reasons for the target belief.

A good metaphor for coherentism is that of a crossword puzzle. The answers in the crossword form the set of our beliefs, each individual answer that we fill in representing a single belief. When we get an answer that fits with an answer that we have already, that fact helps to confirm the correctness of the second answer. But it is equally true that the second answer helps confirm the correctness of the first answer. Each answer in the crossword plays a part in supporting all the other answers, which in turn play a part in supporting it. Just as no belief is epistemically basic, no answer in the crossword is more basic than any other.

How does coherentism solve the regress problem? It rejects the linear model of justification in which beliefs are ordered in some hierarchy, so that lower-level beliefs support higher-level beliefs: belief A justifying belief B, B justifying C, and so on. According to the linear picture, the infinite regress problem is unavoidable unless one adopts externalist foundationalism, i.e, the view that a belief may be non-inferentially justified without the subject having to know or believe that this is so. (Internalist foundationalism is of no help here. For if you need to be justified in believing that a belief is non-inferentially justified, the non-inferentially justified belief gives rise to its own regress.) Coherentism replaces the idea of linear justificatory dependence by the idea of mutual or reciprocal justification. Justificatory 'lines' describe big loops. These circles of justification are said not to be vicious because the justification of a particular belief finally depends, not on other particular beliefs, as the linear conception of justification would have it, but on the overall system and its coherence.

Introduction to Alston

William Payne Alston is emeritus professor of philosophy at Syracuse University. His main research areas are epistemology, philosophy of religion, metaphysics, and philosophy of language.

In *Beyond 'Justification': Dimensions of Epistemic Evaluation* (2004) and *Epistemic Justification: Essays in the Theory of Knowledge* (1989), Alston develops and defends externalist reliabilism and a qualified foundationalism. This position he then applies to the philosophy of religion. Our religious beliefs are said to owe their justification directly to our religious experience, in much the same way that perceptual beliefs about physical objects are immediately justified by perceptual experiences. The religious experiences in question are those incidences when people become aware of God's presence or receive messages from God. The reliabilist and foundationalist conception of perceptual and religious experience is set fourth in *Perceiving God: The Epistemology of Religious Experience* (1991) and in *The Reliability of Sense Perception* (1993).

Another topic on which Alston has written extensively is realism. In *A Realist Conception of Truth* (1996) he defends a notion of truth that is compatible with, but doesn't imply, the correspondence theory, i.e., the view that a proposition is true because and only because it matches or corresponds to the way the world is. And *A Sensible Metaphysical Realism* (2002) suggests that vast stretches of reality are not dependent on conceptualization, but some aspects of it are.

William P. Alston, 'Two Types of Foundationalism'

Foundationalism is often stated as the doctrine that knowledge constitutes a structure the foundations of which support all the rest but themselves need no support. To make this less metaphorical we need to specify the mode of support involved. In contemporary discussions of foundationalism knowledge is thought of in terms of true-justified-belief (with or without further conditions); thus the mode of support involved is justification, and what gets supported a belief.* The sense in which a foundation needs no support is that it is not justified by its relation to other justified beliefs; in that sense it does not "rest on" on other beliefs. Thus we may formulate foundationalism as follows:

I. Our justified beliefs form a structure, in that some beliefs (the foundations) are justified by something other than their relation to other justified beliefs; beliefs that *are* justified by their relation to other beliefs all depend for their justification on the foundations.

Notice that nothing is said about *knowledge* in this formulation. Since the structure alleged by foundationalism is a structure of the justification of belief, the doctrine can be stated in terms of that component of knowledge alone. Indeed, one who thinks that knowledge has nothing to do with justified belief is still faced with the question of whether foundationalism is a correct view about the structure of epistemic justification.

[a] → Two emendations will render this formulation more perspicuous. First, a useful bit of terminology. Where what justifies a belief includes* the believer's having certain other justified beliefs, so related to the first belief as to embody reasons or grounds for it, we may speak of *indirectly (mediately) justified belief*. And, where what justifies a belief does not include any such constituent, we may speak of *directly (immediately) justified belief*. Correspondingly, a case of knowledge in which the justification requirement is

satisfied by indirect (mediate) justification will be called *indirect (mediate) knowledge*; and a case in which the justification requirement is satisfied by direct (immediate) justification will be called *direct (immediate) knowledge*.

Second, we should make more explicit how mediate justification is thought to rest on immediately justified belief. The idea is that, although the other beliefs involved in the mediate justification of a given belief may themselves be mediately justified, if we continue determining at each stage how the supporting beliefs are justified, we will arrive, sooner or later, at directly justified beliefs. This will not, in general, be a single line of descent; typically the belief with which we start will rest on several beliefs, each of which in turn will rest on several beliefs. So the general picture is that of multiple branching from the original belief.

With this background we may reformulate foundationalism as follows (turning the "foundation" metaphor on its head):

b→   II Every mediately justified belief stands at the origin of a (more or less) multiply branching tree structure at the tip of each branch of which is an immediately justified belief.

II can be read as purely hypothetical (*if* there are any mediately justified beliefs, then ...) or with existential import (there are mediately justified beliefs, and ...). Foundationalists typically make the latter claim, and I shall understand the doctrine to carry existential import.

II can usefully be divided into two claims:

(A) There are directly justified beliefs.
(B) A given person has a stock of directly justified beliefs sufficient to generate chains of justification that terminate in whatever indirectly justified beliefs he has.

In other words, (A) there are foundations, and (B) they suffice to hold up the building.

In this paper we shall restrict our attention to A. More specifically, we shall be concerned with a certain issue over what it takes for a belief to serve as a foundation.

I   The Second-level Argument

Let's approach this issue by confronting foundationalism with a certain criticism, a recent version of which can be found in Bruce Aune.[1]

---

[1]   *Knowledge, Mind and Nature* (New York: Random House, 1967).

The line of reasoning behind the empiricist's assumption is, again, that while intra-language rules may validly take us from premise to conclusion, they cannot themselves establish empirical truth. If the premises you start with are false, you will have no guarantee that the conclusions you reach are not false either. Hence, to attain knowledge of the actual world, you must ultimately have premises whose truth is acceptable independently of any inference and whose status is accordingly indubitable. Only by having such premises can you gain a starting point that would make inference worthwhile. For convenience, these indispensable basic premises may be called "intrinsically acceptable." The possibility of empirical knowledge may then be said to depend on the availability of intrinsically acceptable premises.

If this line of thought is sound, it follows that utter scepticism can be ruled out only if one can locate basic empirical premises that are intrinsically acceptable. Although philosophers who attack scepticism in accordance with this approach generally think they are defending common sense, it is crucial to observe that they cannot actually be doing so. The reason for this is that, from the point of view of common experience, there is no plausibility at all in the idea that intrinsically acceptable premises, as so defined, ever exist. Philosophers defending such premises fail to see this because they always ignore the complexity of the situation in which an empirical claim is evaluated.

I have already given arguments to show that introspective claims are not, in themselves, intrinsically infallible, they may be regarded as virtually certain if produced by a reliable (sane, clear-headed) observer, but their truth is not a consequence of the mere fact that they are confidently made. To establish a similar conclusion regarding the observation claims of everyday life only the sketchiest arguments are needed. Obviously the mere fact that such a claim is made does not assure us of its truth. If we know that the observer is reliable, made his observation in good light, was reasonably close to the object, and so on, then we may immediately regard it as acceptable. But its acceptability is not intrinsic to the claim itself . . . I would venture to say that any spontaneous claim, observational or introspective, carries almost no presumption of truth, when considered entirely by itself. If we accept such a claim as true, it is only because of our confidence that a complex body of background assumption – concerning observers, standing conditions, the kind of object in question – and, often, a complex mass of further observations all point to the conclusion that it is true.

Given these prosaic considerations, it is not necessary to cite experimental evidence illustrating the delusions easily brought about by, for example, hypnosis to see that no spontaneous claim is acceptable wholly on its own merits. On the contrary, common experience is entirely adequate to show that clear-headed men never accept a claim merely because it is made, without regard to the peculiarities of the agent and of the conditions under which it is produced. For such men, the acceptability of every claim is always determined by inference. If we are prepared to take these standards of acceptability seriously, we must accordingly admit that the traditional search for intrinsically acceptable empirical premises is completely misguided (41–43).

Now the target of Aune's critique differs in several important respects from the foundationalism defined above. First and most obviously, Aune supposes that any "intrinsically acceptable premises" will be infallible and indubitable, and some of his arguments are directed specifically against these features.* Second, there is an ambiguity in the term 'intrinsically acceptable'. Aune introduces it to mean "whose truth is acceptable independently of any inference," this looks roughly equivalent to our 'directly justified'. However in arguing against the supposition that the "observation claims of everyday" are intrinsically acceptable, he says that "the mere fact that such a claim is made does not assure us of its truth," thereby implying that to be intrinsically acceptable a claim would have to be justified just by virtue of being made. Now it is clear that a belief (claim) of which this is true is directly justified, but the converse does not hold. A perceptual belief will also be directly justified, as that term was explained above, if what justifies it is the fact that the perceiver "is reliable, made his observation in good light, was reasonably close to the object, and so on," *provided it is not also required that the he be justified in believing that these conditions are satisfied.* Thus this argument of Aune's has no tendency to show that perceptual beliefs cannot be directly justified, but only that they cannot enjoy that special sort of direct justification which we may term "self-justification."*

However some of Aune's arguments would seem to be directed against any immediate justification, and a consideration of these will reveal a third and more subtle discrepancy between Aune's target(s) and my version of foundationalism. Near the end of the passage Aune says:

> If we accept such a claim [observational or introspective] as true, it is only because of our confidence that a complex of background assumptions . . . all point to the conclusion that it is true.

And again:

> For such men [clear-headed men], the acceptability of every claim is always determined by inference.

It certainly looks as if Aune is arguing that whenever a claim (belief) is justified it is justified by inference (by relation to other justified beliefs); and that would be the denial of 'There are directly justified beliefs'. But look more closely. Aune is discussing not what would justify the issuer of an introspective or observational claim in his belief, but rather what it would take to justify "us" in accepting his claim; he is arguing from a third-person perspective. Now it does seem clear that *I* cannot be immediately justified in accepting *your* introspective or observational claim as true. If I am so justified it is because I am justified in supposing that you issued a claim of that sort, that you are in a normal condition and know the language, and (if it is an observational claim) that conditions were favorable for your accurately perceiving that sort of thing. But that is only because *I*, in contrast to you, am justified in believing that *p* (where what you claimed is that *p*, and where I have no independent access to *p*) only if I am justified in supposing that you are justified in believing that *p*. My access to *p* is through your access. It is just because *my* justification in believing that *p* presupposes my being justified in believing that you are justified, that my justification has to be indirect. That is why I have to look into such matters as conditions of observation, and your normality. Thus what Aune is really pointing to is the necessity for "inferential" backing for any higher-level belief to the effect that someone is justified in believing that *p*. (I shall call such higher-level beliefs *epistemic beliefs*.) His argument, if it shows anything, shows that no epistemic belief can be immediately justified. But it does nothing to show that the original observer's or introspector's belief that *p* was not immediately justified. Hence his argument is quite compatible with the view that an introspective belief is self-justified and with the view that an observational belief is justified just by being formed in favorable circumstances.

As a basis for further discussion I should like to present my own version of an argument against the possibility of immediate justification for epistemic beliefs – what I shall call the *second-level argument*:

$\boxed{c} \rightarrow$ A1 Where *S*'s belief that *p* is mediately justified, any jurisdiction for the belief that *S is justified in believing that p* is obviously mediate. For one could not be justified in this latter belief unless it were based on a justified belief that *S* is justified in accepting the grounds on which his belief that *p* is based. But even where *S* is immediately justified in believing that *p*, the higher-level belief will still be mediately justified, if at all. For in taking a belief to be justified, we are evaluating it in a certain way.* And, like any evaluative property, epistemic justification is a supervenient property, the application of which is based on more fundamental properties. A belief is justified because it possesses what Roderick Firth has called "warrant-increasing properties."[2] Hence in order

[2] In "Coherence, Certainty, and Epistemic Priority," *Journal of Philosophy*, vol. LXI, 19 (Oct. 15, 1964): 545–557.

for me to be justified in believing that S's belief that p is justified, I must be justified in certain other beliefs, viz., that *S's belief that p* possesses a certain property, Q, and that Q renders its possessor justified. (Another way of formulating this last belief is: a belief that there is a valid epistemic principle to the effect that any belief that is Q is justified.) Hence in no case can an epistemic belief that S is justified in believing that p, itself be immediately justified.

Before proceeding I shall make two comments on this argument and its conclusion.

(1) It may appear that the conclusion of the argument is incompatible with the thesis that one cannot be justified in believing that p without also being justified in believing that one is justified in believing that p. For if being immediately justified in believing that p necessarily carried with it being justified in believing that I am justified in believing that p, it would seem that this latter justification would be equally immediate. I would not shirk from such an incompatibility, since I feel confident in rejecting that thesis. It is not clear, however, that there is any such incompatibility. It all depends on how we construe the necessity. If, e.g., it is that my being justified in believing that p necessarily puts me into possession of the *grounds* I need for being justified in the higher-level belief, then that is quite compatible with our conclusion that the latter can only be mediately justified.

d→ (2) The conclusion should not be taken to imply that one must perform any conscious inference to be justified in an epistemic belief, or even that one must be explicitly aware that the lower-level belief has an appropriate warrant-increasing property. Here as in other areas, one's grounds can be possessed more or less implicitly. Otherwise we would have precious little mediate knowledge.

I have already suggested that the second-level argument is not really directed against II. To be vulnerable to this argument, a foundationalist thesis would have to require of foundations not only that *they* be immediately justified, but also that the believer be immediately justified in believing that they are immediately justified. A position that does require this we may call *iterative foundationalism*, and we may distinguish it from the earlier form (*simple foundationalism*) as follows (so far as concerns the status of the foundations):

Simple Foundationalism: For any epistemic subject, S, there are p's such that S is immediately justified in believing that p.

Iterative Foundationalism: For any epistemic subject, S, there are p's such that S is immediately justified in believing that p and S is immediately justified in believing that he is immediately justified in believing that p.*

It would not take much historical research to show that both positions have been taken. What I want to investigate here is which of them there is most reason to take. Since the classic support for foundationalism has been the regress argument, I shall concentrate on determining which form emerges from that line of reasoning.

II   The Regress Argument

The regress argument seeks to show that the only alternatives to admitting epistemic foundations are circularity of justification or an equally unpalatable infinite regress of justification. It may be formulated as follows:

A2   Suppose we are trying to determine whether S is mediately justified in believing that p. To be so justified he has to be justified in believing certain other propositions, q, r, . . . that are suitably related to p (so as to constitute adequate grounds for p). Let's say we have identified a set of such propositions each of which S believes. Then he is justified in believing that p only if he is justified in believing each of those propositions.* And, for each of these propositions q, r, . . . that he is not immediately justified in believing, he is justified in believing it only if he is justified in believing some other propositions that are suitably related to it. And for each of these latter propositions . . .

Thus in attempting to give a definitive answer to the original question we are led to construct a more or less extensive true structure, in which the original belief and every other putatively mediately justified belief form nodes from which one or more branches issue, in such a way that every branch is a part of some branch that issues from the original belief. Now the question is: what form must be assumed by the structure in order that S be mediately justified in believing that p? There are the following conceivable forms for a given branch:

A. It terminates in an immediately justified belief.

B. It terminates in an unjustified belief.

C. The belief that p occurs at some point (past the origin), so that the branch forms a loop.

D. The branch continues infinitely.

Of course some branches might assume one form and others another.

The argument is that the original belief will be mediately justified only if every branch assumes form A. Positively, it is argued that on this condition the relevant necessary condition for the original belief's being mediately justified is satisfied, and, negatively, it is argued that if any branch assumes any of the other forms, is not.

A. Where every branch has form A, this necessary condition is satisfied for every belief in the structure. Since each branch terminates in an immediately justified belief that is justified without necessity for further justified beliefs, the regress is ended along each branch. Hence justification is transferred along each branch right back to the original belief.

B. For any branch that exhibits form B, no element, even the origin, is justified, at least by this structure. Since the terminus is not justified, the prior element, which is justified only if the terminus is, is not justified. And, since it is not justified, its predecessor, which is justified only if it is, is not justified either. And so on, right back to the origin, which therefore itself fails to be justified.

C. Where we have a branch that forms a closed loop, again nothing on that branch, even the origin, is justified, so far as its justification depends on this tree structure. For what the branch "says" is that the belief that p is justified only if the belief that r is justified, and that belief is justified only if..., and the belief that z is justified only if the belief that p is justified. So what this chain of necessary conditions tells us is that the belief that p is justified only if the belief that p is justified. True enough, but that still leaves it completely open whether the belief that p *is* justified.

D. If there is a branch with no terminus, that means that no matter how far we extend the branch the last element is still a belief that is mediately justified if at all. Thus, as far as this structure goes, wherever we stop adding elements we have still not shown that the relevant necessary condition for the mediate justification of the original belief is satisfied. Thus the structure does not exhibit the original belief as mediately justified.

Hence the original belief is mediately justified only if every branch in the tree structure terminates in an immediately justified belief. Hence every mediately justified belief stands at the origin of a tree structure at the tip of each branch of which is an immediately justified belief.*

Now this version of the argument, analogues of which occur frequently in the literature,* supports only simple foundationalism. It has no tendency to show that there is immediately justified epistemic belief. So long as S *is* directly justified in believing some t for each branch of the tree, that will be quite enough to stop the regress; for all that is needed is that he *be* justified in believing *t* without thereby incurring the need to be justified in believing some further proposition....

... Since immediately justified epistemic belief would do nothing to stop the regress, this kind of regress argument can provide no support for iterative foundationalism.

. . .

IV   Envoi

As we have seen, the main reason for adopting foundationalism is the seeming impossibility of a belief's being mediately justified without resting ultimately on immediately justified belief. And the main reason for rejecting it (at least the main antecedent reason, apart from the difficulties of working it out) is that reason one version of which we found in the quotation from Aune. That is, it appears that the foundationalist is committed to adopting beliefs in the absence of any reasons for regarding them as acceptable. And this would appear to be the sheerest dogmatism. It is the aversion to dogmatism, to the apparent arbitrariness of putative foundations, that leads many philosophers to embrace some form of coherence or contextualist theory, in which no belief is deemed acceptable unless backed by sound reasons.

The main burden of this paper is that with simple foundationalism one can have the best of both arguments; one can stop the regress of justification without falling into dogmatism. We have already seen that Aune's form of the dogmatism argument does not touch Simple Foundationalism. For that form of the argument attacks only the ungrounded acceptance of claims *to know-ledge or justification*; and simple foundationalism is not committed to the immediate justification of any such higher-level claims. But one may seek to apply the same argument to lower-level beliefs. Even simple foundationalism, the critic may say, must allow that some beliefs may be accepted in the absence of any reasons for supposing them to be true. And this is still arbitrary dogmatism. But the simple foundationalist has an answer. His position does not require anyone to accept any belief without having a reason for doing so. Where a person *is* immediately justified in believing that *p*, he may find adequate reasons for the higher-level belief that he is immediately justified in believing that *p*. And if he has adequate reasons for accepting this epistemic proposition, it surely is not arbitrary of him to accept the proposition that *p*. What better reason could he have for accepting it?

Lest the reader dismiss this answer as a contemptible piece of sleight-of-hand, let me be more explicit about what is involved. Though the simple foundationalist requires *some* immediately justified beliefs in order to termin-ate the regress of justification, his position permits him to recognize that all epistemic beliefs require mediate justification. Therefore, for any belief that one is immediately justified in believing, one *may* find adequate reasons for accepting the proposition that one is so justified. The curse (of dogmatism) is taken off immediate justification at the lower level, just by virtue of the fact that propositions at the higher level are acceptable only on the basis of reasons. A foundational belief, *b*, is immediately justified just because some valid epistemic principle lays down conditions for its being justified which do not include the believer's having certain other justified beliefs. But the believer will be justified in believing *that* he is immediately justified in holding *b* only if he has *reasons* for regarding that principle as valid and for regarding *b* as falling under that principle. And if he does have such reasons he certainly cannot be accused of arbitrariness or dogmatism in accepting *b*. The absence of reasons for *b* is "compensated" for by the reasons for the correlated higher-level belief. Or, better, the sense in which one can have reasons for accepting an immediately justified belief is necessarily different from that in which one can have reasons for accepting a mediately justified belief. Reasons in the former case are necessarily "meta" in character; they have to do with reasons for regarding the belief as justified. Whereas in the latter case, though one *may* move up a level and find reasons for the higher-level belief that the original belief is mediately justified, it is also required that one have adequate reasons for the lower-level belief itself.

We should guard against two possible misunderstandings of the above argument. First, neither simple foundationalism nor any other epistemology can guarantee that one will, or can, find adequate reasons for a given epistemic proposition, or for any other proposition. The point rather is that there is nothing in the position that rules out the possibility that, for any immediately justified belief that one has, one can find adequate reasons for the proposition that one is so justified. Second, we should not take the critic to be denying the obvious point that people are often well advised, in the press of everyday life, to adopt beliefs for which they do not have adequate reasons. We should interpret him as requiring only that an *ideal* epistemic subject will adopt beliefs only for good and sufficient reason. Hence he insists that our epistemology must make room for this possibility. And, as just pointed out, Simple Foundationalism does so.

The dogmatism argument may be urged with respect to *showing* that *p*, as well as with respect to accepting the proposition that *p*. That is, the critic may argue that foundationalism is committed to the view that "foundations cannot be argued for." Suppose that in trying to show that *p* I adduce some grounds, and, the grounds being challenged, I try to show that they are true, and . . . in this regress I finally arrive at some foundation *f*. Here, according to the critic, the foundationalist must hold that the most I can (properly) do is simply *assert f*, several times if necessary, and with increasing volume. And again this is dogmatism. But again Simple Foundationalism is committed to no such thing. It leaves something for the arguer to do even here, viz., try to establish the higher-level proposition that he is immediately justified in believing that *f*. And, if he succeeds in doing this, what more could we ask? Unless someone demands that he go on to establish the grounds appealed to in that argument – to which again the simple foundationalist has no objection in principle. Of course, as we saw earlier, the demand that one establish every ground in a demonstration is a self-defeating demand. But the point is that the simple foundationalist need not, any more than the coherence theorist, mark out certain points at which the regress of showing *must* come to an end. He allows the possibility of one's giving reasons for an assertion whenever it is appropriate to do so, even if that assertion is of a foundation.

But, like many positions that give us the best of both worlds, this one may be too good to be true. Although I am convinced that simple foundationalism is the most defensible form of foundationalism, especially if it also divests itself of other gratuitous claims for foundations, such as infallibility and incorrigibility,* I do not claim that it can actually be made to work. Though it escapes the main antecedent objection, it still faces all the difficulties involved in finding enough immediately justified beliefs to ground all our mediately justified beliefs. And on this rock I suspect it will founder. Meanwhile, pending a final decision on that question, it is the version on which both constructive and critical endeavors should be concentrated.

Commentary on Alston

Alston distinguishes between simple (externalist) and iterative (internalist) foundationalism, argues that only simple foundationalism is capable of dissolving the infinite regress argument, and clears simple foundationalism of suspicion of dogmatism, because it adopts beliefs as foundational in the absence of any reasons for regarding them as foundational.

To precisely state the position of foundationalism, a distinction has to be drawn between mediate and immediate justification of belief. According to paragraph $\boxed{a}\rightarrow$, basic beliefs are beliefs that are directly justified in that they are epistemically independent of other beliefs. Mediately justified beliefs, on the other hand, are only justified because they are based upon other beliefs that are themselves justified. Usually an inferential belief has as its basis not just a single belief but a number of beliefs. By tracing the 'flow' of justification from its sources to the target belief we get a tree- or bush-like structure with branches terminating in a single node. Alston employs the tree metaphor in his revised definition of foundationalism in paragraph $\boxed{b}\rightarrow$.

The epistemic dependence constitutive of mediate justification has to be distinguished from other kinds of dependence such as causal dependence and conceptual dependence. Suppose my belief that $2 + 3 = 5$ counts as a basic belief. My having this belief depends on my having numerous other concepts and beliefs. For example, I couldn't have this belief if I didn't possess the concept of a number or if my elementary school teacher hadn't taught me the rules for addition. Given these dependencies, in what respect then is the belief that $2 + 3 = 5$ basic? It is basic in that it is justified not because I infer it from something else I justifiably believe, but simply because it seems obviously true to me. Clearly, which beliefs are directly and which are indirectly justified differs from person to person.

> Does the phrase 'inferential justification' also apply to unconscious reasoning from unconscious premises?

In the paragraph marked $\boxed{d}\!\!\mapsto$ Alston answers in the affirmative. For if only conscious inferences qualified as inferential justification, most, if not all, of our justified beliefs would come out as being basic. The odd exceptions would be beliefs based on reflective reasoning. A more plausible conception of inferential justification operates with the notion of a reconstructible inference. Instead of demanding that a subject must either consciously or unconsciously infer belief A from belief B, inferential justification is characterized in terms of a conditional: if the subject were challenged as to what his justification was for accepting belief A, he would cite belief B.

Next Alston distinguishes between simple and iterative foundationalism. The former is externalist in that a belief may be non-inferentially justified without the subject having to be aware of this fact. Iterative foundationalism, on the other hand, claims that the bearer of an immediately justified belief must be immediately justified in believing that he is immediately justified.

> Why does Alston think that the position of iterative foundationalism is incoherent?

The reason is that beliefs to the effect that someone is immediately justified in believing p cannot themselves be immediately justified. The 'second-level argument' in paragraph $\boxed{c}\!\!\mapsto$ shows that for S to justifiably believe that he is immediately justified in believing p, S must reason from certain other beliefs, such as that the belief that p 'tracks' (in Nozick's sense) the fact that p. If immediate object-level justification calls for higher-level justification (as iterative foundationalism claims) and if higher-level justification is necessarily mediate (as the second-level argument maintains), then immediate justification is a fiction and the foundationalist project collapses.

The second-level argument against iterative foundationalism can be parsed into the following steps:

1. Justification is an evaluative property.
2. Evaluative properties supervene on more fundamental properties.
3. If a property P supervenes on more fundamental properties Q, then S is justified in believing that something x is P only if S is justified in believing that x has Q and that whatever has Q has P.

4. *S* is justified in believing that *S* is justified in believing that *p* only if *S* is justified in believing that the belief that *p* has *Q* and that whatever has *Q* is justified.
5. Hence, *S*'s belief to the effect that *S* is justified in believing that *p* cannot be immediately justified.

In the present context '*x* supervenes on *y*' is more or less synonymous with '*x* depends on *y*'.

As already remarked, the foundationalism–coherentism dialectic arises from the infinite regress problem. The aim of section II is to show that because simple foundationalism is sufficient for solving the infinite regress problem, iterative foundationalism is not only incoherent but unnecessary. According to the regress problem, a belief is justified only by being evidentially supported by some other belief. For the supporting beliefs to justify the target belief, they themselves need to be justified. Hence for any belief to be justified there has to be an infinite sequence of justifications. As Alston explains in paragraph $\boxed{e}\mapsto$, there are four possible kinds of sequences: the infinite, the circular, the sequence terminating in beliefs that are unjustified, and the sequence terminating in an non-inferentially justified belief.

The first possibility commits us to the idea that humans have an infinite number of beliefs. But even if our minds could house an infinite set of beliefs, infinite epistemic chains cannot achieve justification since the justificatory process never comes to an end. The second option is adopted by coherentism, the principal alternative to foundationalism. Without going into the details here – coherentism will be discussed in the second part of this chapter – we can see that, given the linear conception of justification, epistemic chains looping back upon themselves are not going to do the trick. Suppose I am looking at my watch and thereby come to believe that it's Friday. Further suppose that my justification for the belief that today is Friday is my further belief that my watch works reliably on Fridays. Clearly this circular explanation fails to lend support to the target belief. The third possibility is unsatisfactory because it blurs the distinction between justified and unjustified beliefs; any belief could come to count as justified. The only remaining alternative, then, is that epistemic sequences terminate in unconditionally or non-inferentially justified beliefs. Thus the upshot of the regress argument is that if there are any inferentially justified beliefs, there must be some non-inferentially justified ones.

Why does Alston think that iterative foundationalism is useless for solving the epistemic regress problem?

Of the two types of foundationalism, it is simple foundationalism that brings the justificatory sequence to a halt. Iterative foundationalism, instead of stopping the epistemic sequence originating in the target belief, generates another such sequence. This was the lesson of the second-level argument.

After having shown that simple foundationalism is superior to iterative foundationalism, Alston turns to the chief objection to simple foundationalism. The problem with simple foundationalism seems to be that it leads into dogmatism, for it rests the structure of inferentially justified belief upon immediately justified foundations in the absence of reasons for regarding these foundations as acceptable. Often 'dogmatic' is simply a term of abuse, meaning 'uncritical' or 'without sufficient evidence'. In this context, to be dogmatic means to claim knowledge but refuse to attempt to explain how you have it.

When faced with the charge of dogmatism, a simple foundationalist could simply bite the bullet and insist that there is a sharp difference between knowing something and being able to explain how one knows it. (This is similar to the distinction between knowledge conditions and conditions for the attribution of knowledge discussed in the introduction to Chapter 3.) Why should it not be possible to have knowledge but not be able to explain why one has it? There might even be cases where the adoption of a dogmatic attitude can help us to gain knowledge. Dogmatism can be an intellectual virtue.

Is dogmatism a coherent epistemological position?

The problem with embracing dogmatism is that it somehow doesn't seem to be compatible with the aim of epistemology. Epistemology tries to explain and understand how we know things. The thesis that not all knowledge involves epistemological theorizing avoids epistemology while itself being an epistemological thesis. The dogmatist therefore seems to be someone who does epistemology while trying to bypass doing so; or so it could be argued.[1]

In the paragraph marked $\boxed{f}$→ Alston agues that simple foundationalism is not affected by the charge of dogmatism. For although simple foundationalism does not require the bearer of an immediately justified belief that p to have reasons for thinking that he is immediately justified in believing p, it doesn't prevent him from having such reasons. Simple foundationalism doesn't preclude seeking reasons for the higher-level belief that the belief in p is immediately justified. And as the second-level argument shows, *if* one is justified in the higher-level belief, then one is *mediately* justified. The justification of higher-level beliefs demands mediate justification. So when someone is immediately justified in believing that p, he may have reasons for regarding the belief that p as immediately justified and thereby be mediately justified in believing that his belief in p is immediately justified. The charge of dogmatism would only hold, so Alston argues, if simple foundationalism would force us to accept foundational beliefs without argument. But since this is not the case, the objection fails. In Alston's own words: 'The curse (of dogmatism) is taken off immediate justification at the lower level, just by virtue of the fact that propositions at the higher level are acceptable only on the basis of reason' (paragraph $\boxed{f}$→).

[1]   See S. C. Hetherington, *Knowledge Puzzles: An Introduction to Epistemology* (Westview Press, 1996), pp. 5–6.

Introduction to BonJour

Laurence BonJour is professor of philosophy at the University of Washington. His interests are in epistemology, Kant, and British Empiricism. BonJour's first book, *The Structure of Empirical Knowledge* (1985), explains and defends the coherence theory of justification. For many years BonJour was one of the most prominent and sophisticated advocates of coherentism. But while working on his second book, *In Defense of Pure Reason: A Rationalist Account of A Priori Justification* (1998), he defected to the opposite camp. In his new foundationalist incarnation BonJour holds that 'coherentism is pretty obviously untenable, indeed hopeless'.[1] The point of the second book is that simple a priori beliefs (such as the belief that there are no round squares) are self-justified: that the intuitively apprehended necessity of their content provides a reason for thinking that they are true.

The essay reprinted in this volume dates from before BonJour's conversion to foundationalism. Even though the essay speaks up for coherentism, it already shows an acute awareness of the problems with this position. The essay is a preliminary version of Part II of *The Structure of Empirical Knowledge*. A valuable tool for studying BonJour's coherentism is *The Current State of the Coherence Theory* (1989), edited by J. W. Bender, which contains ten critical articles along with BonJour's replies.

Apart from the two books mentioned, BonJour has written a textbook, *Epistemology: Classic Problems and Contemporary Responses* (2002), has co-authored with E. Sosa *Epistemic Justification: Internalism vs. Externalism, Foundations vs. Virtues* (2003), and has co-edited with A. Baker *Philosophical Problems: An Annotated Anthology* (2005).

Laurence BonJour, 'The Coherence Theory of Empirical Knowledge'

. . .

I

The main watershed which divides the coherence theory of empirical knowledge (CTEK) from opposing epistemological views is a familiar problem which I shall call "the regress problem". This problem arises directly out of the justification condition of the traditional explication of knowledge as adequately justified true belief.* The most obvious way in which beliefs are justified is *inferential justification*. In its most explicit form, inferential justi-

---

[1] L. BonJour, 'The Dialectic of Foundationalism and Coherentism', in J. Greco and E. Sosa (eds), *The Blackwell Guide to Epistemology* (1999), p. 139.

fication consists in providing an argument from one or more other beliefs as premises to the justificandum belief as conclusion.* But it is obviously a necessary condition for such inferential justification that the beliefs appealed to as premises be themselves *already* justified in some fashion; that a belief follows from unjustified premises lends it no justification. Now the premise-beliefs might also be justified inferentially, but such justification would only introduce further premise-beliefs which would have to be justified in some way, thus leading apparently to an infinite, vicious regress of epistemic justification. The justification of one belief would require the *logically antecedent* justification of one or more other beliefs, which in turn would require the logically antecedent justification of still further beliefs, etc. The result, seemingly inescapable so long as all justification is inferential in character, would be that justification could never even get started and hence that no belief would ever be genuinely justified.* Any adequate epistemological position must provide a solution to this problem, a way of avoiding the skeptical result – and the character of that solution will determine, more than anything else, the basic structure of the position. . . .

(i) The historically most popular solution has been what may be called 'strong foundationism', one version of the basic foundationist approach to epistemological issues. The basic thesis of foundationism in all of its forms is that certain empirical, contingent beliefs have a degree of epistemic warrant or justification which is non-inferential in character, i.e. which does not derive from other beliefs via inference in a way that would require those other beliefs to be antecedently justified. Strong foundationism is the view that the non-inferential warrant of these beliefs is sufficient *by itself* to satisfy the adequate-justification condition of knowledge and to qualify them as acceptable premises for the inferential justification of further beliefs. Thus these 'basic beliefs' constitute the 'foundation' upon which the rest of our empirical knowledge is based; the regress of justification terminates when such beliefs are reached.

. . .

(ii) The main traditional alternative to strong foundationism is the CTEK. In first approximation, the CTEK involves two main theses. The first is that *all* epistemic justification for individual empirical beliefs is inferential in character and hence that there are no basic beliefs and no foundation for knowledge. The second is the twofold claim (a) that the regress of justification does not go on forever, which would involve an infinite number of distinct beliefs, but rather circles back upon itself, thus forming a closed system; and (b) that the primary unit of epistemic justification is such a system, which is justified in terms of its internal coherence. The main historical proponents of the CTEK were the absolute idealists, though they tended at times to conflate (or confuse) the CTEK with a coherence account of *truth*. A similar view was also held by certain of the logical positivists, especially Neurath and Hempel.[1] Among contemporary philosophers views resembling the CTEK to some extent have been held by Quine, Sellars, and others.[2] To most philosophers, however, the CTEK has seemed to be afflicted with insuperable difficulties.

. . .

II

The underlying motivation for the CTEK is the conviction that all foundationist accounts of empirical knowledge are untenable. The crucial problem is much the same for both versions of foundationism: what is the source or rationale of the non-inferential epistemic warrant which allegedly attaches to a basic belief (in strong foundationism) or to an initially credible belief (in weak foundationism)? If an empirical, contingent belief B, one which is not knowable a priori, is to have such warrant for a given person, it seems that he must have some reason for thinking that B is true or likely to

[1]   The clearest specimen of this idealist view is Brand Blanshard, The Nature of Thought (London, Allen & Unwin, 1939). See also F. H. Bradley, Essays on Truth and Reality (Oxford, Oxford University Press, 1914); and Bernard Bosanquet, Implication and Linear Inference (London, Macmillan, 1920). For the positivists, see Otto Neurath, 'Protocol Sentences', translated in A. J. Ayer (ed.) Logical Positivism (New York, The Free Press, 1959), pp. 199–208; and Carl G. Hempel, 'On the Logical Positivists' Theory of Truth', Analysis II (1934–35), 49–59. The Hempel paper is in part a reply to a foundationist critique of Neurath by Schlick in 'The Foundation of Knowledge', also translated in Logical Positivism, pp. 209–227. Schlick replied to Hempel in 'Facts and Propositions', and Hempel responded in 'Some, Remarks on "Facts" and Propositions', both in Analysis II (1934–35), 65–70 and 93–96, respectively.

[2]   See W. V. O Quine, 'Two Dogmas of Empiricism', in his From a Logical Point of View (Cambridge, Mass., Harvard University Press, 1953); also his Word and Object (New York, John Wiley & Sons, 1960), Chapter I; and Gilbert Harman, 'Quine on Meaning and Existence II', Review of Metaphysics XXI (1967–68), 343–67. Sellars's writings on this subject are voluminous, but the most important are: 'Empiricism and the Philosophy of Mind' (especially Section VIII) and 'Some Reflections on Language Games', both reprinted in his Science, Perception and Reality (London, Routledge & Kegan Paul, 1963); 'Givenness and Explanatory Coherence', Journal of Philosophy LXX (1973), 612–24; and 'The Structure of Knowledge', his unpublished Machette Lectures, given at the University of Texas in the spring of 1971, especially Part 3, 'Epistemic Principles'. The view offered in this paper is closest to Sellars's and is, at certain points, strongly influenced by it, though I am very unsure how much of it Sellars would agree with. Others who have advocated somewhat similar views include Hall, Aune, Harman, and Lehrer. For Hall's view see his Our Knowledge of Fact and Value (Chapel Hill, University of North Carolina Press, 1961). Aune's views are to be found in his book Knowledge, Mind, and Nature (New York, Random House, 1967). For Harman, see his book Thought (Princeton, Princeton University Press, 1973). For Lehrer, see his Knowledge (Oxford, Oxford University Press, 1974).

be true (the degree of likelihood required depending on whether *B* is held to be basic or only initially credible). And it is hard to see what such a reason could consist in other than the justified beliefs both (a) that *B* has some property or feature Φ and (b) that beliefs having the property or feature Φ are likely, to the appropriate degree, to be true. Such justified beliefs would provide the basis for a justifying argument for *B*, and reliance on them would of course mean that *B* was not basic or initially credible after all. But how can a person be justified in accepting a contingent belief if he does not believe, and *a fortiori* does not know, anything about it which makes it at all likely to be true? A standard of epistemic justification which yields this result would seem clearly to have severed the vital connection between epistemic justification and truth, thus leaving itself without any ultimate rationale. It is for reasons of this sort that the CTEK holds that the justification of particular empirical beliefs is always inferential in character, and that there can in principle be no basic (or initially credible) empirical beliefs and no foundation for empirical knowledge.*

This picture of the CTEK, however, though accurate as far as it goes, is seriously misleading because it neglects the systematic or holistic character of the view. The best way to see this is to return to the regress problem.

Having rejected foundationism, the CTEK must hold that the regress of justification moves in a circle (or at least a closed curve), since this is the only alternative to a genuinely infinite regress involving an infinite number of distinct beliefs. But this response to the regress problem will seem obviously inadequate to one who approches the issue with foundationist preconceptions. For surely, it will be argued, such an appeal to circularity does not solve the regress problem. Each step in the regress is an argument whose premises must be justified *before* they can confer justification on the conclusion. To say that the regress moves in a circle is to say that at some point one (or more) of the beliefs which figured earlier as conclusions is now appealed to as a justifying premise. And this situation, far from solving the regress problem, yields the patently absurd result that the justification of such a belief (qua conclusion) depends on *its own* logically prior justification (qua premise): it cannot be justified unless it is *already* justified. And thus neither it nor anything which depends on it can be justified. Since justification is always finally circular in this way according to the CTEK, there can be on that view no genuine justification and no knowledge.

The tacit premise in this seemingly devastating line of argument is the idea that inferential justification is essentially *linear* in character, involving a linear sequence of beliefs along which warrant is transferred from the earlier beliefs in the sequence to the later beliefs via connections of inference. It is this linear conception of inferential justification that ultimately generates the regress problem. If it is accepted, the idea that justification moves in a circle will be obviously unacceptable, and only *strong* foundationism will be left as an alternative. . . . Thus the basic response of the CTEK to the regress problem is not the appeal to circularity, which would be futile by itself, but rather the rejection of the linear conception of inferential justification.*

The alternative is a holistic or systematic conception of inferential justification (and hence of empirical justification in general, since all empirical justification is inferential for the CTEK): beliefs are justified by being inferentially related to other beliefs in the overall context of a coherent system. To make this view clear, it is necessary to distinguish two levels at which issues of justification can be raised. Thus the issue at hand may be merely the justification of a particular belief, or a small set of beliefs, in the context of a cognitive system whose overall justification is taken for granted; or it may be the global issue of the justification of the cognitive system itself. According to the CTEK it is the latter, global issue which is fundamental for the determination of epistemic justification. Confusion arises, however, because it is only issues of the former, more limited, sort which tend to be raised explicitly in actual cases.

At the level at which only the justification of a particular belief (or small set of such beliefs) is at issue, justification appears linear. A given justificandum belief is justified explicitly by citing other premise-beliefs from which it may be inferred. Such premise-beliefs can themselves be challenged, with justification being provided for them in the same fashion. But there is no serious danger of a regress at this level since the justification of the overall epistemic system (and thus of at least most of its component beliefs) is *exhypothesi* not at issue. One thus quickly reaches premise-beliefs which are dialectically acceptable in that context.

If on the other hand no dialectically acceptable stopping point is reached, if the premise-beliefs which are offered by way of justification continue to be challenged, then the epistemic dialogue would, if ideally continued, eventually move in a circle, giving the appearance of a regress and in effect challenging the entire cognitive system. At this global level, however, the CTEK no longer conceives the relation between the various particular beliefs as one of linear dependence, but rather as one of mutual or reciprocal support. There is no ultimate relation of epistemic priority among the members of such a system and consequently no basis for a true regress. The component beliefs are so related that each can be justified in terms of the others; the direction in which the justifying argument actually moves depends on which belief is under scrutiny in a particular context. The apparent circle of justification is not vicious because the justification of particular beliefs depends finally not on other particular beliefs, as in the linear conception of justification, but on the overall system and its coherence.

Thus the fully explicit justification of a particular belief would involve four distinct steps of argument, as follows:

1. The inferability of that particular belief from other particular beliefs, and further inference relations among particular beliefs.
2. The coherence of the overall system of beliefs.
3. The justification of the overall system of beliefs.
4. The justification of the particular belief in question, by virtue of its membership in the system.

According to the CTEK, each of these steps depends on the ones which precede it. It is the neglecting of steps 2 and 3, the ones pertaining explicitly to the cognitive system, that is the primary source of the linear conception of justification and thus of the regress problem. This is a seductive mistake. . . .

 Thus the problem of giving an adequate account of coherence is one which may safely be neglected by the sort of preliminary defense of the CTEK which is offered here. There are, however, some essential points concerning the concept which should be noted. First, coherence is not to be equated with consistency. A coherent system must be consistent, but a consistent system need not be very coherent. Coherence has to do with systematic connections between the components of a system, not just with their failure to conflict.* Second, coherence will obviously be a matter of degree. For a system of beliefs to be justified, according to the CTEK, it must not be merely coherent to some extent, but more coherent than any currently available alternative.* Third, coherence is closely connected with the concept of explanation. Exactly what the connection is I shall not try to say here. But it is clear that the coherence of a system is enhanced to the extent that observed facts (in a sense to be explicated below) can be explained within it and reduced to the extent that this is not the case. Since explanation and prediction are at the very least closely allied, much the same thing can be said about prediction as well.

The problems relating to the other problematic transition in the schematic argument, that from step 2 to step 3, are more immediately serious. What is at issue here is the fundamental question of the connection between coherence and justification: why, if a body of beliefs is coherent, is it thereby epistemically justified? The force of this question is best brought out by formulating three related objections to the CTEK, centering on this point, which are usually thought to destroy all plausibility which it might otherwise have:

(I) According to the CTEK, the system of beliefs which constitutes empirical knowledge is justified *solely* by reference to coherence. But coherence will never suffice to pick out one system of beliefs, since there will always be many other alternative, incompatible systems of belief which are equally coherent and hence equally justified according to the CTEK.

(II) According to the CTEK, empirical beliefs are justified only in terms of relations to other beliefs and to the system of beliefs; at no point does any relation to the world come in. But this means that the alleged system of empirical knowledge is deprived of all *input* from the world. Surely such a self-enclosed system of beliefs cannot constitute empirical knowledge.

(III) An adequate epistemological theory must establish a connection between its account of justification and its account of *truth*; i.e., it must be shown that justification, as viewed by that theory, is *truth-conductive*, that one who seeks justified beliefs is at least likely to find true ones. But the only way in which the CTEK can do this is by adopting a coherence theory of truth and the absurd idealistic metaphysics which goes along with it.

Of these three objections, (III) is the most basic and (I) is the most familiar. It is (II), however, which must be dealt with first, since the answer to it is essential for dealing with the other two objections. Fundamentally, the point made in (II) must simply be accepted: there must be some sort of input into the cognitive system from the world. Thus the answer to (II) must consist in showing how the CTEK can allow for such input. . . .

III

It may be thought that the suggestion that there is room in the CTEK for an appeal to observation involves an immediate contradiction in terms. For surely, the argument might go, it is essential to the very conception of observation that observational beliefs are *non-inferential* in character; and it is equally essential to the conception of the CTEK, as explained above, that *all* justified beliefs are *inferential*. Thus the CTEK can accord no significant epistemic role to observation (which surely constitutes an immediate *reductio ad absurdum* of the theory).

But this argument is mistaken. It rests on a confusion between two quite different ways in which a belief may be said to be inferential (or non-inferential). In the first place, there is the issue of how the belief was arrived at, of its *origin* in the thinking of the person in question: was it arrived at via an actual process of reasoning or inference from other beliefs or in some other way? In the second place, there is the issue of how the belief is *justified* or *warranted* (if at all): is it justified by virtue of inferential relations to other beliefs or in some other way? Thus there are two distinct senses in which a belief may be inferential (and corresponding senses in which it may be non-inferential). And the immediate force of the above objection rests on a failure to distinguish these senses, for it is in the *first* sense (inferential or non-inferential *origin*) that an observational belief is paradigmatically non-inferential; while it is in the *second* sense (inferential or non-inferential *warrant*) that the CTEK insists that all justified beliefs must be inferential. And there is nothing absurd about the idea that a belief might be arrived at in some non-inferential way (e.g., as a hunch) and only subsequently justified, via inference.

. . .

I begin with objection (II), which alleges that a consequence of the CTEK is that empirical knowledge has no *input* from the world. In light of the discussion of observation, it should now be clear that the CTEK can allow for input into the cognitive system from the world, while insisting that this input must be understood in *causal* rather than epistemic terms. The world impinges upon the system of knowledge by causing cognitively spontaneous beliefs of various sorts, but these beliefs are epistemically justified or warranted only from within the system, along the lines set out above. And, in principle at least, any sort of causal impact of the world that is capable of producing such beliefs in a reliable way is capable of being justified as a species of observation.

. . .

The answer to objection (I), the alternative coherent systems objection, is already implicit in the foregoing discussion. For once it is clear that the CTEK involves the possibility that a system which is coherent at one time may be rendered incoherent by subsequent observational input, and once the requirement is accepted that any putative system of empirical knowledge must allow for this possibility, objection (I) in effect divides into two parts. Part one is the claim that *at a given moment* there may be many equally coherent empirical systems among which the CTEK provides no basis for decision. This claim is correct, but does not provide any basis for a serious objection, since the same thing will be true for any theory of knowledge imaginable. The important issue is whether these equally coherent systems will remain equally coherent and still distinct under the impact of observation in the long run.* Thus the second and crucial part of objection (I) will be the claim that even in the long run, and with the continuing impact of observation, there will be multiple, equally coherent empirical systems among which it will not be possible to decide. But, once the role of observation in the CTEK is appreciated, there seems little if any reason to accept this claim. The role of observation undercuts the idea that such alternatives can be simply constructed at will: such systems might be coherent at the beginning, but there is no reason to think that they would remain so as observations accumulate. This point is obvious enough if the observational components of the different systems involve the same concepts. But even if the observational components, or even the entire systems, involve different concepts so that they are not directly commensurable, there is no reason to think that one objective world will go on providing coherent input to incompatible systems in the long run.*

This brings us to objection (III), surely the most penetrating and significant of the three. Objection (III) contends that the CTEK will be unable to establish the vital connection between justification and truth, will be unable to show that its account of justification is truth-conducive, unless it also adopts the coherence theory of *truth*. It is certainly correct that a connection of this sort must be established by any adequate epistemology, even though this issue is rarely dealt with in a fully explicit fashion. Truth is after all the *raison d'etre* of the cognitive enterprise. The only possible ultimate warrant for an account of epistemic justification must therefore consist in showing that accepting such an account and seeking beliefs which are in accord with it is likely to yield the truth or at least more likely than would be the case on any alternative account. And the objection is also right that one who adopts a coherence theory of justification is in danger of being driven dialectically to espouse the coherence theory of truth as well. For the easiest and most straightforward way to establish a connection between a coherence account of justification and truth itself is to simply identify truth with justification-in-the-long-run, i.e. with coherence-in-the-long-run. Essentially this move was made by the absolute idealists and, in a different way, by Peirce. I assume here that such a coherence theory of truth is mistaken, that truth is to be understood at least roughly along the lines of the traditional correspondence theory. But if this is right, then the only way finally to justify the CTEK and answer objection (III) is to provide an argument to show that following the epistemic standards set by the CTEK is, in the long run, *likely* at least to lead to correspondence.*

I believe that it is possible to give such an argument, though I cannot undertake to provide a detailed account of it here. The main difficulty is an extrinsic one: no one has succeeded so far in giving an adequate account of the correspondence theory of truth,* and such an account is an indispensable ingredient of the envisaged argument. It is possible, however, to provide a rough sketch of the way in which the argument would go, given a very rough and intuitive conception of the correspondence theory: a proposition is true if it accords with an actual situation in the world, and otherwise false. (The argument is relative to the assumption that the observation requirement can be satisfied; if there were no possibility of reliable input from the world, then no set of epistemic standards would be likely to yield the truth.)

Suppose then that we have a hypothetical cognitive system which is coherent and satisfies the observation requirement as stipulated above, but fails to accord with reality. Our task is to show that such a system is unlikely to *remain* coherent (and continue to satisfy the observation requirement) unless it is revised in the direction of greater accord with reality. The way in which such revision *might* take place is obvious enough. If the lack of accord between the system and reality involves observable matters, then if the appropriate observations are actually made, they will produce inconsistency or incoherence within the system and force its revision. If the observations themselves are not rejected by such a revision, then the effect is to bring the system more into accord with reality. And this process *might* be repeated over and over until complete accord with reality is achieved in the very long run.

This, as I say, is what *might* happen. But is it *likely* to happen? The best way to show that it is likely to happen is to consider in turn each of the various seemingly plausible ways in which it might fail to happen, despite the lack of accord between system and reality stipulated above, and show that these are all *un*likely.

First. The process described above, whereby the system is revised in the direction of greater accord with the world, depends essentially on the occurrence of observational beliefs which conflict with other parts of the system and thus force the revision of the system. But any such revision involves a choice as to which of the conflicting beliefs to retain, and the system will come to accord more closely with reality only if this choice results in the retention of the observational beliefs and the exclusion of their competitors. Thus the most obvious way in which such revision in the direction of truth might fail to occur is that the choice be made consistently in favor of the non-observational beliefs in question, rejecting the observational beliefs. In the short run, it is quite likely that such a revision would produce a more justified result than would the alternative choice in favor of observation. But this could not happen in the long run. For if an inquirer or community of inquirers were to follow in the long run such a policy, deliberate or not, of resolving most such decisions in favor of the antecedent system and against the observational belief, this would inevitably have the effect of undermining the law that such observations are reliable and thus eventually violating the observation requirement. Thus this first possibility may be ruled out.

Second. Another way in which the envisaged revision in favor of truth might fail to take place is that, although the situations in the world which conflicted with the system were in fact observable, it might be the case that the inquirer or inquirers in question were simply never in the proper position to make the requisite observations, and so the conflict between the system and world would never be discovered. This possibility cannot be completely ruled out. But the longer the period of inquiry in question becomes, the more unlikely it is that this situation would continue, and this unlikelihood is increased as the supposed discrepancy between system and world is made larger.

Third. So far the assumption has been that the lack of accord between system and world involves aspects of the world which are observable. But suppose that this is not the case, that the aspects of the world in question are unobservable. There are various ways in which this might be so. First, and most basically, it might be the case that the aspects in question simply had no causal effects which were detectable by the sense organs or sensitive faculties of our community of inquirers, so that there would be no way that such inquirers could learn to observe those aspects. Second, it might be the case that, although the aspects in question did have causal impact on our inquirers, these inquirers simply had not learned to make observations of the appropriate sort. Third, it might be the case that although the aspects in question were in principle observable by our inquirers, there were barriers of some sort which prevented them from actually making the observations. Such barriers would include distance in space or time, impossibly hostile environments of various sorts, etc.

This sort of situation must be acknowledged as possible and even likely. The question is whether it could be overcome, given only the resources allowed by the CTEK, and if so, how likely it is that such an overcoming would occur.* The answer to the first part of the question is that it *could* be overcome, in either of two ways. In the first place, the unobservability of the aspects of the world in question might be overcome: the barriers might be transcended, the inquirers might learn to make the requisite observations, and/or new instruments might be developed which would create an appropriate causal linkage between these aspects and the sense organs of our observers. . . . All of these things could happen, but there is no way to show that they are likely to happen in general. Thus the more important way in which the situation of unobservability might be overcome is by the development of *theories* concerning the unobservable aspects of the world. It is via theory construction that we come to know about the unobservable aspects of the world.

But is there any reason to think that such theory construction is likely to take place? The only possible answer on behalf of the CTEK, as indeed on behalf of any theory of knowledge, is that if enough aspects of the world are observable and if the unobservable aspects of the world have enough causal impact on the observable ones, then a fully coherent account of the observable aspects will in the long run lead to theories about the unobservable aspects. The main consideration here is that coherence essentially involves both prediction and explanation. An account of the observable world which was unable to predict and explain the observable effects of unobservable entities and processes would be to that extent incoherent. Thus to suppose that an ideally coherent account could be given of the observable aspects without any mention of the unobservable aspects would be in effect to suppose both that the world divides into two parts with no significant causal interaction between the two, and that this division coincides with that between the observable and the unobservable. And this is surely unlikely, even if one does not bring in the fact that the observable/unobservable line is not fixed once and for all.*

. . .

The foregoing considerations are an attempt to make plausible the following conclusion: it is highly unlikely, though not impossible, that a cognitive system which failed to accord with the world and which satisfied the observation requirement would be coherent and remain coherent under the impact of new observation, unless it was gradually revised in the direction of greater accord with the world. This is so because all of the apparent ways in which such revision could fail to take place represent highly unlikely situations.[3] This is obviously only a sketch of a line of argument which would have to be greatly elaborated in various ways to be really adequate. Here it is intended only to suggest the sort of answer which the CTEK can make to objection (III), how it can establish the truth-conduciveness of its view of justification, without resorting to the desperate expedient of the coherence theory of truth.

Thus the standard objections to views like the CTEK turn out to be in fact far less conclusive than has usually been thought, and it is reasonable to suppose that they can be successfully answered, once the role of observation in the theory is fully understood and appreciated. This in turn suggests that views like the CTEK are potentially viable accounts of empirical knowledge, worthy of far more serious attention than they have usually been given.*

Commentary on BonJour

The coherence theory of justification holds that what makes a belief justified is its coherence with the system of beliefs held by the subject. A belief is justified in virtue of its membership in a coherent system of beliefs. Unlike foundationalism, there are no beliefs whose justification is independent of other beliefs in the system. Epistemic support is symmetrical and reciprocal.

In paragraph [b]→ BonJour develops an objection to foundationalism similar to Alston's second-level argument: given that a belief can only count as justified if the bearer of the belief has some reason for thinking it is true, the justification of so-called basic beliefs is not self-sufficient but involves inferential relations to other beliefs. (But Alston has shown that there is another version of foundationalism,

[i]→ 3   There are of course other logically possible ways in which a lack of accord could exist between a cognitive system and reality without observation operating to correct the system in the ways suggested. The assumption operative here and in the earlier discussion of objection (I) is that a mechanism for producing cognitively spontaneous beliefs is unlikely to yield coherent results in the long run unless it genuinely reflects objective reality. It is certainly not necessary that this be so: coherent results might conceivably be produced by hallucination, by a Cartesian demon, or even by pure chance. The claim here is only that all of these things are unlikely to happen, that each would represent an improbable coincidence relative to the envisaged situation.

namely, simple or externalist foundationalism, which doesn't fall prey to this objection.)

We saw that foundationalism is a response to the regress problem: only if one stipulates non-inferentially justified beliefs can one hope to put an end to the regress of justification. As the paragraphs marked $\boxed{a} \mapsto$ and $\boxed{d} \mapsto$ explain, coherentism solves the regress problem by replacing the linear picture of justification by a holistic picture.

> **How can BonJour claim that the coherentist conception of justification does not move in a circle?**

BonJour distinguishes between a circular and a holistic conception of coherence. According to circular coherence, belief B_1 is justified in virtue of belief B_2, which in turn gets its support from $B_3, \ldots B_{n-1}$, which is justified by B_n, which finally is justified by B_1. There are two things to notice about this circular process. First, it is implausible to hold that the justification of B_1 'depends on *its own* logically prior justification' and that 'it cannot be justified unless it is *already* justified' (paragraph $\boxed{c} \mapsto$). Moving in a circle doesn't justify anything. Second, circular coherentism, like foundationalism, presupposes a linear conception of justification, according to which justification is a one-way street between single beliefs.

According to holistic coherentism, the relations of justification do not involve a linear or asymmetrical order of dependence among the beliefs in question. Instead justification is holistic in character, with all of the beliefs in a system mutually supporting each other and none being epistemically prior to the others. The reason holistic justification is not circular is because it rejects the linear conception of justification.

Since the notion of coherence is central to coherentism, in paragraph $\boxed{f} \mapsto$ BonJour attempts to explain what is meant by coherence.

> **What exactly is coherence?**

BonJour acknowledges that it is difficult to spell out the notion of coherence in detail. Still, he provides a sketch of a definition. First, a minimal condition for coherence is logical consistency. A system of beliefs is consistent if they can all be true at the same time. Consistency is not a sufficient but only a necessary condition for coherence. To see this, consider a set of beliefs that are highly unlikely to be true at the same time. For example, the system of beliefs might include the belief that I will spend my next summer vacation in England and the belief that it will be sunny every day. These beliefs are not logically inconsistent, but it is highly unlikely that they are both true.

> **Granted BonJour's claim that logical consistency is a necessary condition for coherence, how likely is it that the belief system of any human being is coherent?**

It is fair to assume that all of us hold at least some beliefs that are inconsistent with each other or at least imply things that are inconsistent with one another. And, to make matters worse, frequently we are not aware of such inconsistencies because the affected beliefs belong to distant 'regions' of our belief systems. In response to this argument, BonJour would probably distinguish between approximate and ideal justification and hold that ordinarily we only approximate justification.[1]

Clearly logical consistency is not sufficient for coherence since coherence requires positive connections and not just the absence of conflict. The most important kinds of positive connections are inferential and explanatory relations. For example, the beliefs that Socrates is a human, that humans are mortal, and that Socrates is mortal are connected by the inferential rule known as *modus Barbara*. The common types of explanatory connections are induction and deduction. In deductive reasoning, the conclusion follows necessarily from the premises, so that it is logically impossible for the premises to be true and the conclusion to be false. An inductive argument, on the other hand, does not guarantee its conclusion but only makes it probable.

BonJour distinguishes between a local and a global level of justification. Local justification concerns particular beliefs while global justification concerns the belief system as a whole. The local and the global level mutually include each other. The justification of a particular belief depends on the coherence of the overall system of belief, and the overall system can only be coherent if the particular beliefs cohere with one another.

The full justification of a particular belief involves the four stages outlined in paragraph e →. First, the target belief coheres with other particular beliefs in the system. Second, the system of beliefs as a whole is coherent. A belief can only be justified if it is a member of a coherent belief system. Third, it is not enough that the system of beliefs be coherent but the subject must be justified in believing that it is coherent. Arguably this is the most problematic stage, for it involves an explanation of why holistically coherent beliefs are likely to be true. We will return to this issue. And, fourth, the target belief is justified in virtue of its membership in the coherent system.

According to BonJour, for a belief to be justified it is not enough that it is a member within a coherent system. To be justified in believing something, a person must also (be able to) *recognize* that the belief stands in this relationship to other beliefs. For unless the person has access to the coherentist justification of his beliefs, he 'has no reason for thinking that the belief is at all likely to be true'.[2] Having access to one's justification means, according to BonJour, having a further justified belief to the effect that the target belief is likely to be true.

Given the third stage of the justifying argument, to be justified in holding belief *B*, I must justifiably believe that *B* is a member of my system of beliefs and that that system as a whole is justified in the coherentist sense. Given BonJour's internalism,

[1]   See L. BonJour, 'Replies and Clarifications', in J. W. Bender (ed.), *The Current State of the Coherence Theory* (Kluwer, 1989), p. 285.
[2]   *The Structure of Empirical Knowledge* (Harvard University Press, 1985), p. 31.

being justified in believing that my belief system as a whole is justified (in the coherentist sense) means that I hold beliefs about the epistemic properties of my belief system. An example of such a meta-belief states that my belief system is coherent and that epistemic justification consists in coherence. But now the question is this: what justifies meta-beliefs about the coherence of the entire set of beliefs? Meta-beliefs cannot themselves be justified in the internalist and coherentist fashion. Since meta-beliefs concern the coherence of the belief system it would be circular and question-begging to appeal to the coherence of the belief system for *their* justification. But how should meta-beliefs be justified if not in virtue of their membership in a coherent system?

In chapter 5 of *The Structure of Empirical Knowledge*, BonJour attempts to solve this problem by introducing a *doxastic presumption*. ('Doxa' is Greek for 'belief' and a 'doxastic presumption' is a presumption regarding one's beliefs.) The doxastic presumption (with respect to myself) is the proposition that my meta-beliefs are, by and large, correct. As the label 'doxastic presumption' indicates, it is neither justified in the internalist sense, nor is it self-justified in the foundationalist sense. The point is that, rather than being epistemically entitled to hold my meta-beliefs as mostly true, I cannot help but to hold them true. The meta-belief to the effect that my belief system as a whole is coherent is simply 'a basic and unavoidable feature of cognitive *practice*'.[3]

In the paragraph marked $\boxed{g} \to$ BonJour presents three standard objections brought against coherentism: the alternative coherent system objection, the input objection (or isolation objection), and the problem of truth. BonJour's strategy is to begin with the input objection and then use his response to that objection as the basis for responding to the other two.

Coherentism has it that justification consists in internal relations among beliefs within a system, not beliefs and the world. A coherent system of beliefs might therefore have nothing to do with the world it purports to describe. As far as coherence is concerned, it doesn't seem to matter what the world is like. If a coherent system of beliefs represents the world accurately, this is only a lucky coincidence. And since accidentally true beliefs do not qualify as knowledge, coherentism cannot account for empirical knowledge.

To resolve this input objection, BonJour reminds us of the difference between that which causes a belief and that which justifies a belief. Just because a belief is justified in virtue of the relations to other beliefs in the system doesn't mean that beliefs cannot be causally generated by the world. In this context, BonJour talks about 'cognitively spontaneous beliefs'. The mark of these beliefs is that they arise without being inferred from any other beliefs. The world has an effect on the coherent belief system by giving rise to cognitively spontaneous beliefs.

---

[3] *The Structure of Empirical Knowledge* (Harvard University Press, 1985), p. 104. Today this move strikes BonJour as 'pretty desperate'. See his 'The Dialectic of Foundationalism and Coherentism', in J. Greco and E. Sosa (eds), *The Blackwell Guide to Epistemology* (Blackwell, 1999), p. 126.

The alternative coherent system objection holds that there may be many mutually incompatible coherent systems that are equally coherent. Even though some such coherent system could provide a correct account of the world while the others do not, coherentism is unable to choose this coherent system as being more justified than the others. So, assuming that astronomy and astrology are each equally coherent, the coherentist is not more justified in believing the former rather than the latter.

In response to this objection, BonJour acknowledges that two belief systems may be equally coherent at some particular time, but that this tie is likely to be broken in the long run and with the continuing impact of cognitively spontaneous beliefs.

What, if anything, guarantees in the long run that two equally coherent belief systems will not remain equally coherent?

Either BonJour clandestinely resorts to the foundationalist idea that cognitively spontaneous beliefs are epistemically privileged or he simply assumes the falsity of scepticism. Yet as long as scepticism is in the field of competitors, one cannot assume, as BonJour does, that mutually incompatible yet equally coherent belief systems will eventually differ with respect to their degrees of internal coherence. We will return to this point.

A general problem with coherentism is the so-called problem of truth. The objection states that coherence may be a necessary but not a sufficient condition for justification because, by itself, it does not allow one to distinguish truth from deluded but coherent theories or belief systems. Fairytales, dreams, and hallucinations may sometimes be coherent. A completely internal and subjective notion of justification, such as coherence, cannot bridge the gap between true belief, which might be no more than a lucky guess, and knowledge, which must be grounded in some connection between internal subjective conditions and empirical data. Coherentism must somehow show that coherently justified beliefs are more likely to be true than beliefs that are not justified in this way. (We have already touched upon the problem of truth in connection with Sosa's text.)

One attempt to connect up coherence with truth is the adoption of a coherence theory of truth, that is, the view that a belief is true if and only if it coheres with a set of beliefs. If truth is defined in terms of coherence, it is a definitional truth that coherence is truth-conducive. The obvious problem with the coherence theory of truth is, however, that it is not clear why it shouldn't be possible for a belief to enjoy coherentist justification and nevertheless be false. In paragraphs $\boxed{a} \mapsto$ and $\boxed{h} \mapsto$ BonJour rejects the coherence theory of truth and instead adopts the correspondence theory of truth, which states that a belief that p is true if and only if it corresponds with the fact that p. The correspondence theory captures our commonsense intuition that truth depends on something in the world to make it true.

BonJour mentions in passing that the correspondence theory of truth poses unresolved problems.

Can you think of some of the problems that are raised by the correspondence theory of truth?

Unless we know what a fact is and what it is for a belief to correspond to a fact, the correspondence theory of truth is explanatorily vacuous. But since it is difficult to explain what is a fact without using the concept of truth, it is doubtful that the correspondence theory provides a non-circular account of truth. Moreover, is the correspondence between a proposition p and the fact that p one of identity, close resemblance, or simply rough correlation? Let p stand for the proposition that the car is red. Unlike the car, the proposition p cannot be weighed, seen, or driven. So in what respect can p 'correspond' to the red car?

Let's return to the problem of truth. What reasons are there for thinking that the coherence of beliefs increases their likelihood to be true? BonJour's answer is complex and extends over the last nine paragraphs of the essay. Imagine a system of beliefs that (i) continually receives perceptual input (and hence meets the 'observation requirement') and (ii) remains coherent and stable over a period of time. How can we explain the long-term coherence of such a belief system? Three explanations suggest themselves. First, the stable coherence of the belief system is a lucky coincidence. Second, the coherence of the belief system is due to a demon manipulating the agent's mind. Third, the coherence and stability of the belief system is due to most of the beliefs being true. BonJour's thesis is that correspondence with reality provides the most probable explanation of the fact that the overall belief system remains coherent while the agent continually accepts cognitively spontaneous beliefs. A system of beliefs that remains coherent over the long run and continues to satisfy the observation requirement is likely to correspond to an independent reality.

Do you agree with BonJour's claim that the explanation in terms of truth is the best explanation of long-term coherence?

Imagine the following competing explanation: a demon causes the agent to have cognitively spontaneous beliefs, which contribute to the coherence of the agent's belief system. (In the footnote at $\boxed{i} \mapsto$ BonJour sketches a similar demon explanation.) Now why is this demon explanation supposed to be less probable than the explanation in terms of truth? BonJour's response is that the presence of a demon who feeds us coherence-conducive perceptual beliefs is 'unlikely to happen' and that it would 'represent an improbable coincidence' (passage $\boxed{i} \mapsto$). But the problem with this response is that it assumes, without argument, that scepticism is probably false. Obviously the sceptic challenges this assumption. As in the case of the alternative coherent system objection, it seems that BonJour is begging the question against the sceptic.

After having thought about the question whether coherentist justification is truth-conducive, reconsider the last two paragraphs of the commentary on Sosa in Chapter 3. Does Sosa's epistemology create a Gettier problem at the second level?

6

Scepticism in Context

Introduction to the Problem

Almost nobody thinks that scepticism is true. That does not mean scepticism is not important. Its relevance is methodological. By understanding whether and how sceptical arguments fail, we learn something about knowledge.

Scepticism comes in many shapes and colours. *Academic* (from Plato's academy in ancient Greece) scepticism embodies a positive claim: we do not know about the nature of reality independent of our own immediate experience. *Pyrrhonian* (Pyrrho was an ancient sceptic) scepticism is more cautious. It does not deny that we have knowledge. Instead, it recommends suspension of judgement. The readings in this chapter are concerned with academic scepticism only.

Academic sceptics differ among themselves in the scope of their scepticism. A global sceptic maintains we can know *nothing* or next to nothing about *anything*. Local sceptics, on the other hand, maintain that even if knowledge is possible elsewhere, it is, for special reasons, not available in this or that selected area. Favourite areas for local scepticism are knowledge of the external world, of other minds, of the past, of God, or moral truths. Both texts in this chapter are concerned with scepticism about the external world.

Sceptical theories differ not only in scope, but in theme. Sceptical arguments can either be directed against knowledge (you cannot know propositions of type A) or justification (it is not even reasonable to believe propositions of type A) or both at once. Still another difference concerns the order or level of one's scepticism. First-order (or direct) scepticism is the thesis that you cannot know that propositions of type A (e.g., propositions about the external world) are true. Second-order (or iterative) scepticism is the weaker thesis that we cannot know (or justifiably believe) that we have (first-order) knowledge of A-type propositions. Maybe you know that p, maybe you do not, but you cannot know that you know that p. Second-order scepticism is true if first-order scepticism is, but not vice versa. The readings in this chapter focus on first-order scepticism.

Scepticism about the external world is the thesis that the evidence we have for our beliefs about the external world falls short of what is needed for knowledge (or even justification in more aggressive forms of scepticism). The evidence is never logically conclusive. Error is always possible. So in order to minimize the possibility of mistake, it seems reasonable to demand that someone, in order to know, must be able to exclude sources of error and deception. According to the sceptic, though, this is exactly what we cannot do. There is no sure way of telling that we are causally hooked up (via perception, say) to the facts in the way we think we are. The rationality of our beliefs about an independently existing world might be nothing but the coherence of a dream or a clever deception by some malevolent demon. To put a more contemporary spin on the sceptical hypothesis, our perceptual evidence for an external world is consistent with our being disembodied brains wired to a properly programmed computer. If the computer stimulated us to have exactly the experiences we now have, our beliefs would be false but our evidence would nonetheless be the same. How can we know this is not the case? (The brain-in-a-vat scenario was discussed by Nozick in Chapter 1.)

The point of sceptical hypotheses is to highlight the fact that all our evidence for an external world resides in the subjective character of our experience. Everything in our experience could be exactly the way it now is even if the world were completely different from the way we judge it to be. Experience is our only source of information about the world, but experience does not rule out alternative possibilities. It would seem, therefore, that nothing can be known for certain on the basis of this experience. If we cannot, by appealing to experience, show we are not dreaming, then experience is not a sufficiently secure basis for knowing we are not dreaming. And if we cannot know we are not dreaming, we cannot know we are perceiving a mind-independent reality.

As traditionally understood, the argument for external-world scepticism can be summed up as follows:

(1) I don't know that the sceptical hypothesis is false.
(2) If I know that p, then I know that the sceptical hypothesis is false.
(3) Therefore, I don't know that p,

where 'p' stands for any proposition about the external world. The second premise relies on the *principle of closure under known implications*, which states that for S to know that p, S must be able to rule out those propositions of which S knows that they are incompatible with p. If knowing p implies knowing that the sceptical hypothesis is false (premise (2)), then, since you don't know that the sceptical hypothesis is false (premise (1)), you don't know that p. This argumentative structure is called *modus tollens*.

Epistemologists have developed a host of strategies to rebut scepticism. We have already encountered (in Chapter 2) one anti-sceptical strategy, namely externalism about knowledge. Externalism is the view that to know something the subject needs reliable, non-accidentally produced, true belief but he need not know that he has non-accidental true belief. The externalist definition of knowledge promises to avoid the justificatory regress that seems to be an inevitable ingredient of scepticism. The sceptic typically asks how one can know that sense experience is a reliable guide to what is going on in the external world. The externalist acknowledges that he does not know that it is, but this does not matter; this does not undermine his knowledge. To know something on the basis of experience, a person does not have to know that experience is a reliable indicator of the truth. It just has to *be* a reliable indicator of the truth. If experience is reliable, it gives us knowledge. If it is not, then it does not. Thus, second-level scepticism may be in order (we cannot know whether we know), but arguments for first-order scepticism, arguments designed to show that we *cannot* know there is an external world, are refuted. We *do* know if our experience is related in the appropriate way to the reality it causes us to believe in.

Advocates of internalism argue that this response to scepticism is not satisfactory, for it only shows that it is *possible* that our beliefs about the external world amount to knowledge. A satisfactory response to scepticism, the internalist thinks, must establish that we in fact possess knowledge.

The two readings in this chapter represent two different contextualist responses to scepticism. According to Dretske's *relevant alternative account of knowledge*, a claim to know that *p* is made within a certain framework of alternatives that are incompatible with *p*. To know that *p* is to be able to rule out these alternatives to *p*. The closure principle (premise (2)) demands that to know that *p* one needs to be able to rule out *all* known alternatives to *p*. But, if to know that *p*, one had to rule out each and every known possibility of not-*p*, one would be required to have evidence against some utterly wild and weird cases, as long as they are logically possible and one is aware of them conflicting with *p*. This is too strong a requirement for knowledge. A more plausible view is that to know that *p* it is sufficient that one be able to rule out *some* – namely the *relevant* – alternatives to *p*. So it is possible to know a proposition without knowing another proposition entailed by it, which amounts to the denial of the closure principle.

In Williams's view, the sceptic erroneously assumes *epistemological realism*, that is, the thesis that a belief's epistemic status depends on its content, rather than on contextual features of how the belief is held. Epistemological realism also supposes that there is a hierarchy of epistemic priority, so that beliefs of some kinds (e.g., beliefs about the world) always depend on beliefs of other kinds (e.g., beliefs about sensory experience) for their evidence, again independently of context. Williams proposes to replace epistemological realism with a version of contextualism that holds that truths about what justifies what vary from context to context depending on the aims and standards that define the context. Since in most everyday contexts it would be inappropriate to try to answer the sceptical challenge, scepticism is unable to undermine our ordinary knowledge.

Introduction to Dretske

Fred Dretske is emeritus professor at Stanford University and senior research scholar at Duke University. His interest centres on the intersection of epistemology and philosophy of mind.

In *Knowledge and the Flow of Information* (1981), Dretske develops (among other things) a version of reliabilism in terms of information. Knowledge is said to be information-caused belief. For a belief to carry the information that *p*, it is not sufficient that it be caused by a reliable process that just happens to carry the information that *p*. The very properties of the process that are responsible for its carrying the information that *p* also have to be responsible for reliably causing the belief that *p*. In other words, the knower must be able to discriminate between the information-generating properties of the source of her belief and other irrelevant properties, so that she would not have formed her belief in the absence of these information-relevant properties. The relevant alternative account of knowledge, set forth in the text below, was developed within the context of information-theoretic reliabilism. Yet it is possible to understand (and appreciate) the relevant alternative theory without knowing about information-theoretic reliabilism.

Other books by Dretske are *Seeing and Knowing* (1969) and *Perception, Knowledge and Belief: Selected Essays* (2000). *Explaining Behavior: Reasons in a World of Causes* (1988), addresses the question of the role of mental content in causal explanations of behaviour. The thesis is that it is in virtue of S's belief being a belief about *p* and S's desire being a desire for *q* that the belief and the desire can be used to explain S's behaviour. *Naturalizing the Mind* (1995) develops a naturalistic theory of the phenomenal, the what-it-is-like aspects of the mind. The central idea is that the phenomenal aspects of perceptual experiences are the same as external, real-world properties that experience represents objects as having.

A valuable tool for understanding Dretske's epistemology and philosophy of mind is *Dretske and His Critics* (1991), edited by B. McLaughlin, which contains nine critical essays and Dretske's responses.

Fred Dretske, 'The Pragmatic Dimension of Knowledge'

Knowing that something is so, unlike being wealthy or reasonable, is not a matter of degree. Two people can both be wealthy, yet one be wealthier than the other; both be reasonable, yet one be more reasonable than the other. When talking about people, places and topics (*things* rather than facts), it makes sense to say that one person knows something *better than* another. He knows the city better than we do, knows more Russian history than any of his colleagues, but doesn't know his wife as well as do his friends. But *factual* knowledge, the knowledge *that* something is so, does not admit of such comparisons.[1] If we both know that today is Friday, it makes no sense to say that you know this better than I. A rich man can become richer by acquiring more money, and a person's belief (that today is Saturday, for example) can be made more reasonable by the accumulation of additional evidence, but if a person already knows that today is Friday, there is nothing he can acquire that will make him know it better. Additional evidence will not promote him to a loftier form of knowledge – though it may make him *more certain* of something he already knew. You can boil water beyond its boiling point (e.g., at 300°F) but you are not, thereby, boiling it better. You are simply boiling it at a higher temperature.

[a]→   In this respect factual knowledge is *absolute*. It is like being pregnant: an all or nothing affair. One person cannot be *more* pregnant, or pregnant *better than* someone else. Those who view knowledge as a form of justified (true) belief typically acknowledge this fact by speaking, not simply of justification, but of *full, complete*, or *adequate* justification. Those qualifications on the sort of justification required to know something constitute an admission that knowledge is, whereas justification is not, an absolute idea. For these qualifiers are meant to reflect the fact that there is a certain threshold of justification that must be equalled or exceeded if knowledge is to be obtained, and *equalling or exceeding this threshold* is, of course, an absolute idea. I can have a better justification than you, but my justification cannot be more adequate (more sufficient, more full) than yours. If my justification is complete in the intended sense, then your justification cannot be more complete.

Philosophers who view knowledge as some form of justified true belief are generally reluctant to talk about this implied threshold of justification. Just how much evidence or justification, one wants to ask, is *enough* to qualify as an adequate, a full, or a complete justification? If the level or degree of justification is represented by real numbers between 0 and 1 (indicating the conditional probability of that for which one has evidence or justification), any threshold less than 1 seems arbitrary. Why, for example, should a justification of 0.95 be good enough to know something when a justification of 0.94 is not adequate? And if one can know *p* because one's justification is 0.95 and know *q* because one's justification is similarly high, is one excluded from knowing *p and q* because the justification for their joint occurrence has (in accordance with the multiplicative rule in probability theory) dropped below 0.95?

[1]   I know we sometimes say things that suggest a comparison of this sort (e.g., No one knows better than I that there are a lot of mosquitos in the Northwest Territories), but I take such constructions to be describing, not better knowledge, but more direct, more compelling, kinds of evidence.

Aside, though, from its arbitrariness, any threshold of justification less than 1 seems to be *too low*. For examples can easily be given in which such thresholds are exceeded without the justification being *good enough* (by ordinary intuitive standards) for knowledge. For example, if the threshold is set at 0.95, one need only think of a bag with 96 white balls and 4 black balls in it. If someone draws a ball at random from this bag, the justification for believing it to be white exceeds the 0.95 threshold. Yet, it seems clear (to me at least) that such a justification (for believing that a white ball has been drawn) is *not* good enough. Someone who happened to draw a white ball, and believed they drew a white ball on the basis of this justification, would not know that they drew a white ball.

Examples such as this suggest (though they do not, of course, prove) that the absolute, non-comparative, character of knowledge derives from the absoluteness, or conclusiveness, of the justification required to know. If I know that the Russians invaded Afghanistan, you can't know this better than I know it because in order to know it I must already have an optimal, or conclusive justification (a justification at the level of 1), and you can't do better than that. I have explored this possibility in other papers, and I do not intend to pursue it here.[2] What I want to develop in this paper is a different theme, one that (I hope) helps to illuminate our concept of knowledge by showing how this absolute idea can, despite its absoluteness, remain sensitive to the shifting interests, concerns and factors influencing its everyday application. In short, I want to explore the way, and the extent to which, this absolute notion exhibits a degree of contextual relativity in its ordinary use.

. . .

b⟶ If knowledge is absolute in this way, then there should be similar objections to its widespread application to everyday situations. Powerful magnification (i.e., critical inquiry) *should*, and with the help of the skeptic *has*, revealed 'bumps' and 'irregularities' in our evidential posture with respect to most of the things we say we know. There are always, it seems, possibilities that our evidence is powerless to eliminate, possibilities which, until eliminated, block the road to knowledge. For if knowledge, being an absolute concept, requires the elimination of *all* competing possibilities (possibilities that contrast with what is known), then, clearly we seldom, if ever, satisfy the conditions for applying the concept.

This skeptical conclusion is unpalatable to most philosophers. . . .

Knowledge *is* an absolute concept . . . , though, I do not derive skeptical conclusions from this fact. . . .

Absolute concepts depict a situation as being completely devoid of a certain sort of thing: *bumps* in the case of flatness and *objects* in the case of emptiness. The fact that there can be *nothing* of this sort present for the

[2] 'Conclusive reasons', *Australasian Journal of Philosophy* (May 1971) and *Seeing and Knowing* (University of Chicago Press, 1969).

concept to be satisfied is what makes it an absolute concept. It is why if *X* is
empty, *Y* cannot be emptier. Nonetheless, when it comes to determining
what *counts* as a thing of this sort (a bump or an object), and hence what
counts against a correct application of the concept, we find the criteria or
standards peculiarly spongy and relative. What counts as a thing for assessing the emptiness of my pocket may not count as a thing for assessing the
emptiness of a park, a warehouse, or a football stadium. Such concepts, we
might say, are *relationally absolute*; absolute, yes, but only relative to a certain
standard. We might put the point this way: to be empty is to be *devoid of all
relevant things*, thereby exhibiting, simultaneously, the absolute (in the word
'all') and relative (in the word 'relevant') character of this concept.

If, as I have suggested, knowledge is an absolute concept, we should
expect it to exhibit this kind of *relationally* absolute character. This, indeed, is
the possibility I mean to explore in this paper. What I propose to do is to use
what I have called relationally absolute concepts as a model for understanding knowledge. In accordance with this approach (and in harmony with an
earlier suggestion) I propose to think of knowledge as an evidential state in
which *all relevant alternatives* (to what is known) *are eliminated*. This makes
knowledge an absolute concept but the restriction to *relevant* alternatives
makes it, like *empty* and *flat*, applicable to this epistemically bumpy world we
live in.

Why do this? What are the advantages? A partial catalog of benefits
follows:

. . .

(3) Thirdly, we get a better perspective from which to understand the
persisting and undiminished appeal of skeptical arguments. Most philosophers have experienced the futility of trying to convince a devoted skeptic,
or just a newly converted freshman, that we *do* know there are tables and
chairs *despite* the possibility of dreams, hallucinations, cunning demons and
diabolical scientists who might be toying with our brain on Alpha Centuri
(Nozick's example). Somehow, in the end, we seem reduced to shrugging
our shoulders and saying that there are certain possibilities that are just too
remote to worry about. Our evidence isn't good enough to eliminate these
wilder hypotheses because, of course, these wild hypotheses are carefully
manufactured so as to *neutralize* our evidence. But dismissing such hypotheses as too remote to worry about, as too fanciful to have any impact on our
ordinary use of the verb 'to know', is merely another way of saying that for
purposes of assessing someone's knowledge that this is a table, certain
alternative possibilities are simply not relevant. We are doing the same
thing (or so I submit) as one who dismisses chalk dust as irrelevant, or too
insignificant, to worry about in describing a classroom as empty. What it is
important to realize, especially in arguments with the skeptic, is that the
impatient dismissal of his fanciful hypotheses is not (as he will be quick to
suggest) a mere *practical* intolerance, and refusal to confront, decisive

objections to our ordinary way of talking. It is, rather, a half conscious attempt to exhibit the *relationally* absolute character of our cognitive concepts.

(4) Finally, this approach to the analysis of knowledge gives us the kind of machinery we need to handle the otherwise puzzling examples that are becoming more frequent in the epistemological literature. Consider yet one more example (one *more* because this one, I think, combines elements of several of the more familiar examples). An amateur bird-watcher spots a duck on his favorite Wisconsin pond. He quickly notes its familiar silhouette and markings and makes a mental note to tell his friends that he saw a Gadwall, a rather unusual bird in that part of the midwest. Since the Gadwall has a distinctive set of markings (black rump, white patch on the hind edge of the wing, etc.), markings that no other North American duck exhibits, and these markings were all perfectly visible, it seems reasonable enough to say that the bird-watcher *knows* that yonder bird is a Gadwall. He can see that it is.

Nevertheless, a concerned ornithologist is poking around in the vicinity, not far from where our bird-watcher spotted his Gadwall, looking for some trace of Siberian Grebes. Grebes are duck-like water birds, and the Siberian version of this creature is, when it is in the water, very hard to distinguish from a Gadwall duck. Accurate identification requires seeing the birds in flight since the Gadwall has a white belly and the Grebe a red belly – features that are not visible when the birds are in the water. The ornithologist has a hypothesis that some Siberian Grebes have been migrating to the midwest from their home in Siberia, and he and his research assistants are combing the midwest in search of confirmation.

Once we embellish our simple story in this way, intuitions start to diverge on whether our amateur bird-watcher does indeed know that yonder bird is a Gadwall duck (we are assuming, of course, that it *is* a Gadwall). Most people (I assume) would say that he did *not* know the bird to be a Gadwall if there actually were Siberian Grebes in the vicinity. It certainly sounds strange to suppose that he could give assurances to the ornithologist that the bird he saw was *not* a Siberian Grebe (since he knew it to be a Gadwall duck). But what if the ornithologist's suspicions are unfounded. None of the Grebes have migrated. Does the bird-watcher still not know what he takes himself to know? Is, then, the simple presence of an ornithologist, with his false hypothesis, enough to rob the bird-watcher of his knowledge that the bird on the pond is a Gadwall duck? What if we suppose that the Siberian Grebes, because of certain geographical barriers, *cannot* migrate. Or suppose that there really are no Siberian Grebes – the existence of such a bird being a delusion of a crackpot ornithologist. We may even suppose that, in addition to there being no grebes, there is no ornithologist of the sort I described, but that people in the area believe that there is. Or *some* people believe that there is. Or the bird-watcher's *wife* believes that there is and, as a result, expresses skepticism about his claim to know that what he saw was a Gadwall duck. Or, finally, though no one believes any of this, some of the locals are interested in whether or not our bird-watcher *knows* that there are no look-alike migrant grebes in the area.

Somewhere in this progression philosophers, most of them anyway, will dig in their heels and say that the bird-watcher really *does* know that the bird he sees is a Gadwall, and that he knows this despite his inability to justifiably rule out certain alternative possibilities. . . .

e ⟶ Most philosophers will dig in their heels here because they realize that if they don't, they are on the slippery slope to skepticism with nothing left to hang onto. . . . One of the ways to prevent this slide into skepticism is to acknowledge that although knowledge requires the evidential elimination of all relevant alternatives (to what is known), there is a shifting, variable set of relevant alternatives. It may be that our bird-watcher does know the bird is a Gadwall under normal conditions (because look-alike grebes are not a relevant alternative), but does not know this if there is a suspicion, however ill-founded it may be, that there exist look-alike grebes within migrating range. This will (or should) be no more unusual than acknowledging the fact that a refrigerator could truly be described as empty to a person looking for something to eat, but *not* truly described as empty to a person looking for spare refrigerator parts. In the first case 'empty' implies having no food in it; in the second it implies having no shelves, brackets and hardware in it.

These, then, are some of the advantages to be derived from this approach to the analysis of knowledge. They are, however, advantages that can only be harvested if certain questions can be given reasonable answers: in particular (a) what makes a possibility relevant? (b) If, in order to know, one must rule out all relevant alternatives, how is this 'elimination' to be understood? What does it take, evidentially, to 'rule out' an alternative? (c) Is it possible, as this type of analysis suggests, for one to know something at one time and, later, not know it (due to the introduction of another relevant alternative) without forgetting it? (d) Can one make it easier to know things by remaining ignorant of what are, for others, relevant possibilities?

These, and many more questions, need answers if this framework for the analysis of knowledge is to be anything more than suggestive. Since I cannot here (or anywhere else, for that matter) provide answers to all these questions, I will try, in the time remaining, to fill in some of the large gaps.

f ⟶ Call the *Contrasting Set (CS)* the class of situations that are necessarily eliminated by what is known to be the case. That is, if S knows that p, then q is in the *CS* (of p) if and only if, given p, necessarily not-q. In our bird-watcher's example, the bird's being a Siberian Grebe (or any kind of grebe at all) is in the *CS* of our bird-watcher's knowledge, or putative knowledge, that it is a Gadwall duck. So is its being an elephant, a hummingbird, a holographic image, or a figment of his imagination. Furthermore, let us call the set of possible alternatives that a person must be in an evidential position to exclude (when he knows that *p*) the *Relevancy Set* (*RS*). In saying that he must be in a position to exclude these possibilities I mean that his evidence or justification for thinking these alternatives are *not* the case must be good enough to say he *knows* they are not the case. Items in the *CS* that are not in the *RS* I shall call irrelevant alternatives. These are items which, though their existence is incompatible with what is known to be the case, the knower *need not* (though he may) have a justification for thinking do not exist. Under normal conditions (the kind of conditions that I assume prevail in the world today) the possibility of something's being a look-alike grebe, though it is a member of the contrasting set, is not a member of the relevancy set of a bird-watcher's knowledge that what he sees is a Gadwall duck (in the kind of circumstances I described).[3] On the other hand, its being an eagle, a Mallard, or a Loon *are* members of the relevancy set since if the bird-watcher could not eliminate these possibilities (sufficient unto knowing that it was not an eagle, a Mallard or a loon) on the basis of the bird's appearance and behavior, then he would not know that it was a Gadwall.

What we are suggesting here is that the *RS* is always a proper subset of the *CS* and, moreover, may not be the same *RS* from situation to situation even though what is known remains the same. The situation can be diagrammed as follows:

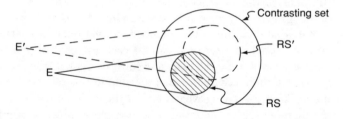

Figure 1

The solid lines indicate a *RS* and the corresponding piece of evidence that would be required to know with this *RS*. With a different *RS* (*RS'*), indicated by dotted lines, different evidence would be required. If Siberian Grebes are in the Relevancy Set, then additional, more elaborate, evidence is required to know that yonder bird is a Gadwall than in the normal situation. Since the bellies are of different color, one might, for example, be able to tell that it was a Gadwall by watching it in flight. The point, however, is that something more would be needed than was available in the original, normal situation.

---

[3] Though there are grebes, and some of them look like ducks, there are (to the best of my knowledge) no Siberian Grebes that look like Gadwall ducks. This part of my story was pure invention.

In terms of this kind of diagram, a skeptic could be represented as one who took $RS = CS$ in all cases. One's evidence must be comprehensive enough to eliminate all contrasting possibilities – there being no irrelevant alternatives.

Once the mistake is made of identifying RS with CS the pressure (on non-skeptics) for lowering the standards of justification (requisite for knowing) becomes irresistible. For if in order to know that P one must be justified in rejecting *all* members of the CS (not just all members of the RS), then one can no longer expect very impressive levels of justification for what people know to be the case. If the evidence our bird-watcher has for believing the bird to be a Gadwall duck (wing markings, etc.) is also supposed to justify the proposition that it is *not* a look-alike grebe, then, obviously, the justifi-cation is nowhere near conclusive. What some philosophers seem inclined to conclude from this is that knowledge does not require conclusive evidence. The reasoning is simple: the bird-watcher knows it is a Gadwall; he doesn't have conclusive reasons (he can't exclude the possibility that it is a look-alike grebe); therefore knowledge does not require conclusive reasons. But this, I submit, is a fallacy, a misunderstanding of what needs to be conclusively excluded in order to know. Such reasoning is analogous to arguing that to be empty an object can have a few hundred things in it, and to conclude this on the basis of the undeniable fact that empty classrooms, warehouses, and buildings generally have at least a hundred things in them.

But what determines the membership of a relevancy set? A relevancy set, you will recall, is a set of situations each member of which contrasts with what is known to be the case, and must be evidentially excluded if one is to know. Are there criteria for membership in this set? I'm now going to stick my neck out by saying what some of the considerations are that determine the membership of these sets. I do not expect much agreement.

(1) The first point has to do with the way we use contrastive focusing to indicate the range of relevant alternatives. I have discussed this phenom-enon in another place, so let me give just one example to illustrate the sort of thing I have in mind.[4] Someone claiming to know that Clyde *sold* his typewriter to Alex is not (necessarily) claiming the same thing as one who claims to know that Clyde sold his typewriter *to Alex*. The sentence we use to express what they know is the same, of course, but they reflect, and are designed to reflect, different relevancy sets. A person who knows that Clyde *sold* his typewriter to Alex must be able to rule out the possibility that he *gave* it to him, or that he *loaned* it to him, or (perhaps) that he merely *pretended* to sell it to him. But he needs only a nominal justification, if he needs any justification at all, for thinking it was Alex to whom he sold it. He has to be right about its *being* Alex, of course, but he isn't claiming to have any special justification for thinking it was Alex rather than, say, his twin

4   In 'Contrastive statements', *The Philosophical Review* (October 1972).

brother Albert. On the other hand, the person who knows that Clyde sold his typewriter *to Alex* is claiming to know that it wasn't Albert and is, therefore, expected to be in possession of evidence bearing on the identity of the recipient. But, in this second case, the knower needs only a nominal justification for the belief that Clyde *sold* him the typewriter rather than, say, loaned it to him. He certainly needn't be able to exclude the possibility that the entire transaction was a sham designed to fool the IRS.

(2) A second point, related to the first, is the way the subject term chosen to give verbal expression to what is known often functions to restrict the range of relevant alternatives.[5] Once again, an example will have to suffice. If I say that I could tell that your sister was amused by my funny story, I do not thereby claim to know that she is really your sister, really a human being (rather than a cleverly contrived robot), or really the sort of creature that could experience amusement. These possibilities, though certainly relevant to the truth of what I say in the sense that if they were realized I would not know what I say I know, are not possibilities that I need be in an evidential position to exclude to know that your sister was amused by my joke. I was, as it were, *taking it for granted* that she was your sister (hence, a human being, a creature that could experience amusement), and I was claiming to know something about the thing so referred to. On the other hand, if I said that I could tell that the object in the corner (that happened to be your sister) was amused by my funny story, the possibility that it is a robot becomes a relevant alternative, one that I am (by this choice of words) accepting epistemic responsibility for excluding.

(3) Thirdly, in saying that we know we often reveal, either directly or indirectly, *how* we know. I could *see* that the tire was flat, could tell (by the way they *behaved*) that they were in love, *heard* them making plans to go, learned (from the *newspapers*) that the auto workers went out on strike, and used *my pocket calculator* to get the answer. The *way* we come to know, the channel (so to speak) over which we obtain our information, is, I submit, always the locus of irrelevant alternatives. . . .

(4) Fourthly, some people, I am sure, would insist that a pertinent factor influencing the size and membership of the relevancy set is the importance (for speaker and listeners) of what is known or of someone's knowing it. . . .

There is, I admit, some appeal to this point, but I think it mistaken. . . .

(5) Finally, we come to the difficult question, the question of when an alternative (not otherwise excluded as irrelevant by one of the considerations already discussed) is just *too remote* to qualify as relevant. In the case of our bird-watcher, some philosophers, thinking to turn the tables on the skeptic (by drastically diminishing the relevance set), have suggested that an

[5] I tried to describe the way this works with perceptual claims in: *Seeing and Knowing* (Chicago, 1969), pp. 93–112.

alternative only becomes relevant when there are positive reasons for thinking it is, or may be, realized. Doubt can also be irrational, and if there are no reasons to doubt, mere possibilities are irrelevant to whether what is believed is known.

This, obviously, is an over-reaction. The Wisconsin lakes could be loaded with migrant Siberian Grebes without the bird-watcher having any reason to think that such look-alike birds actually existed. His lack of any reason to doubt, his ignorance of the possibility that what he sees is a grebe and not a Gadwall, is irrelevant. The mere possibility is in this case enough to show he doesn't know.

This shows that having a reason (evidence) to think X is a genuine possibility is not a necessary condition for X's being a relevant alternative. Perhaps, though, it is sufficient. Perhaps, that is, a reasonable (justified) belief that yonder bird *might* be a look-alike grebe (whether or not this belief is true) is enough to make its being a look-alike grebe a relevant possibility.

. . .

. . . The difference between a relevant and an irrelevant alternative resides, not in what we happen to *regard* as a real possibility (whether reasonably or not), but in the kind of possibilities that actually exist in the objective situation. Whether or not our bird-watcher knows that the bird he sees is a Gadwall depends on whether or not, in some objective sense, it could be a look-alike grebe (or any other similar looking creature). If, as a matter of fact, there are no look-alike grebes, that settles the matter. He knows it is a Gadwall. If there are grebes, but due to certain geographical barriers, they are confined to their Siberian habitat, then, once again, the possibility of the bird's being a grebe, though remaining a logical possibility, is not a relevant possibility. They, the grebes, cannot migrate to the midwest.

If, however, there are grebes, and they can migrate, but just have not done so, the case becomes more ambiguous. I think, however, that we now have a genuine possibility, a relevant alternative. By hypothesis the bird-watcher does not know it is not a migrant grebe, and however improbable this possibility may be, there is nothing the bird watcher has (either in the look of the bird or in general background information) that excludes the possibility that what he is looking at is a migrant grebe. He does not, therefore, know it to be a Gadwall. He will, no doubt, say he knows. And everyone else may agree and, as a result, think *they* know (having been told by someone who knows). But the truth lies elsewhere. It is, I suggest, tantamount to saying that the bottle is empty when there is a drop left. No one is going to quarrel with this description since all the relevant implications (e.g., we can't make another martini) are true. But the claim itself is false.

Commentary on Dretske

Dretske starts out by arguing that knowledge is an absolute or non-scaling concept. Knowledge doesn't allow for degrees. If you and I know p, we know it equally well. Sure, you may have some background knowledge concerning p that I lack. But by knowing *more* about p you don't have *better* knowledge that p. Justification, unlike knowledge, does allow for degrees. Your reasons for believing p may be better than mine either because you have more reasons than I do or because your reasons are conclusive while mine are indecisive.

> Given that knowledge implies justification, how is it possible that knowledge is an absolute concept while justification is a relational concept?

As Dretske explains in the paragraph marked $\boxed{a}\!\mapsto$, the absoluteness of knowledge can be combined with the relational nature of justification by stipulating a threshold of justification. In this proposal, a belief qualifies as knowledge if its justification meets or exceeds a certain threshold. Meeting or exceeding a threshold is an absolute affair, like knowing. So even though justification is a matter of degree, the introduction of a threshold allows for clear yes-or-no answer to the question 'Is S justified in believing that p?'.

But how should we go about fixing a threshold of justification? A person's degree of justification can be represented by a real number between 0 and 1. At one extreme, when S's reason for thinking that p guarantees the truth of p, the justification is 1. At the other extreme, the probability of p being true given that S has reasons for thinking that p is true may be the same as if S did not have any reasons. In this case the justification is 0. In the middle, the probability of p being true given S's justification may be 50 per cent, in which case we may say that the justification is 0.5.

Whenever the threshold of justification is less than 1, there are going to be cases where a justified belief is only accidentally true and therefore does not qualify as knowledge. For, after all, the justification condition is supposed to prevent accidentally true beliefs from counting as knowledge. So unless justification guarantees the truth of the target proposition, the possibility of sceptical hypotheses and Gettier cases undermines every knowledge claim. But if the threshold of justification is set at 1, justified belief becomes a very rare commodity indeed. Our reasons for holding a proposition true are hardly ever conclusive. Justification typically leaves open the possibility of falsehood (see paragraph $\boxed{b}\!\mapsto$). So we seem to be caught in a predicament: no matter how we set the threshold of justification we end up with a counter-intuitive result.

Dretske's solution to this dilemma is to say that absolute concepts (such as knowledge) can be sensitive with regard to different contexts. To see how absolute concepts can exhibit a degree of contextual relativity, consider the concept *flat*. 'Flat' is an absolute concept – something is flat only if it is not at all bumpy. Nevertheless this concept is sensitive with respect to different contexts, since it is the context that determines what counts as a 'bump' in the sense that it has to be taken into account. A road may be flat although it has bumps that, if they were found on a kitchen counter, would prevent the kitchen counter from counting as flat. 'Flat' is what in paragraph $\boxed{c}\rightarrow$ is called a *relationally absolute concept*: it is absolute, but only relative to a specified standard.

> How does the account of 'flat' as a relationally absolute concept apply to the concept of knowledge?

Dretske suggests that every knowledge claim implies a host of contrastive cases, i.e., cases incompatible with the truth of the target proposition. For instance, knowing that there is a glass of water entails that there is a glass, that there is a glass of drinkable liquid, that there is a material object, and that no malevolent demon is falsely causing me to believe that there is a glass of water. Depending on the context in which a knowledge claim is made, different contrastive cases are to the fore and hence different kinds of evidence are needed to qualify the knowledge claim as knowledge. When the issue is whether there are any beverages left, the claim to know that there is a glass of water is easier to justify than when solipsism or scepticism are at issue. So whether someone is justified in believing that p (and hence knows p) depends on the context to which his assertion that p is a response. Something may be evidence for some proposition relative to one context while failing to be evidence for that very same proposition in another. Questions about whether someone knows p, considered in isolation from the circumstances in which the questions about p arise, cannot be answered.

According to the relevant alternative theory, to know that p one doesn't have to rule out *all* possibilities in which one would be wrong with regard to p, but only those that are relevant in a given situation. Knowledge is said to be 'an evidential state in which all relevant alternatives (to what is known) are eliminated' (paragraph $\boxed{d}\rightarrow$). Because knowledge is a non-scaling concept, each and every relevant alternative to p must be eliminated. Yet what counts as a 'relevant' alternative is context-sensitive. So, just as to be flat means to be free of *relevant* bumps, to know that p means that one's reasons rule out the *relevant* alternatives to p.

> According to paragraph $\boxed{e}\rightarrow$, what speaks in favour of the relevant alternative account of knowledge is that it provides a response to the sceptical challenge. What does this response consist in?

To understand the anti-sceptical force of the relevant alternative account of knowledge, let's remind ourselves of the sceptical argument. The sceptic argues that we have no way of knowing that sceptical hypotheses are false and concludes, therefore, that we do not know anything about the external world. This reasoning typically employs the principle of closure under known entailment: if S knows that p, and S knows that p entails q, then S knows that q. The proposition that you are now reading a book (p) logically implies the falsity of the sceptical counter-possibility that you are a brain in a vat (q). If you are aware of this implication, the closure principle yields the consequence that if you know that p, then you know q; and since you cannot rule out the possibility that you are a brain in a vat, you do not know q. So you do not know that p – that you are reading. Conclusion: scepticism is true.

Dretske thinks that the closure principle is too strict to be convincing. If knowing that p would require the elimination of *every* known alternative to p, as suggested by the closure principle, we could never know anything about the world around us. A more plausible view might be that knowledge requires the elimination of only *relevant* alternatives and that sceptical alternatives are normally not relevant. Closure does not hold in general.

Consider the following example[1]: at the zoo, you see some striped animals in a cage marked 'zebras'. Your evidence justifies the belief that these animals are zebras. You know that to be a zebra means to not be a painted mule. But your evidence does not count towards these animals not being painted mules since you would have exactly the same evidence were it a hoax. Does this mean that you don't know that these animals are zebras? Dretske answers in the negative. His idea is that in *ordinary* cases of claiming to know that some animals in the zoo are zebras the possibility that they are painted mules is not relevant. Thus, you can truthfully claim to know that they are zebras despite your inability to rule out this fanciful alternative. Scepticism is powerless to undermine everyday empirical knowledge. But in some exceptional circumstances, the painted-mules hypothesis may become a relevant alternative. And when the painted-mule case is not just a member of the contrastive set (CS) but of the relevance set (RS), then you cannot know that what you are seeing are zebras unless you have eliminated the possibility that these animals are cleverly disguised mules (see paragraph $\boxed{f} \mapsto$).

Prima facie it seems that the relevant alternative account begs the question against the sceptic. For the theory of relevant alternatives simply claims that sceptical hypotheses are usually not relevant and therefore don't have to be eliminated for us to acquire empirical knowledge. Whether the theory of relevant alternatives *is* question begging depends on how the notion of relevance is explicated. Ideally the definition of relevance does not already presuppose the falsity of scepticism.

What makes an alternative relevant? What standards do the alternatives raised by the sceptic fail to meet? It has proven to be difficult to answer these questions with any degree of precision and generality. Generally speaking, there is an objective and a subjective reading of the concept of relevance. In the objective reading, the relevance of an alternative has to do with the objective probability of its realization. If there are hoaxing zoos in one's vicinity, then this could render it a relevant alternative that what looks like a zebra is in fact a disguised mule. It doesn't matter whether one is aware of the prevalence of hoaxing zoos. In the subjective reading, an alternative is relevant if the believer takes it to be probable. Here relevance depends on the

---

[1]   F. Dretske, *Perception, Knowledge and Belief* (Cambridge University Press, 2000), p. 39.

assumptions, purposes, and intentions of the subject who makes the knowledge claim and on the 'community' in which he operates.[2]

Some philosophers hold that the relevance of an alternative is dependent on the conversational context of not only the epistemic subject but also the attributor, i.e., the person describing the epistemic subject as a knower or a non-knower. This view is called *contextualism*, in the narrow sense of the word. Contextualists usually hold on to the closure principle.

Does Dretske endorse the subjective or the objective interpretation of relevance?

In the end, Dretske seems to want to integrate the objective and the subjective dimension of relevance. In $\boxed{h}\to$ and the following paragraphs Dretske opts for an objective reading of relevance. Relevant alternatives are those that 'actually exist in the objective situation'. What speaks in favour of this objective reading is that when we are interested in acquiring *empirical* knowledge what matters is the world, not us and our conversational context. Given the objective notion of relevance, it may be impossible to tell, from a first-person perspective, whether or not one is justified in believing something. Dretske's ornithologist, for example, due to his ignorance of the presence of Siberian Grebes, mistakenly takes himself to be justified in believing that he is seeing Gadwall ducks, which he cannot tell from Grebes.

Dretske declares that even if, as a matter of fact, Siberian Grebes have never migrated to Wisconsin, as long as they 'can migrate', one cannot know that something is a Gadwall duck unless one can eliminate the possibility that it is a Siberian Grebe. There are general problems of determining what counts as a physical (as opposed to a purely logical) possibility in a certain situation. Depending on which parameters are held constant, different situations count as physically possible.

Knowledge is not only relative to extra-evidential circumstances but also to subjective features such as the conversational context. In $\boxed{g}\to$ and the following paragraphs Dretske suggests that which alternative is relevant is also determined by contrastive focusing. In knowing that Oscar *killed* Bert (knowing that what Oscar did to Bert was kill him) I don't necessarily have to know that *Oscar* killed Bert (know that it was *Oscar* who killed Bert). And thus I can justifiably believe that Oscar *killed* Bert without having evidence to rule out the (irrelevant) alternative that Bert was killed by someone other than Oscar.

What, if anything, speaks in favour of combining the subjective and the objective dimension of relevance?

If the subject doesn't consider an alternative that is very likely, objectively speaking, he fails to know because it is accidental that the counter-possibility wasn't actual and that he got it right. And if the subject doesn't take into account some of the subjective

---

[2]   For a comparison of the relevant alternative theory with contextualism see 'Dretske's Replies', in B. McLaughlin (ed.), *Dretske and his Critics* (Blackwell, 1991), pp. 192–6.

possibilities, he fails to meet the justification condition for knowledge. Thus it seems that an alternative is relevant when the objective probability of its realization is high *and* when it is pertinent to the subject's conversational context.

One of the obstacles for the kind of anti-sceptical strategy put forward by Dretske is the powerful intuition many people have in support of the closure principle. Dretske admits that developing examples in which closure is violated is not enough to refute closure because the denial of closure 'is sufficiently counterintuitive to render controversial most of the crucial examples'.[3] Yet the relevant alternative analysis of knowledge is not committed to denying closure *tout court*. Just because one cannot know that one isn't a brain in a vat by way of knowing that one is seeing a zebra doesn't mean that one cannot, for example, know that one is petting a mammal on the basis of knowing that one is petting a zebra. In fact, if one couldn't know *any* of the known consequences of the things one knows, reasoning in general would be in jeopardy. So it seems that the relevant alternative theory is incomplete until we are given a general criterion to differentiate between benign and inappropriate applications of the closure principle.[4]

Introduction to Williams

Michael Williams is professor of philosophy at Johns Hopkins University. His main areas of research are epistemology (with special reference to scepticism), philosophy of language, and the history of modern philosophy.

In his first book, *Groundless Belief: An Essay on the Possibility of Epistemology* (1977), Williams criticizes the empiricist idea that our knowledge of the world rests on a perceptual or experiential foundation. His second book, *Unnatural Doubts: Epistemological Realism and the Basis of Scepticism* (1992), argues for the provocative thesis that there is no such thing as 'knowledge of the external world', the kind of knowledge the Cartesian sceptic questions. Only if we assume the problematic doctrine of epistemological realism does the phrase 'knowledge of the external world' constitute a theoretically coherent kind of knowledge. Williams suggests replacing epistemological realism with a version of contextualism. The essay reprinted in this volume contains many of the ideas that make up *Unnatural Doubts*.

Most recently Williams has written *Problems of Knowledge: A Critical Introduction to Epistemology* (2001). Rather than simply introducing a configuration of positions, this book develops his own epistemology. Last but not least, Williams has edited *Scepticism* (1993), a large collection of seminal essays.

---

[3] *Perception, Knowledge and Belief* (Cambridge University Press, 2000), p. 40.
[4] In 'The Case Against Closure', in M. Steup and E. Sosa (eds), *Contemporary Debates in Epistemology* (Blackwell, 2005), pp. 20–4, Dretske sketches such a criterion in terms of the difference between heavyweight and lightweight implications.

Michael Williams,
'Realism and Scepticism'

I

It is a longstanding philosophical opinion that metaphysical realism is an essential ingredient in the case for scepticism.* However, as I see things, the source of scepticism lies in realist commitments of another sort entirely, commitments carried by a doctrine I call 'epistemological realism'. This is what I want to explain.*

II

Realism seems to open the way to scepticism because it seems to make it impossible to account for the necessary truth-conduciveness of epistemic justification.*

. . .

a→ . . . If we explain truth and justification in wholly disparate terms – one as a relation between beliefs and the world and the other as a relation between beliefs and other beliefs – we have no hope of accounting for the necessary truth-conduciveness of justification, hence no way of explaining how knowledge is possible. Realism, it seems, leads inevitably to scepticism.

III

. . .

IV

. . .

. . . [C]oherence theories treat justification holistically. An individual belief derives its credibility from its place in a coherent total belief-system, and the factors that determine coherence – typically such things as comprehensiveness and explanatory integration – even if they supervene on relations between particular beliefs in a system, have to do with the character of the system as a whole. I take holism to be essential to coherence theories properly so called. And just as the conception of truth as a property of beliefs or a belief – world relation is an addition to the negative thesis that truth is not an epistemic notion, so this holistic conception of the justification is an addition to the thesis that nothing can justify a belief except another belief.

...

b→ It is precisely in virtue of their holistic character that coherence theories invite sceptical challenges. In our earlier discussion of truth, we saw that the sceptical argument did not presuppose any positive form of realism, however minimal. What did appear to be crucial, however, was the legitimacy of asking questions about justification at a very high level of generality or abstraction. This is where coherence theories of justification make their contribution: for by analysing justification in terms of features belonging to our system of beliefs as a whole, they offer a way of making sense of the sceptic's characteristically global requests for justification and, more importantly still, reinforce the thought that we have a useful notion of 'our system of beliefs' or 'our knowledge of the world', such that we might reasonably be expected to offer some kind of defence of its epistemological status.

Contextualist theories, by contrast, though they share with coherence theories the negative thesis that nothing can justify a belief except another belief, have no use for such notions as 'our total view' or 'our system of beliefs'. In other words, they are distinguished by their rejection of the radical holism that is definitive of coherence theories proper. This is not to say that contextualists understand the way credibility attaches to beliefs atomistically. It may well be that, in specific contexts of inquiry, beliefs are evaluated or sustained on the basis of their systematic connections with other beliefs: justification may be, so to speak, locally or contextually holistic. But this local or contextual holism needs to be kept distinct from the strong holism, characteristic of coherence theories of justification, according to which a belief owes its credibility to its being embedded in a suitably coherent 'total view'* or (global) system of beliefs.

I think we can see right away that this contrast may have implications for our sceptical problem. A coherence theory of justification makes it seem perfectly proper to seize on any random 'belief' or set of beliefs and ask 'Justifiable or not?' This simply means: 'Can the belief or beliefs in question be embedded in a suitably coherent total view?' However, on a contextualist view of justification, the propriety of such questions is much less obvious. For a contextualist, there is no straightforward matter of fact as to whether c→ a given belief or proposition, abstractly viewed, is or is not 'justified'. For a contextualist, questions of justification arise only in the face of specific difficulties, hence only in contexts of inquiry where *not* everything is open to question. The contextualist agrees with the coherentist that nothing can justify a belief except another belief. However, he does not see that a fully general account of how 'getting some beliefs to fit in with others' favours truth is either possible or required. Everything depends on the beliefs in question and the kind of fit. The characteristic generality of sceptical demands for justification begins to look suspicious.

So, although our sceptical problem survives deflation of the notion of truth, it is not at all clear that it survives contextualization of the notion of justification. The problem demands that justification be understood in a way that allows us to make sense of demands for justification imposed at an unusually high level of generality and in abstraction from all specific, directed forms of inquiry. Even when sceptical attention is focused on more restricted kinds of beliefs, the kinds are very broad and have no clear relations to more ordinary divisions by subject-matter. 'Beliefs about the past' is not co-extensive with 'history' nor 'beliefs about the external world' with 'physics'. Sceptical argument requires a conception of justification that makes such classifications seem reasonable. This is what is right about the claim that the sceptical challenge to connect coherence with truth rests on an essentialist conception of justification. 'Justified beliefs' must constitute a theoretically coherent kind. On a contextualist view of justification they do not. . . .

d→ But how exactly does a contextualist view of justification work to undermine or defuse our sceptical problem? The most obvious suggestion appeals to a contrast between local and global demands for justification. For a contextualist, only local demands are admissible and, with this restriction in place, there is no longer any problem about combining a realistic account of truth, of any degree of strength indeed, with a rejection of the idea of verification by confrontation. Challenged on the truth of a given belief, I can appeal to my own experience, to the testimony of others, to whatever tests, experiments or investigations I or other people have carried out, and so on. Should the evidential value – the truth-conduciveness – of whatever I cite itself come under suspicion, we have a further matter for empirical investigation. How reliable an observer am I in the relevant circumstances? Is my friend's testimony generally trustworthy? How accurate are these instruments? How often does this test produce false positives? And so on. So long as questions about evidential value remain at this level of specificity, we will feel no temptation to suppose that we can justify a given belief by appeal to something other than further beliefs. Neither will we be tempted to reconstrue truth in epistemic terms or to feel that the evidential value, the truth-conduciveness, of a given justifying move must have some kind of a priori basis. A problem arises only if we admit the sceptic's demands for some kind of global account of the truth-conduciveness of 'the test of coherence', precisely what a contextualist view of justification says we need not do.

However, a blunt appeal to the contrast between local and global demands for justification does not go to the heart of the matter.* It leaves too many questions hanging to be a satisfying explanation of how the sceptic goes wrong.

For one, at what point do demands for justification become too general? How local must they be to remain admissible? Lacking an index of improper generality that is independent of our becoming vulnerable to scepticism, we have a dismissal of sceptical questions but no real account of what is wrong with them.

For another, how does a contextualist view of justification go beyond a point any sceptic will readily concede: that to get on with various ordinary, more specific forms of inquiry, we have to rely on all sorts of assumptions? No one denies that, for everyday practical (and even theoretical) purposes, we have to ignore fundamental epistemological questions. But this does not mean either that such questions are badly posed or that sceptical answers to them are incorrect.

And finally, sceptical questions can be very general without being global. Even the challenge to connect coherence with truth concedes, for the sake of argument, that we know what we believe and how our beliefs hang together. So it does not violate the contextualist stricture on attempts to validate everything we believe, all at once. The sceptical problem that results from failure to meet this challenge is not therefore going to be defused by ruling out global demands for justification. We must look beyond the simple local/global distinction for the anti-sceptical potential in a contextualist understanding of verification.

V

The most significant feature of the contextualist understanding of justification is that it is anti-realist, or anyway non-realist, with respect to the typical objects of epistemological theorizing – knowledge, justified belief and the like. In this way, it is opposed both to foundationalist and coherence theories of the traditional kind, which are committed to what I call 'epistemological realism'. This is not, I must stress, realism with respect to what we claim to know, but *realism with respect to the objects of epistemological inquiry.**

We can begin with foundationalist accounts of justification, where commitment to epistemological realism is most immediately visible. The doctrine of the given, which contextualists and coherence theorists agree in rejecting, does not capture all that is distinctive about foundationalism. Rather, the root idea of foundationalism lies in the doctrine of epistemological priority. Beliefs are seen as partitioned into broad epistemological classes arranged in an epistemological hierarchy, an 'order of reasons' that cuts across ordinary subject-matter divisions. This hierarchy is not seen by the foundationalist as imposed for the purpose of carrying out some particular, restricted theoretical project. Rather, he takes it to capture the fundamental, underlying, and fully objective structure of empirical justification, a structure that determines what kinds of belief can, in the last analysis, be taken to provide warrant for others. On this view, beliefs stand in definite and objective epistemological relations, independently of how they are embedded in particular, specific contexts of inquiry. Foundationalism is therefore not just a doctrine about the formal structure of empirical inference: it embodies a definite realism with respect to relations of justification.* Beliefs, we might say, stand in *natural* epistemological relations, and the classes they fall into, depending on their place in the order of reasons, constitute *natural epistemological kinds*.

As I see it, then, the most significant feature of a contextualist understanding of justification is not that it tries to place 'global' epistemological questions under interdict, but that it amounts to a decisive rejection of epistemological realism. For a contextualist, a belief has no intrinsic epistemological character or status. Accordingly, there are no invariant epistemological relations or natural epistemological kinds. If this is right, there is nothing compelling about the ways beliefs get classified for the purposes of sceptical arguments. Of course we *can* partition our beliefs into, say, those having to do with the external world and those having to do only with 'experience'. However, unless this partition corresponds to some fundamental and objective epistemological asymmetry, failure to show in some fully general way how the latter can serve to ground the former will have no special significance. It will not imply that we never know anything about the external world.

We noticed earlier that sceptical arguments classify beliefs in ways that cut across ordinary subject-matter divisions. They do so because the principles of classification are epistemological through and through. Beliefs are sorted according to their potential for certainty, to whether they can be justified immediately or only inferentially, and so on. This kind of sorting stands or falls with epistemological realism. If there are no natural epistemological kinds, there is no reason even to try to sort beliefs this way. So when a sceptic raises questions about beliefs about the past, beliefs about the external world or, at the limit of abstraction, justified beliefs, a contextualist will be unmoved: not because the sceptic's questions are too general or because his negative verdict is a priori unacceptable, but because he has failed to identify a coherent object of assessment.

This answers our questions about the contextualist reply to scepticism. The first question was 'How general is too general?' In particular, is there a criterion for improper generality in epistemological questions independent of their tendency to suggest sceptical answers? However, we can sidestep all such questions, for the issue is not generality as such, but the peculiar kind of generality achieved by reliance on a purely epistemological classification of beliefs.* The contextualist's objection is not to the generality of the sceptic's questions but to their implicit reference to natural epistemological kinds.

The second question was: how is contextualism different from the uncontroversial point that, to get on with ordinary, specific investigations, we have to make all kinds of assumptions? I think we can now see that this 'uncontroversial' point is tendentious. As Wittgenstein remarks,

It isn't that the situation is like this: we just can't investigate everything, and for that reason we are forced to rest content with assumption. If I want the door to turn, the hinges must stay put.

Exempting some things from doubt, in a particular context, reflects
neither practical incapacities nor epistemological insouciance: it is rather a
function of the direction of inquiry. The idea that, in giving an inquiry
a definite direction, we are making assumptions which, theoretically speaking, ought to be justified, even if present interests and practical limitations
deter us from making the effort, derives its force entirely from the picture
of an underlying structure of empirical knowledge, present in and presupposed by all particular attempts at investigation. Abandon that picture and
we see that loosening the hinges does not yield a more rigorous approach to
our original topic: rather it amounts to *changing the subject*. To entertain
doubts about the reality of the past is not to insist on a more rigorous
approach to history, as perhaps to advocate formal proof is to insist on a
more rigorous approach to mathematics. Entertaining such doubts leads to a
wholly different set of problems, epistemological rather than historical,
failure to solve which in no way impugns the legitimacy of historical
research.

This leads to the third objection, which was that the sceptic need not try
to question everything we believe. As we might put it now, his examination
of our knowledge of the world has its own hinges: contextualism thus
cannot amount to an objection to scepticism, because the sceptic creates a
context in which his highly general questions make perfectly good sense.
That, however, is the point: he *creates* a context; whereas, for his conclusions
to have the significance he wants them to have, his questions have to be
responsive to objective epistemological constraints, not to self-imposed
limitations. The contextualist thinks that, to the extent it succeeds at all,
the sceptic's approach to classifying beliefs is completely artificial. The
sceptic claims to be investigating the presuppositions of all ordinary inquiries
and arguments when in fact he is only inventing a conundrum.

VI

The relevance of this line of criticism to the sceptical problem we have been
most concerned with may not be immediately obvious. Can it be used to
defuse the demand that we connect coherence with truth?

Epistemological realism is less immediately visible in coherence theories
of justification. We might be tempted to conclude that it is not present at
all, ... For a hallmark of coherence theories is their rejection of any general
doctrine of epistemic priority. How, then, can they be committed to such
things as natural epistemological kinds?

However, here we must remember that even a coherence theorist is committed to thinking that, in talking of 'justified beliefs', he identifies some clear object for analysis and assessment. So his epistemological classifications may be less fine-grained than or in some other way different from those of the foundationalist. But this does not mean that he escapes epistemological realism.

One dimension of the coherentist's realistic understanding of justification has to do with the factors that determine coherence, understood holistically. Coherence theorists usually concede that there is more to coherence than logical consistency: our beliefs must not just be compatible with one another, they must 'hang together'. However this idea of explanatory coherence, as it is generally called, is far from easy to grasp. Explanation seems to be a paradigm of a context-sensitive or interest-relative relation, which is why attempts at purely formal accounts of it have met with little success. Whether some particular facts can be taken to be a good explanation of a given fact seems to depend crucially on what particular questions are on the table. But the coherentist's notion of explanation cannot be like this. The explanatory relations that contribute to coherence must be seen as context-independent, as holding between our various beliefs in virtue of their content alone. Like the foundationalist's hierarchical relations, they are taken to be fully objective. Only taken this way can they contribute to the 'coherence' of our 'total view'.

Seen this way, the foundationalist and coherence theorist agree that there is an objective structure of empirical knowledge while differing as to its character. The foundationalist appeals to an epistemological hierarchy, while the coherence theorist focuses on more complex explanatory inter-relations between beliefs. However, I think it would be a mistake to represent the coherence theorist as unqualifiedly hostile to the doctrine of epistemological priority. I think that coherentists are as committed to this doctrine as foundationalists. True, for coherentists, rational change of belief is not a matter of accommodating our beliefs to certain privileged beliefs. Rather we make overall revisions in the light of the factors that determine coherence. But such a view does not so much eliminate epistemic privilege as relocate it: in general criteria as opposed to particular factual beliefs.* Even for the coherence theorist, the regress of justification has to stop somewhere and, for him, it stops with the criteria of coherence. Coherence theorists are committed to a criterial conception of justification.

But this is not all. There is a way in which the coherence theorist is committed, not just to a variant of the foundationalist's epistemological realism, but to the very same doctrine. If there is to be a serious sceptical question about the relation between coherence and truth, we must allow that it is possible for us to know what, in general, we believe, and how our beliefs cohere, even if we do not know that any of them are true. In this sense, then, even for a coherence theorist, knowledge of our beliefs is epistemologically prior to knowledge of the world. And this priority must be objective, if failure to solve the sceptical problem is to amount to a negative assessment of our knowledge of the world. . . .

If we reject epistemological realism, we will be unmoved by the demand that we connect 'justification' with truth. We will hold that this demand seems pressing to coherence theorists proper only because they have already mistakenly construed justification holistically and criterially. We will be dubious about the need for any general account of the relation between the factors relevant to justification and truth because we will be dubious about the very notion of 'the factors relevant to justification'. We will see no reason to think of 'justified belief' or 'empirical knowledge' as objects of uniform theoretical analysis. Accordingly, we will be reluctant to concede that the sceptic, in his insistence that we assess the totality of our knowledge, or our knowledge of the world, has picked out anything for assessment. The fact that there is some fairly stable linguistic usage with respect to terms like 'know' proves nothing: think of Bacon on 'heat' . . . Stable linguistic contrasts do not guarantee the existence of natural or theoretically significant kinds: Bacon's 'hot' things includes fires and spices. What takes us from a merely nominal to a natural or theoretical kind is the idea of an underlying structure. In epistemology, the study of 'knowledge', the idea of such a structure is fleshed out by the foundationalist's epistemic hierarchy or the coherentist's criteria of 'global' coherence.

Highlighting the coherentist's critical conception of justification is perhaps the way to throw into sharpest relief the differences between coherentism and contextualism. To reject epistemological realism is to become dubious about the idea of purely epistemological questions, questions about justification that are to be raised and answered in the absence of all background, factual information. A contextualist never thinks of justifying a belief or statement as simply a matter of showing that it satisfies some set of purely epistemic criteria. This view is typical of the genuine coherentist and it is this view that, by treating questions of justification as detachable from all background factual beliefs, makes it seem possible to call into question the legitimacy of all our beliefs, or all our beliefs about the world, all at once.

For an anti-realist about the objects of epistemological inquiry, there will be no question of identifying the factors relevant to justification in abstraction from all specific subject-matters and contexts of inquiry. But we have already seen that, so long as questions about justification remain relatively local and specific, there is no problem in principle about how to explain the evidential value of whatever we cite in support of a belief that has come into question: generally, the explanation will be straightforwardly empirical and will treat evidence as a reliable indicator of the truth of whatever it is cited as evidence for. What makes this kind of explanation legitimate is the contextualist's rejection of the coherentist's criterial conception of justification.

So the contextualist conception of justification, while receptive to the view that nothing can justify a belief except another belief, is hostile to questions about the credibility of our beliefs taken as a whole and, as a result, sees no need for anything like a completely general relation between coherence and correspondence, still less one that can be shown to hold a priori. Whether or not this hostility is in the end well-founded, the point remains that (metaphysical) realism does not threaten us with scepticism when combined only with what I initially identified as minimal negative coherentism, the thesis that nothing can justify a belief except another belief. The key ingredient in sceptical argument is *epistemological* realism.

Commentary on Williams

Scepticism claims that all the evidence for our beliefs about the external world resides in our beliefs about sensory experiences. Yet everything in our experience could be exactly the way it now is even if the external world were completely different from the way we take it to be. For example, it could seem to me as if I am now reading a book even if I was dreaming. Perceptual experience is our only source of information about the world, but experience does not rule out alternative possibilities. Our evidence for the nature of the external world is inconclusive and falls short of what is needed for knowledge.

For the argument for external-world scepticism to go through, we have to make two assumptions:

(i)   Beliefs about sensory experience are the only evidence for beliefs about the external world.
(ii) Even if the external world were radically different from how we think it is, our beliefs about sensory experience could be the same as they are now.

Given these assumptions, we are in the situation of having sensory experiences from which alone we must construct the picture of the world around us. But since the external world is logically independent of the experiences, knowing the experiences gives us no reason to believe anything about the world.

To endorse the idea that we could have the very beliefs about sensory experiences we are having now even if the world were completely different is to be committed to *metaphysical realism*. Crudely put, metaphysical realism is the view that the world exists independently of our experience or our knowledge of it. Both metaphysical realism and scepticism hold that it is always possible that the 'real' world differs radically from the way it appears to us and from the way we conceive of it. Anti-realism, on the other hand, denies the existence of this 'real' world that lies behind the world that we know. The recognizable world is the only world.

While acknowledging the role metaphysical realism plays for scepticism (see paragraph [a]→), Williams argues that scepticism assumes another contentious kind of realism, namely epistemological realism.

What is epistemological realism?

Epistemological realism is the view that there is a hierarchy of epistemic priority among classes of beliefs, in the sense that one class of beliefs constitutes the evidential base for another class of beliefs. Which class of belief belongs to which camp depends only on the belief contents. The 'context of inquiry' plays no role in the division of beliefs into privileged and problematic classes and the assignment of justificatory roles. According to the foundationalist version of epistemological realism, for example, beliefs fall into two classes: those that need support from others and those that support others and do not stand in need of justification. The existence of such relations of epistemic dependence is understood as a basic metaphysical fact, which is why Williams labels this doctrine a form of 'realism'.

In addition to stipulating context-independent relations of justificatory priority among classes of beliefs, epistemological realism claims that these classes have a context-independent existence. According to epistemological realism, the objects of epistemological inquiry constitute genuine kinds of things – 'natural epistemological kinds' (paragraph $\boxed{e}\mapsto$). Phrases such as 'our system of beliefs', 'beliefs about the external world', and 'beliefs about the past' are thought to pick out definite objects with a unified structure; they are treated on a par with natural kind terms like 'tiger' and 'gold' (see paragraph $\boxed{b}\mapsto$).[1] If 'our knowledge of the world' were nothing but a loose aggregate of more or less unrelated things, the sceptic's attempt to assess the totality of our beliefs about the external world would be a non-starter.

External-world scepticism presupposes epistemological realism in its foundationalist form. To see this, consider assumption (i). What this assumption says is that beliefs about the external world, in virtue of their content alone, must depend for justification on the evidence of beliefs about sensory states and perceptual experiences. Each and every belief about the external world owes its justification to a member of the set of sensory experiences. So while assumption (ii) is committed to metaphysical realism, assumptions (i) (and (ii) presuppose epistemological realism.

Although coherentism is usually seen as the principal alternative to foundationalism, Williams claims that it is also committed to epistemological realism.

Why is coherentism said to presuppose epistemological realism?

The answer to this question can be found in section VI. First, coherentism assumes that the phrase 'justified beliefs' picks out a natural epistemological kind. Second, the inferential and explanatory relations that constitute coherence are taken by coherentists to be context-independent and as holding solely in virtue of the contents of the

[1]   The idea behind natural kinds is that nature is itself divided into different species or kinds. The notion of a natural kind is contentious. Some philosophers have pointed out that there is good evidence that many natural kind terms cut things up into groupings that are arbitrary, so that the question arises whether there are any real grounds for belief in a special category of natural kinds at all.

beliefs involved (see passage $\boxed{h}\!\rightarrow$). Third, while foundationalism attributes a privileged status of epistemic priority to beliefs about sensory experience, coherentism takes the criteria of coherence to be epistemically prior. Fourth, the so-called *problem of truth* (which was discussed in the context of BonJour's essay) presupposes that knowledge of the coherence of one's belief system is epistemologically prior to knowledge of the world.

> Assuming Williams is right in claiming that scepticism is committed to epistemological realism, in what way does this discovery undermine scepticism?

One could simply deny epistemological realism and conclude that scepticism is wrong. However, Williams's strategy is more subtle. He argues that because the sceptic's argument depends on the contentious doctrine of epistemological realism, scepticism is not innocent and intuitive but is a theoretically loaded, artificial, and 'unnatural' problem. (Hence the title of his book, *Unnatural Doubts*.) Like Dretske, Williams accuses the sceptic of shifting the ordinary standards of justification.

The sceptic asks us to assess the totality of our beliefs about the world from an external standpoint. He then goes on to argue that we have no justification for anything we ordinarily believe about the world. Williams asks whether we have any understanding of the project of 'assessing our beliefs about the world' that is independent of our familiarity with the sceptical argument. He answers in the negative. We do not have an intuitive understanding of the project of assessing all of our empirical beliefs at once. Rather, it is only because there are arguments for external-world scepticism and because we are familiar with them that we can make sense of the idea of assessing our empirical beliefs as a whole. So, contrary to first impression, scepticism depends on theoretical commitments that are not forced on us by our ordinary ways of thinking about justification. 'The sceptic claims to be investigating the presuppositions of all ordinary inquiries and arguments when in fact he is only inventing a conundrum' (paragraph $\boxed{g}\!\rightarrow$). And once the intuitive plausibility of the sceptical problem is called into question, the sceptic loses his inbuilt dialectical advantage and the burden of proof is shifted from the opponent's shoulders to his own: the sceptic has to motivate the less-than-compelling doctrine of epistemological realism (plus foundationalism) before the anti-sceptic has to show that empirical knowledge is indeed possible. Until epistemological realism has been adequately motivated, the contextualist 'will be unmoved' by scepticism (paragraph $\boxed{f}\!\rightarrow$).

But is it actually the case that anyone who raises the problem about our knowledge of the external world must presuppose the elaborate theoretical construction called 'epistemological realism' and 'foundationalism'?

> Do you find Williams's move against the sceptic convincing?

If scepticism were theoretically loaded in the way suggested by Williams, wouldn't it be a miracle that undergraduates are gripped by Descartes's dream argument long before they are introduced to foundationalism and epistemological realism? Does this mean that undergraduates don't fully understand the sceptical challenge? Or is Williams wrong in thinking that the priority of experiential beliefs over beliefs about the external world is not intuitive and unnatural?

Suppose there *is* an intimate relation between scepticism, on the one hand, and epistemological realism in its foundationalist form, on the other. For this insight to warrant the conclusion that sceptical doubts are unnatural doubts, our understanding of the sceptical problem must presuppose epistemological realism and foundationalism. But couldn't it be argued that epistemological realism and foundationalism are presuppositions not of our understanding of scepticism but of our attempt to respond to scepticism? The idea that beliefs about sensory experience constitute the justificatory base for beliefs about the external world comes into play *after* the sceptical challenge has been understood and when one tries to answer the question of how we can know anything about the world.[2]

> How would you characterize Williams's positive position which he labels 'the contextualist theory of justification'?

Contextualism entails the falsity of epistemological realism. It is not the case that beliefs fall into context-independent classes that determine the order of justification. 'Questions of justification arise only in the face of specific difficulties, hence only in contexts of inquiry where *not* everything is open to question' at once (paragraph $\boxed{c} \mapsto$). Abstracting from contextual details, there is no fact of the matter as to what sort of evidence justifies a given proposition. Like Dretske, Williams holds that what justifies what varies from context to context. 'There are no invariant epistemological relations' (paragraph $\boxed{e} \mapsto$). The context determining the order of justification is made up of the subject of inquiry, the evidence available for the belief in question as well as other conversational factors. For example, while a pupil may be entitled to justify his belief that Mount Everest is the highest mountain by citing a textbook, this justificatory procedure cannot be used by a geologist engaged in a debate with a colleague who claims to have arguments to the effect that K2 is slightly higher.

As paragraph $\boxed{d} \mapsto$ explains, contextualism does not allow us to call all of our beliefs about the physical world into question at once. There is a limit on the amount of beliefs that can be questioned at any given time. We can doubt *any* empirical belief but we cannot doubt *every* empirical belief at the same time. Given the context-relativity of justification, the sceptic's demand for a justification of all of our beliefs about the external world in general, independent of any particular context, is simply a misconception.

---

[2]   This point is borrowed from B. Stroud, 'Epistemological Reflection on Knowledge of the External World', *Philosophy and Phenomenological Research* 56 (1996), p. 350.

Essay/Examination Questions

These questions cover all of the topics in this book. Some readers may want to use these questions to acquire practice with writing in examination conditions. Alternatively, readers may wish to pick a question and write an essay on it in their own time, using the publications suggested in 'Further Reading' as appropriate.

1   What is the Gettier problem? Why did the Gettier problem cause such a revolution in epistemology? How effective are Gettier examples in attacking the standard account of knowledge?

2   According to the defeasibility theory of knowledge proposed by Lehrer and Paxson (and discussed by Pollock), knowledge is undefeated justified true belief. What is a defeated justification?

3   Why have attempts to provide a conceptual analysis of 'S knows that p' not been fully successful? What does this tell us about the concept of knowledge? Is it reasonable to expect that philosophers will ever come up with the correct analysis of the concept of knowledge, or is it impossible to define 'knowledge'?

4   Explain the difference between internalism and externalism, regarding both justification and knowledge.

5   Why might Goldman's version of process reliabilism be considered to combine internalist and externalist elements?

6   Explain three objections to process reliabilism. Do you think that any of these objections show that process reliabilism is mistaken?

7   Explain how the ordinary concept of justification motivates internalist theories of justification.

8   Discuss the charge of doxastic involuntarism levelled against epistemic deontologism. Is belief indeed an involuntary affair?

9   Discuss Sosa's distinction between animal knowledge and reflective knowledge. What is your assessment of Sosa's attempt to reconcile internalism and externalism?

10 Is it possible to justify that most of what you have ever learnt through testimony is true, where this justification does not in any way rest on knowledge acquired by you through testimony?

11 Under what conditions, and with what controls, should an adult listener believe what he is told, on some particular occasion?

12 Explain the difference between the reductionist and the anti-reductionist view of testimony.

13 What is the 'infinite regress problem' of justification? Explain two strategies for dealing with this problem.

14 How can the coherence theory of justification avoid the criticism (usually launched by foundationalists) that it is circular to use belief A as part of one's justification for belief B, if B is (part of) one's justification for A?

15 Discuss the three main criticisms of coherentism. How might the coherentist respond to these objections?

16 Review Alston's second-level argument against iterative foundationalism. How does the simple foundationalist attempt to get around this argument? Do you think it is successful?

17 What does it mean to say that knowledge is closed under known logical implication? Why do philosophers such as Dretske think that it is implausible to suppose that the closure principle governs our ordinary concept of knowledge?

18 Discuss this statement: The sceptic's claim that no one knows anything is self-defeating since, if it is true, the sceptic cannot know it is true.

19 Explain the position of epistemological realism and the role Williams thinks it plays in the sceptic's argument. Is epistemological realism part of our intuitive understanding of such notions as justification and knowledge? If not, what follows from this for the assessment of scepticism?

20 Consider Dretske's and Nozick's discussion of the relevant alternative account of knowledge. What makes an alternative relevant? Is this anti-sceptical strategy successful?

Further Reading

Readers wishing to delve more deeply into the issues discussed in this book may use my anthology *Knowledge: Readings in Contemporary Epistemology* (2000), co-edited with Fred Dretske. The two books complement each other in that *Knowledge* features 41 texts and little commentary while this book features 12 texts and extensive commentary. With the exception of two texts (Nozick and Foley), the readings are different. Both books are organized around the five main questions of epistemology (explained in the general introduction on pp. 1–2) and contain six chapters or parts, respectively. Chapter 1 of this book corresponds to Part I of *Knowledge*, Chapters 2 and 3 to Part II, Chapter 4 to Part V, Chapter 5 to Part III, and Chapter 6 to Part IV.

Reference Books

J. Dancy and E. Sosa (eds), *A Companion to Epistemology* (Blackwell, 1993).
J. H. Fetzer and R. F. Almeder, *Glossary of Epistemology/Philosophy of Science* (Paragon House, 1993).
J. Greco and E. Sosa (eds), *The Blackwell Guide to Epistemology* (Blackwell, 1999).
P. K. Moser (ed.), *The Oxford Handbook of Epistemology* (Oxford University Press, 2002).
I. Niiniluoto, M. Sintonen, and J. Wolenski (eds), *Handbook of Epistemology* (Kluwer, 2004).
M. Steup and E. Sosa (eds), *Contemporary Debates in Epistemology* (Blackwell, 2005).

1   Defining Knowledge

E. Adams, 'Subjunctive and Indicative Conditionals', *Foundations of Language* 6 (1970), pp. 89–94. Accessible discussion of the difference between these types of conditionals.
N. Everitt and A. Fisher, *Modern Epistemology: A New Introduction* (McGraw-Hill, 1995), chs 2–4. Introduction to the Gettier problem and many of the contemporary attempts to define propositional knowledge.

J. A. Fodor, M. Garrett, E. Walker, and C. Parkes, 'Against Definitions', *Cognition* 8 (1980), pp. 263–367. Argues that no interesting concept can be analysed by a set of individually necessary and jointly sufficient conditions.

G. Harman, *Thought* (Princeton University Press, 1975), chs 7–9. A broad study of the nature of knowledge, with particular emphasis on indefeasibility theories.

F. Jackson (ed.), *Conditionals* (Oxford University Press, 1991), introduction and chs 1 and 2. Difficult but rewarding discussions of the nature of counterfactual conditionals.

F. Jackson, *From Metaphysics to Ethics: A Defense of Conceptual Analysis* (Oxford University Press, 1998). The subtitle says it all. Should be read in connection with Fodor's 'Against Definitions'.

M. Kaplan, 'It is Not What You Know that Counts', *Journal of Philosophy* 82 (1985), pp. 350–63. Argues that the Gettier challenge is irrelevant to responsible inquiry.

S. Luper-Foy (ed.), *The Possibility of Knowledge: Nozick and His Critics* (Rowman & Littlefield, 1987). Contains essays assessing Nozick's analysis of knowledge and evidence and his approach to scepticism.

W. Lycan, 'On the Gettier Problem', in S. Hetherington (ed.), *Epistemology Futures* (Oxford University Press, 2005). A review of recent literature on the Gettier problem and a defence of the no-false-premise view.

G. Pappas and M. Swain (eds), *Essays on Knowledge and Justification* (Cornell University Press, 1978). Collection of articles on various solutions to the Gettier problem, including the indefeasibility approach and the causal theory of knowledge.

M. D. Roth and L. Galis (eds), *Knowing: Essays in the Analysis of Knowledge* (Random House, 1970). A collection of articles centring around the Gettier problem.

R. K. Shope, *The Analysis of Knowing: A Decade of Research* (Princeton University Press, 1983). A detailed study of the history of the Gettier problem and the major kinds of analysis of knowledge.

R. K. Shope, 'The Analysis of Knowledge', in I. Niiniluoto, M. Sintonen, and J. Wolenski (eds), *Handbook of Epistemology* (Kluwer, 2004), pp. 283–329. Review of the literature on the Gettier problem since the publication of Shope's *The Analysis of Knowing*.

M. Swain, *Reasons and Knowledge* (Cornell University Press, 1981). A detailed advancement of the position that knowledge is indefeasibly true, justified belief.

T. Williamson, *Knowledge and Its Limits* (Oxford University Press, 2000), ch. 1. Argues that instead of analysing knowledge in terms of belief, the concept of knowledge should be used to elucidate the concept of belief.

L. Zagzebski, 'The Inescapability of Gettier Problems', *Philosophical Quarterly* 44 (1994), pp. 65–73. Argues that as long as knowledge is defined as true belief plus something else that is reliably but not inviolably connected with truth, Gettier counterexamples to the definition can always be generated.

2   Justification and Truth

W. P. Alston, 'How to Think about Reliability', *Philosophical Topics* 23 (1995), pp. 1–29. This is, in part, a response to Feldman's 'Reliability and Justification'.

R. Baergen, *Contemporary Epistemology* (Harcourt Brace College, 1995), ch. 4. A clear presentation of the pros and cons of reliabilism.

L. BonJour, *The Structure of Empirical Knowledge* (Harvard University Press, 1985), ch. 3. The *locus classicus* of the meta-incoherence objection to reliabilism.

E. Conee and R. Feldman, 'The Generality Problem for Reliabilism', *Philosophical Studies* 89 (1998), pp. 1–29. A recent formulation of the generality problem.

J. S. Crumley, *An Introduction to Epistemology* (Mayfield, 1999), ch. 3. Another clear presentation of the pros and cons of reliabilism.

R. Feldman, 'Reliability and Justification', *Monist* 68 (1985), pp. 159–74. A penetrating discussion of the generality problem.

A. Goldman, *Epistemology and Cognition* (Harvard University Press, 1986). A presentation of process reliabilism for justification and knowledge, with much discussion of related developments in cognitive psychology.

H. Kornblith (ed.), *Epistemology: Internalism and Externalism* (Blackwell, 2001). A collection of articles on the internalism–externalism issue.

K. Lehrer and S. Cohen, 'Justification, Truth, and Coherence', *Synthese* 55 (1983), pp. 191–207. An early statement of the new evil-demon problem.

A. Plantinga, *Warrant: The Current Debate* (Oxford University Press, 1993). A critique of reliabilism, foundationalism, and coherentism.

F. F. Schmitt, *Knowledge and Belief* (Routledge, 1990). A comprehensive elaboration and defence of process reliabilism.

W. J. Talbott, *The Reliability of the Cognitive Mechanism* (Garland, 1990). A comprehensive elaboration and defence of process reliabilism.

3   Duties and Virtues

R. Almeder, *Blind Realism* (Rowman & Littlefield, 1992), ch. 2. A sustained defence of internalism, including a detailed discussion of Alston's position.

W. P. Alston, *Epistemic Justification: Essays in the Theory of Justification* (Cornell University Press, 1989), part II. A careful examination of epistemic deontologism. Alston defends internalism but rejects deontologism.

S. Bernecker, 'Prospects of Epistemic Compatibilism', forthcoming in *Philosophical Studies*. Argues against Sosa's virtue perspectivism that internalism and externalism cannot be combined by bifurcating justification and knowledge into an object-level and a meta-level and assigning externalism and internalism to different levels.

R. M. Chisholm, *Theory of Knowledge* (2nd edition, Prentice-Hall, 1977), ch. 1. An early formulation of deontological internalism.

R. Feldman, 'Epistemic Obligations', *Philosophical Perspectives* 2 (1988), pp. 240–56. A defence of epistemic deontologism against the charge of doxastic involuntarism.

R. Feldman, *Epistemology* (Prentice-Hall, 2003), ch. 4. A presentation and defence of evidentialism.

A. I. Goldman, 'Internalism Exposed', *Journal of Philosophy* 96 (1999), pp. 271–93. A powerful attack on internalism. Steup's 'A Defense of Internalism', reprinted in this volume, is a response to Goldman's paper.

J. Greco, *Putting Skeptics in Their Place: The Nature of Skeptical Arguments and Their Role in Philosophical Inquiry* (Cambridge University Press 2000), ch. 7. Presents a version of reliabilism-based virtue epistemology that differs from Sosa's virtue perspectivism.

J. Greco, 'Virtues in Epistemology', in P. Moser (ed.), *The Oxford Handbook of Epistemology* (Oxford University Press 2002), pp. 287–315. A comprehensive and accessible introduction to reliabilism-based virtue epistemology.

J. Greco (ed.), *Ernest Sosa and His Critics* (Blackwell, 2004). Twenty-two critical essays on Sosa's epistemology and metaphysics together with Sosa's replies.

A. Plantinga, *Warrant and Proper Function* (Oxford University Press, 1993). A development of a non-reliabilist version of externalism. Justified beliefs are said to be the result of 'properly functioning' cognitive faculties.

M. Steup, *An Introduction to Contemporary Epistemology* (Prentice-Hall, 1996), ch. 4. A presentation and defence of epistemic deontologism.

M. Steup and E. Sosa (eds), *Contemporary Debates in Epistemology* (Blackwell, 2005), part 2. Head-to-head debates about internalism and epistemic deontology.

L. T. Zagzebski, *Virtues of the Mind: An Inquiry into the Nature of Virtue and the Ethical Foundations of Knowledge* (Cambridge University Press, 1996). Presents a virtue theory that is designed to apply both to ethics and to epistemology.

4 Knowledge by Hearsay

R. Audi, *Epistemology: A Contemporary Introduction to the Theory of Knowledge* (Routledge, 1998), part I. Discussion of various sources of knowledge. Regarding testimony, Audi argues that it doesn't generate knowledge but merely transmits knowledge.

A. Bezuidenhout, 'Is Verbal Communication a Purely Preservative Process?', *Philosophical Review* 107 (1998), pp. 261–88. Argues that Burge is committed to a 'code conception of communication' and opts for an inferential model. Given this model, Burge's claim that beliefs based on testimony can in principle be justified a priori must be rejected.

C. A. J. Coady, *Testimony: A Philosophical Study* (Clarendon Press, 1992). A historically orientated comprehensive treatment of testimony. Coady sides with Reid's anti-reductionism.

J. Dancy, *Introduction to Contemporary Epistemology* (Blackwell, 1985), part III. Discussion of sources of knowledge.

M. J. Frápolli and E. Romero, *Meaning, Basic Self-Knowledge, and Mind: Essays on Tyler Burge* (CSLI Publications, 2003). A survey of Burge's philosophy of mind and epistemology.

M. Hahn and B. Ramberg (eds), *Reflections and Replies: Essays on the Philosophy of Tyler Burge* (MIT Press, 2003). Contains critical essays on anti-individualism and Burge's replies.

D. Hume, *An Enquiry Concerning Human Understanding* (1777), ed. L. A. Selby-Bigge, revised P. H. Nidditch (Oxford University Press, 1975), sec. 10. The *locus classicus* of reductionism.

M. Kusch and P. Lipton, 'Testimony: a Primer', *Studies in the History and Philosophy of Science* 33 (2002), pp. 209–17. A useful bibliographical essay.

T. Reid, *An Inquiry into the Human Mind* (1764), ed. T. Duggan (Chicago University Press, 1970), ch. 6, sec. 24. The *locus classicus* of anti-reductionism.

P. F. Strawson, 'Knowing from Words', in B. K. Matilal and A. Chakrabarti (eds), *Knowing from Words* (Kluwer, 1994), pp. 23–7. Argues that because perception, memory, and testimony are interdependent, any one of them cannot be reduced to the others.

M. Welbourne, *The Community of Knowledge* (Aberdeen University Press, 1986). Defends the idea that the nature of knowledge is to be communicable by say-so.

5   Foundations or Coherence?

R. Audi, *The Structure of Justification* (Cambridge University Press, 1993), part I. Exposition of the foundationalism–coherentism dispute and defence of internalist foundationalism.

J. W. Bender (ed.), *The Current State of the Coherence Theory: Critical Essays on the Epistemic Theories of Keith Lehrer and Laurence BonJour, with Replies* (Kluwer, 1989). Contains, among other things, ten critical articles on BonJour's coherentism along with BonJour's replies.

P. Butchvarov, *The Concept of Knowledge* (Northwestern University Press, 1970). A defence of foundationalism regarding perceptual knowledge.

R. M. Chisholm, *The Foundations of Knowing* (University of Minnesota Press, 1982) chs 1 and 10. A collection of essays, some of which address foundationalism.

J. S. Crumley, *An Introduction to Epistemology* (Mayfield Publishing, 1999), chs 4 and 5. A clear presentation of foundationalism and coherentism.

E. Falves, *A Defense of the Given* (Rowman & Littlefield, 1996). Justification is said to be conferred by infallible beliefs about our perceptual experiences.

R. Fumerton, *Metaepistemology and Skepticism* (Rowman & Littlefield, 1995), chs 4 and 5. A defence of foundationalism and criticism of coherentism.

S. Haack, *Evidence and Inquiry* (Oxford University Press, 1993). An attempt to reconcile foundationalism with coherentism, 'foundherentism'. Haack pays special attention to the connections between epistemology and philosophy of science.

K. Lehrer, *Theory of Knowledge* (Westview Press, 1990), chs 3–7. Discussion of foundationalism and coherentism with defence of the latter.

K. Lehrer, *Self-Trust: A Study of Reason, Knowledge, and Autonomy* (Oxford University Press, 1997). Argues for a kind of coherentism that combines internalist and externalist features.

C. I. Lewis, *An Analysis of Knowledge and Valuation* (Open Court, 1946). A development of an internalist foundationalist position.

M. S. McCleod, *Rationality and Theistic Belief: An Essay in Reformed Epistemology* (Cornell University Press, 1993). Challenges Alston's claim that God can be directly perceived.

T. J. McGrew, *The Foundations of Knowledge* (Littlefield Adams, 1995). Another defence of foundationalism.

P. K. Moser, *Knowledge and Evidence* (Cambridge University Press, 1989). A defence of foundationalism about perceptual knowledge.

N. Rescher, *The Coherence Theory of Truth* (Oxford University Press, 1973). Despite its title, this book defends a coherence theory of justification.

M. Steup and E. Sosa (eds), *Contemporary Debates in Epistemology* (Blackwell, 2005), part 2. Head-to-head debates about the regress problem, coherentism, and immediate justification.

6   Scepticism in Context

S. Bernecker, 'Believing that You Know and Knowing that You Believe', in R. Schantz (ed.), *The Externalist Challenge* (de Gruyter, 2004), pp. 369–76. Critical discussion of anti-sceptical arguments from semantic externalism by Putnam and Dretske.

S. E. Boër, 'Meaning and Contrastive Stress', *Philosophical Review* 88 (1979), pp. 263–98. A critique of Dretske's theory of contrastive stress.

M. F. Burnyeat (ed.), *The Skeptical Tradition* (University of California Press, 1983). Essays on sceptical arguments in the classical texts of philosophy from Plato to Kant.

J. W. Cornman, K. Lehrer, and G. S. Pappas, *Philosophical Problems and Arguments: An Introduction* (4th edition, Hackett, 1992), part 2. An analysis of the logical structure of the sceptic's argument.

K. DeRose and T. A. Warfield (eds), *Skepticism: A Contemporary Reader*, parts 3 and 4. Apart from a helpful introduction, the book contains many important articles.

C. Hookway, *Scepticism* (Routledge, 1990). Presents an historical perspective on scepticism by considering contrasting views, such as those of Sextus Empiricus, Descartes, and Hume, on why scepticism is important.

P. Klein, 'Skepticism', in P. Moser (ed.), *The Oxford Handbook of Epistemology* (Oxford University Press, 2002), pp. 336–61. A comprehensive and up-to-date discussion of epistemic closure and contextualism.

B. McLaughlin (ed.), *Dretske and His Critics* (Blackwell, 1991). Nine critical essays on Dretske's epistemology and philosophy of mind plus Dretske's responses.

D. Pritchard, 'Recent Work on Radical Skepticism', *American Philosophical Quarterly* 39 (2002), pp. 215–57. A survey of the literature that appeared in the late 1980s and 1990s.

M. D. Roth and G. Ross (eds), *Doubting: Contemporary Perspectives on Skepticism* (Kluwer, 1990). A collection of important articles.

J. Schaffer, 'From Contextualism to Contrastivism', *Philosophical Studies* 119 (2004), pp. 73–103. Carefully distinguishes between contextualism and contrastivism (a version of the relevant alternative theory) and argues for the latter.

M. Steup and E. Sosa (eds), *Contemporary Debates in Epistemology* (Blackwell, 2005), part 1. Head-to-head debates about epistemic closure, contextualism, and the prospects of refuting scepticism.

P. F. Strawson, *Skepticism and Naturalism: Some Varieties* (Columbia University Press, 1985). Suggests an anti-sceptical strategy which consists in offering good reason for ignoring scepticism rather than trying to refute it. The reason offered is that beliefs about the external world are indispensable to us.

B. Stroud, *The Significance of Philosophical Scepticism* (Oxford University Press, 1984). A careful study of the motives for, and responses to, Cartesian scepticism.

B. Stroud, *Understanding Human Knowledge: Philosophical Essays* (Oxford University Press, 2002). A collection of important epistemological papers. Ch. 9 is a critical discussion of Williams's version of contextualism.

P. Unger, *Ignorance: A Case for Scepticism* (Clarendon Press, 1975). Argues for the extreme sceptical view that not only can nothing ever be known, but no one can ever have any reason at all for anything.

L. Wittgenstein, *On Certainty* (Blackwell, 1969). A wide-ranging work that seems to defend a version of foundationalism.

P. Yourgrau, 'Knowledge and Relevant Alternatives', *Synthese* 55 (1983), pp. 175–90. A critique of the relevant alternative approach to scepticism.

Index